I WILL MAKE MYSELF LIKE THE MOST HIGH!

Jesse D. Rhodes

Copyright © 2013 by Jesse D. Rhodes

I WILL MAKE MYSELF LIKE THE MOST HIGH!
by Jesse D. Rhodes

Printed in the United States of America

ISBN 9781628395129

All rights reserved solely by the author. The author guarantees all contents are original and do not infringe upon the legal rights of any other person or work. No part of this book may be reproduced in any form without the permission of the author. The views expressed in this book are not necessarily those of the publisher.

Unless otherwise indicated, Bible quotations are taken from The Holy Bible, New International Version. Copyright © 1973, 1978, and 1984 by International Bible Society. Used by permission of Zondervan Publishing House.

www.xulonpress.com

ACKNOWLEDGMENTS

How does one adequately thank almighty God for all He does and shows us? A simple *thank you* seems so inadequate, yet I'm left to humbly stand in awe of all that God has shown me concerning the end-times. Shortly after I was saved in 1992, God placed it on my heart to study all that was written or recorded concerning the end-times. Each time I was left with an emptiness that the entire truth was not being revealed. After all my studies, I still could not find anyone who could adequately explain Daniel's 2,300-, 1,290-, and 1,335-day prophecies. No one could properly place all three figures on a time line that made any sense. Additionally, no one seemed interested in the true meaning behind the fourth terrifying beast of chapter 7 in Daniel. Also, it seemed that everyone wanted to overlay the trumpet judgments with the bowl judgments. Yet in my heart I sensed there was a gap of time and distance between the trumpet and bowl judgments.

Finally, after much seeking and asking for God to reveal to me the truth of the end-times, He had me set aside all the books and tapes and sermons and He granted my request. To my amazement, He revealed the truth of Daniel and Revelation, verse by verse, prophecy by prophecy. Although He has been gracious to allow me to peer into the future, like Daniel and John in the book of Revelation, I still find myself overwhelmed by His wisdom and His choosing me to relay these revelations to the world. I can only humbly thank Him for His wisdom in Christ Jesus, who saved me from my sin, and for the power of the Holy Spirit, who leads the humble into all truth and righteousness. He is truly an awesome God.

Every Christian needs one true Christian friend. God delivered that friend to me in the person of Jim Altmaier. Like a doubting Thomas, soon after God showed me the truth behind Daniel and Revelation, I humbly asked that God give me confirmation of all that He had shown me. He sent Jim into my life to serve as that confirmation. Jim lives for the Lord based on the premise that *steel sharpens steel*. Together we have held each other to a high standard when it comes to spiritually discerning the Word of God. Jim has kept me focused on seeking the truth and the will of God in all areas of my life. The publishing of this book is a direct result of his confirming faith. To him and his wife, Joan, I will be forever greatly indebted.

When anyone sets out to embark on an unknown adventure or project, it is essential to have a system of support for those times when doubt creeps into your mind and you wonder if you're accomplishing God's will. My wife, Linda, is truly a gift from God that I don't deserve. From the very beginning, she has been a solid supporter of the publishing of this book. She ensured I had all the necessary tools to see this project to completion. More than that, she lives her life in a constant state of readiness should the Lord return. She alone has affected my growth as a Christian more than anyone else in the world. Without her faith and belief in me, I would not have accomplished the publishing of this book. To her I owe the deepest debt of gratitude and love.

CONTENTS

INTRODUCTION

CHAPTER

1. UNDERSTANDING GOD'S END-TIME PLAN 15
2. OPENING THE SEVEN SEALS 33
3. THE GREAT REBELLION 89
4. SATAN'S REVELATION: "I AM THE CHRIST!" 113
5. THE DAY OF THE ANTICHRIST 189
6. THE DAY OF THE LORD..216

ILLUSTRATIONS

FIGURE 1-1.	DANIEL ESTABLISHES THE TEN-YEAR END-TIME PERIOD	32
FIGURE 2-1.	JOHN USES DANIEL'S ESTABLISHED TEN-YEAR END-TIME PERIOD TO CONSTRUCT REVELATION	35
FIGURE 2-2.	SHOWING HOW THE FIRST FOUR SEAL JUDGMENTS LINE UP WITH THE KINGDOMS ENVISIONED BY DANIEL IN CHAPTER 7	45
FIGURE 2-3.	THE STRUCTURE OF REVELATION AND JOHN'S USE OF JUXTAPOSITION IN REVELATION 7:9–17	55

FIGURE 2-4.	HOW THE RUSSIAN INVASION BEGINS DANIEL'S SEVENTIETH WEEK— THE TRIBULATION PERIOD	58
FIGURE 2-5.	EZEKIEL'S PROPHECIES LINE UP WITH REVELATION AND DANIEL	66
FIGURE 2-6.	REVELATION, EZEKIEL, AND DANIEL COINCIDE WITH DANIEL'S 2,300-, 1,290-, AND 1,335-DAY PROPHECIES	72
FIGURE 2-7.	THE KING OF THE NORTH DELUDES THE WORLD INTO BELIEVING HE IS THE MAN OF SIN	76
FIGURE 2-8.	WHY THE CHURCH CONFUSES THE KING OF THE NORTH'S ECONOMIC PROGRAM AS BEING THE MARK OF THE BEAST	87
FIGURE 3-1.	COMPARING THE SEAL AND TRUMPET JUDGMENTS	92
FIGURE 3-2.	THE MAN OF SIN BEGINS HIS REBELLION (2 THESSALONIANS 2:3–12)	97
FIGURE 4-1.	DAYS BEFORE THE SEVENTH TRUMPET IS BLOWN	117
FIGURE 4-2.	HOW DANIEL USES THE CONCEPT OF JUXTAPOSITION IN CHAPTER 11 TO SEAL HIS BOOK UNTIL THE TIME OF THE END (DANIEL 12:9)	136
FIGURE 4-3.	HOW REVELATION 12 DETAILS SATAN'S PLAN TO DESTROY ISRAEL AND THE CHURCH AT THE BEGINNING OF DANIEL'S SEVENTIETH WEEK	144

FIGURE 4-4.	DIFFERENCES BETWEEN THE KING OF THE NORTH AND KING OF THE SOUTH, WHO BECOMES THE MAN OF SIN	148
FIGURE 4-5.	THE FOURFOLD PROPHECIES OF MATTHEW 24	183
FIGURE 5-1.	DANIEL'S 2,300-, 1,290-, AND 1,335-DAY PROPHECIES AND METHOD FOR CALCULATING THE DAY OF THE RAPTURE	192
FIGURE 5-2.	SHOWING THE ORDER IN WHICH JESUS BRINGS HOME THE SAINTS	210
FIGURE 6-1.	THE POWERFUL DELUSION THAT ALLOWS SATAN TO PROCLAIM, "I AM THE CHRIST!" (ISAIAH 14:12–15)	241

INTRODUCTION

Daniel 10:21: But first I will tell you what is written in the Book of Truth.

Revelation 10:2: He was holding a little scroll, which lay open in his hand.

Revelation 10:3: When he shouted, the voices of the seven thunders spoke.

2 Thessalonians 2:9–12: The coming of the lawless one will be in accordance with the work of Satan displayed in all kinds of counterfeit miracles, signs and wonders, and in every sort of evil that deceives those who are perishing. They perish because they refused to love the truth and so be saved. For this reason God sends them a powerful delusion so that they will believe the lie and so that all will be condemned who have not believed the truth but have delighted in wickedness.

Revelation 10:7: But in the days when the seventh angel is about to sound his trumpet, the mystery of God will be accomplished, just as he announced to his servants the prophets.

A Book of Truth . . . a little scroll . . . seven thunders speaking and prophesying . . . a trumpet blast accomplishing the mystery of God that was revealed to His servants the prophets . . .

The deep hidden mystery of God is the fact that there is coming a period of time when Satan will attempt to appear as God to all of mankind, including the true believers of Jesus Christ, or the church. Instead of coming to us in the form of a beast, Satan will come to us acting and looking as if he is a spiritual giant, performing all kinds of lying signs and wonders, claiming to be God. But underneath the sheep's clothing that he wears, Daniel and John reveal Satan will be the ultimate religious beast mankind has ever known. Isaiah 14:12–15 gives us insight into the reality of Satan's devious plan:

> How you have fallen from heaven, O morning star, son of the dawn! You have been cast down to the earth, you who once laid low the nations! You said in your heart, "I will ascend to heaven; I will raise my throne above the stars of God; I will sit enthroned on the mount of assembly, on the utmost heights of the sacred mountain. I will ascend above the tops of the clouds; I will make myself like the Most High." But you are brought down to the grave, to the depths of the pit.

This is not a prophecy that has already been fulfilled. It is a future end-time prophecy yet to be completed by Satan. John sees and writes about the fulfillment of this prophecy in Revelation 12:12: "But woe to the earth and the sea, because the devil has gone down to you! He is filled with fury, because he knows that his time is short."

The books of Daniel and Revelation simply describe the mysterious details of Satan's plot to delude mankind into believing he is God. Although he will convince many that he is God, the fulfillment of this prophecy is Satan's last-ditch attempt to destroy all of mankind—especially the Jews and the church. Although he will be a wolf in sheep's clothing, he will appear to mankind as an angel of light—a caring, loving, and forgiving messiah.

He accomplishes this goal by first indwelling a man that appears as a terrifying beast to the world. Many will believe this terrifying beast is the Man of Sin, but this person is only a powerful delusion that lures people into Satan's scheme. When Satan destroys this man, the path will be paved for Satan to indwell the "little horn" of Daniel

Introduction

7:8 and appear as a saving messiah to the world. This is the ultimate delusion that God allows to be sent to the entire world—including the church.

With discernment and God-given wisdom, this book reveals what has been, up until now, a perplexing mystery throughout the church age: that powerful delusion God willed in the Book of Truth thousands of years ago, penned on the little angel's scroll, and spoke to John through the seven thunders.

Step by step, we will explore the events leading up to that time when Satan will be able to proclaim, "I am the Christ!" The apostles tell us we should not be in darkness or ignorant of the lying signs and wonders (2 Thess. 2:9) that Satan uses to delude the entire world into believing he is the Messiah.

With God-given discernment, wisdom, and interpretation of Scripture, this book will give startling evidence that Satan's plan to portray himself as God is, surprisingly, no mystery at all.

This book will help you understand all the delusions Satan creates in order to be successful in his bid to portray himself as a loving and caring messiah. We will unravel all prophecies recorded in Daniel, Ezekiel, Isaiah, and Revelation that reveal the events that must take place at the end of the church era.

No generation has had a need to know or understand the dark prophecies uttered by the seven thunders or the bitter message written on the angel's little scroll.

No generation, that is, until now!

CHAPTER 1

UNDERSTANDING GOD'S END-TIME PLAN

Daniel 2:21–22 informs us it is almighty God who "gives wisdom to the wise and knowledge to the discerning. He reveals deep and hidden things."

Daniel was given specific visions of end-time events that play a vital role in the fulfillment of end-time prophecies. We must rely upon God-given discernment of these visions to understand the truth behind God's most powerful delusion: allowing Satan to portray himself as God through the little horn of Daniel 7:8. It is useless to try to understand the deep prophecies recorded in Revelation until we completely understand all of Daniel's visions. His book lays the foundational time line for the structure of Revelation.

UNSEALING DANIEL'S PROPHETIC PARABLES AND VISIONS

God imparted many secrets of the end-times to Daniel, but he was told that a complete understanding of his writings would not come "until the time of the end" (Dan. 12:4).

God revealed deep and hidden things about the end-times to Daniel that were specifically meant to remain that way until the last generation came into existence. Since God Himself must give us understanding—or unseal Daniel—it makes sense that no other generation would discern the deep and hidden things relayed by Daniel. Using several unique writing styles, God purposely sealed the understanding of Daniel's book. God has purposely waited to reveal the understanding of Daniel to us—the last generation! Daniel 12:4 explains that God would reveal the understanding of Daniel during a time when "many will go here and there to increase knowledge." The Internet, developed only in this generation's lifetime, is the method by which many go here and there to increase knowledge.

Although God did not directly seal Revelation, its complete understanding cannot be properly interpreted until God unseals Daniel. The message spoken by the seven thunders and secretly written on the angel's little scroll keeps the full knowledge of God's strong delusion sealed until the time of the end. That's because their message is revealed in the unsealing of Daniel's writings.

Daniel provides the time line by which all end-time Scripture must fit for proper understanding. If a person attempts to establish the length of time it takes to complete the events related by John in Revelation, using Revelation as a foundation, all end-time events become distorted. Attempting to make Daniel's events fit into the wrong time line leads us to be deluded with theories, which are nothing more than man-made myths that attempt to fill in the gaps of undiscerned, misunderstood, and misinterpreted events. This book will do away with all the myths and reveal the meaning of all prophecies that pertain to the events of the end-times. We will correctly unseal Daniel, which will give us complete understanding of Revelation, and discern all the events that lead up to the time when Satan can boastfully exclaim, "I am the Christ!"

FACING THE HOUR OF TRIAL

Why would God choose this moment in mankind's history to unseal Daniel's writings? Why is it critical for this particular generation to properly understand Daniel's message and the book of Revelation?

This generation is the end-time generation. We represent the end-time church—the Laodicea church (Rev. 3:14–22). Just as John relayed the words of Jesus in Revelation 3:17, we have become a

Understanding God's End-Time Plan

generation that has become deluded by our wealth and luxurious lifestyles. We are a church generation that claims to be so wealthy we have need of nothing—not even the truth.

We have become deluded with this attitude. We have allowed the teaching of end-time events to take on a more positive course. The idea of never having our faith tried has sounded pleasing to our itching ears.

Revelation 3:16 stands against this positive-thinking approach. Jesus warns the last church generation that He is going to put us through a time of rebuke and discipline. In parable-like fashion, He describes it as spitting us out of His mouth. In short, we make Him sick! We've mistaken our prosperity as the sole sign of our godliness. We have forgotten that salvation through Jesus Christ results in eternal life and not necessarily untold riches in this lifetime. For all our wealth achieved through positive thinking and prosperity preaching, Jesus sees us as actually being "wretched, pitiful, poor, blind and naked" (Rev. 3:17). These words are used to describe the unsaved!

Essentially, Jesus is telling us that we've become so useless to the kingdom of God that we are virtually on the edge of being cast into hell. But instead of casting us into hell, God's great mercy calls for a different plan to help us realize the truth behind salvation. The clue as to where Jesus spits us is found in the letter John was told to write to the church at Philadelphia. Through proper discernment, we learn that we are spit out to endure an hour of trial that is coming upon the last church generation.

Jesus informed the true believers of the church at Philadelphia that an hour of testing would come upon the entire world. He went on to promise the believers of that church generation that He would keep them from "the hour of trial that is going to come upon the whole world to test those who live on the earth" (Rev. 3:10).

He then proceeded to have John send a letter of rebuke to the end-time church generation represented by the church at Laodicea. Using the concept of juxtaposition, He directly tells one generation of believers they will not have to endure the hour of trial and indirectly tells the last generation what He has planned for them—an hour of trial! He does not promise to keep the Laodicea church generation from the hour of trial. Jesus tells the Laodicea church in Revelation 3:19 that the hour of trial (without directly mentioning it) is a time of discipline. Although He loves us, we are not beyond being rebuked, disciplined, and having our faith tried.

When we discern the reality of Scripture, we must understand that God does nothing without first warning mankind of His intentions. God wants to ensure we understand Daniel and how it serves as a foundational time line for those entering the hour of trial and for the multitude who will come out of the great tribulation after the rapture of the church.

All the strong delusions concerning the time of the end are recorded in the Bible and have been given to His servants the prophets. An angel confirmed this to John in Revelation 10:7. The complete details of God's strong delusion have been with mankind all along, but hidden from our understanding until now, as we near the end of the church age and face the hour of trial.

WHO'S BEING REVEALED?

The Gospels—Matthew, Mark, Luke and John—tell us Jesus was God revealing Himself to mankind. Jesus paid the price of that proclamation with His life on Calvary. As a result, the sins of any believer of His proclamation are forgiven, and they can receive eternal life.

Therefore, neither Daniel nor Revelation reveals God. Daniel 7:8 reveals how the little horn, empowered by Satan, attempts to reveal himself as being God to an unsuspecting and undiscerning generation.

Likewise, John's book is not called Revelation because God has yet to reveal Himself to mankind. Jesus has already accomplished the revealing of God to the world. Instead, John's book supports Daniel's book and is the revelation of how Satan—through the Man of Sin (or little horn of Daniel 7:8)—attempts to reveal himself as being God in the flesh.

According to 2 Thessalonians 2:3–12, this is the strong delusion that mankind—including the church—must still face in the near future.

The revelation of Jesus as God is found in Matthew 16:16 through Peter's exclamation, "You are the Christ, the Son of the living God." Jesus immediately confirms this revelation in verse 17 by proclaiming, "Blessed are you, Simon son of Jonah, for this was not revealed to you by man, but by my Father in heaven."

The Holy Spirit of God revealed Jesus Christ as the Messiah, or God in the flesh, to Peter. Since Jesus' ascension to heaven, the Holy Spirit of God has been convicting people of Peter's revelation for over two thousand years. This is the plan of God's salvation—coming through the person of Jesus Christ. True Christians who have repented of their sin and accepted by faith that Jesus Christ is God find salvation today through the power of the Holy Spirit. When accepted by faith, the revelation of Jesus as God is experienced by the believer and is confirmed by two witnesses: the Word of God (the Gospels) and the Holy Spirit of God (who dwells inside each believer).

This is the power and promise of the gospel, inspired by the Spirit of God and written through the hand of man. When accepted by faith, the Holy Spirit of God immediately reveals that Jesus Christ is God to the hearts and minds of new believers. When they faithfully confess that Jesus Christ is Lord, to the glory of God the Father, each believer is promised eternal life.

Therefore, the revelation of the person of God is not a future event. Since today is the day of salvation, there is no need for a future revelation of God—who is Jesus Christ—to His believers or to mankind as a whole. Essentially, although we have not physically seen Him, we know who God is at the moment we confess our sins and ask Jesus to be Lord of our lives.

Therefore, it is absurd to believe Jesus would have John write about His future revelation. Although John writes about the second coming of Jesus Christ to earth with His saints, the person of God was not some deep hidden mystery to John. John saw God in the flesh—Jesus! John saw God in His glorified, transfigured body—Jesus! John saw God on earth and in heaven in all His glory—Jesus! And so did Daniel.

The title of John's book, Revelation, must be correctly interpreted in the context of Scripture. Revelation 1:1 tells us that God gave Jesus a revelation, meaning "message," concerning the events of the end-times. Jesus gave the message to an angel to give to John. John in turn was told to give it to the world. The message that terrified John—after hearing the seven thunders speak—was the fact that God was going to allow Satan to successfully portray himself as God in the flesh, or as a victorious messiah. John was astonished because people were successfully being deluded by Satan's appearance as a heaven-sent messiah.

The book of Revelation simply provides the last generation the details of how Satan is allowed to pull off this strong delusion of portraying himself as God. It further relates how Satan convinces the world to believe his lie. That's why it is called "Revelation." It is a message from God specifically designed to be discerned and understood by the end-time generation, the true believers of Jesus Christ.

The Bible clearly states God's intent to send the world a strong delusion because the world continues to reject the truth—that Jesus is God. Since God has already sent His Son Jesus, all that's left for God to send is this strong delusion, allowing the son of perdition, or Satan, to come to mankind in such a way that he will appear as a victorious messiah. This delusion is God's wrath on an unbelieving world. Satan's appearance as God in the flesh will be so powerful that Jesus, in Matthew 24, declared even the true believers of His own church, or the elect, could be easily fooled.

In the book of Revelation, Jesus tells about His intention to spit, or cast, the end-time church into the hour of trial. Then He proceeds to give John the details of how mankind becomes deluded into believing Satan is God. The coming of a messiah was portrayed as tasting sweet in John's mouth as he began to read the message of the angel's little scroll. But John soon realized that the little scroll unraveled the mysteries of Daniel's writings. As he digested the scroll, he was astonished as he began to understand this strong delusion sent to the world by God. As John digested the truth and heard the message of the seven thunders, the bitter revelation that Satan was successfully posing as the Messiah made John's stomach turn sour.

THE CONCEPT OF JUXTAPOSITION

Before we study the details of God's strong delusion, we must explain a certain writing style used by Daniel and John. The concept is called *juxtaposition*. It's the placing of future events beside or within the details of a current event, then backing up and telling the details that make the future event a reality.

Juxtaposition is frequently used in movies, books, and stories. Writers begin by first showing an event that leaves the viewer in suspense. For example, the writer may tell of a mysterious murder. After writing about this event, the author goes back in time and shows the events leading up to the mysterious killing. Near the end, the author merges the story together and then goes on to reveal the reason the person was killed and who killed the person. This style of writing is used to add suspense and intrigue.

The movie *Forrest Gump* is an excellent example of juxtaposition. The movie begins by showing Forrest sitting on a bench. That's the first five minutes of the movie. The next hour and a half, Forrest proceeds to tell the events that led up to his sitting on the bench. Near the end of the movie, we're brought back to the same scene we saw at the beginning of the movie, Forrest sitting on the bench. At this time, we find that it is a bus bench, and Forrest is waiting for the bus so he can meet with Jenny. From that point on, the mystery of the plot is revealed, and then the movie ends.

Daniel uses this concept in chapters 2 and 11. John uses this concept in chapter 3 of Revelation, as well as in chapters 7, 12, and 14. Mankind's inability to discern the use of this style of writing is how God has kept the understanding of both books and end-time events surrounding His strong delusion sealed from previous generations. Now that He has decided to impart this wisdom to us in this book, we can begin to unravel the details of God's mystery.

THE KINGDOM DIVIDES

In chapter 2, Daniel describes five kingdoms—Babylon, Media, Persia, Greece, and Rome—that would dominate the world up to and including the time Jesus walked on earth. Daniel then jumps forward in time to briefly describe an end-time kingdom that will attempt to dominate the world just prior to the beginning of the hour of trial—a kingdom of iron and clay. After indicating this kingdom would not hold together, Daniel concludes chapter 2 by showing how Jesus destroys this end-time kingdom when He returns to earth.

If this were a movie, the camera would fade to black. That's because Daniel is using the concept of juxtaposition at the end of chapter 2. Once Daniel has shown this end-time kingdom being destroyed, from chapter 3 through the rest of his book, Daniel writes exclusively about the future end-time events leading up to Satan posing as the Messiah (through the little horn of Daniel 7:8). Here is where the misunderstanding of Daniel begins. Previous generations have missed Daniel's placing of a future event within the context of describing past events, only to back up and use his life's circumstances as parables to describe the road to that future event.

Daniel shows the second coming of Jesus Christ at the end of chapter 2. Immediately in chapter 3, he begins to describe, via parables and visions, the details of how this end-time kingdom forms and then splits apart. Writing chapters 3 through 6 as parables, Daniel proceeds to relate the same message John was told to relate by Jesus in the last book of the Bible. Daniel reveals the strong delusion God is going to send to the world before Jesus returns. Now that we understand how this concept works in Scripture, we can proceed by understanding the timing of Daniel's parables against the events of Revelation. Once this is discerned, we will be able to unfold the events in Revelation chronologically over a ten-year period of time, not seven years as has been falsely taught. I will prove throughout this book that the events described by John in Revelation cover a ten-year period of time.

To start, let's take a short overview of the book of Daniel. The deeper details of each parable will be unfolded later as needed when we unravel the web of intrigue and mystery in the book of Revelation.

THE FIRE OF HEAVEN'S SALVATION

In Daniel 3, we see where Daniel's friends, Shadrach, Meshach, and Abednego, are thrown into a fiery furnace for refusing to worship the statue of the pagan king Nebuchadnezzar, king of Babylon. We will find that this chapter tells us much about the 144,000 sons of Israel in Revelation 7, when it appears as though they are destroyed by the Man of Sin when he calls fire down from heaven for their failing to worship him as God. Chapter 3 of Daniel is a parable of an end-time event.

BOUND BY IRON AND BRONZE

In chapter 4, Daniel writes another prophetic end-time parable. He uses the ancient kingdom of Babylon to represent a specific end-time nation. Daniel begins the description of this end-time nation by interpreting a dream about a tree that grows large and strong and touches the sky. God blesses this end-time nation in the same way He raised up ancient Babylon. The nation represented by the tree is America.

In the course of his parable, Daniel relates how America becomes entangled in Satan's evil scheme. Daniel tells us that America falls for Satan's delusion; that is, the tree is cut down. The tree's stump becomes bound by iron and bronze. This is a representation of America becoming bound to two different end-time kingdoms—one of iron and the other of bronze—both of which are under the control of Satan. Becoming bound means to join in alliance or agreement with these kingdoms.

This parable is a continuation of showing how the last kingdom described in chapter 2 splits apart, forming two different kingdoms. One kingdom will become known as the iron kingdom. The nations of clay that break away from this iron kingdom will form an alliance that will become known as the bronze kingdom.

Both kingdoms are evil. The king of the iron kingdom will serve as a terrifying beast to the world and delude the world into believing he is the Man of Sin, although he is not. Once the world is convinced of this delusion, Satan can destroy this king in his own bid to establish himself as the Messiah through the real Man of Sin, or the little horn of Daniel 7:8. By accomplishing this powerful delusion, Satan's real Man of Sin, or the little horn of Daniel 7:8, is allowed to appear as a victorious messiah, having destroyed the man everyone believes is the Man of Sin. God sends this powerful delusion to test the people of the world.

THE SECRET POWER OF LAWLESSNESS

Before Satan can appear to the world as being God in the flesh, he has to discredit everything God has already done in the person of Jesus Christ. Until now, Satan has been unsuccessful in discrediting Jesus' first coming to earth to offer forgiveness for sin. If, however, Satan can rise to power by appearing as a messiah, he believes he can then successfully convince mankind that Jesus was no more than a strong delusion.

This is Satan's ultimate goal during the end-times. He wants to convince mankind that he is the Messiah. This requires him to offer some kind of physical salvation, knowing it will eternally destroy those who accept. To be successful, he has to discredit Jesus' first coming. He also has to negate Jesus' second coming as well. To be successful, Satan must delude mankind into believing he has overpowered and destroyed the Man of Sin (portrayed by the terrifying beast). If he can convince mankind that the beast of Revelation has been destroyed, the way is paved for Satan to then appear as a victorious messiah.

To achieve his ultimate goal of destroying all of mankind, Satan begins his bid by establishing the person he wants everyone to believe is the Man of Sin. As verified by John in Revelation 13:2, Satan temporarily gives his evil authority and power to the upcoming king of the iron kingdom, having him appear to the world as being the devil, or the beast of Revelation.

When Satan destroys this king, he sets up his bronze kingdom or the kingdom of the Man of Sin, referenced by John in Revelation 13:3 as a beast whose fatal wound had been healed. This would be the kingdom of the little horn of Daniel 7:8. In these two verses, John transitions from one king (the terrifying beast of Daniel 7:7) to another king (the little horn of Daniel 7:8 who has suffered a wound but has been healed). It is through this second king that Satan will successfully appear as God revealing Himself to mankind for the first and only time. When he accomplishes this goal, Satan will then convince mankind that Jesus, in accordance with Scripture, was no more than a strong delusion that he sent to the world. This then opens the door for Satan, posing as God, to destroy all those people (or Christians within the church) who have believed the supposed lie that Jesus was God.

In Matthew 24:23–25, Jesus forewarns us not to fall for the powerful delusion that Satan creates:

> At that time if anyone says to you, "Look, here is the Christ!" or, "There he is!" do not believe it. For false Christs and false prophets will appear and perform great signs and miracles to deceive even the elect—if that were possible. See, I have told you ahead of time.

Second Thessalonians 2:6–12 reveals that Satan must precede himself by the king of the iron kingdom (from here on referred to as the king of the North in accordance with Daniel 11). People must be convinced that the terrifying beast of Daniel 7:7, or king of the North, is the Man of Sin before they can be deluded into believing Satan, through the little of horn of Daniel 7:8, is God.

The king of the North's rise to power and appearance as being the Man of Sin must take place before Satan can possess the little horn of Daniel 7:8 and appear to the world as the Messiah. The king of the North is the secret power of lawlessness that is already at work in accordance with 2 Thessalonians 2:7. His rise to power is what's holding Satan back. It's not the Holy Spirit of God, living in each true believer of Jesus Christ, who holds Satan back from attempting to reveal himself as the Messiah. It's the king of the North's rise to power and subsequent delusion as appearing to be the Man of Sin that actually holds Satan back from appearing to the world as the messiah through the little horn of Daniel 7:8. Within the context of the following scriptures, all explanations in brackets and all emphases are mine.

2 Thessalonians 2:6: And now you know what is holding him [Satan] back, so that he may be revealed [as God] at the proper time.

2 Thessalonians 2:7: For the secret power of lawlessness is already at work [Satan's waiting for the king of the North to delude the world into believing he is the Man of Sin]; but the one [king of the North] who now holds it back [Satan's appearance as God] will continue to do so till he [king of the North] is taken out of the way [destroyed by Satan during the sixth trumpet war described by John in Revelation so Satan can appear to the world as a victorious messiah coming to redeem mankind].

2 Thessalonians 2:8: And then the lawless one will be revealed [Satan, through the little horn of Daniel 7:8, appears to the world as being God; thus the title of John's book, Revelation], whom the Lord Jesus will overthrow with the breath of his mouth and destroy by the splendor of his coming.

2 Thessalonians 2:9–10: *The coming of the lawless one [Satan's appearance as being the Messiah through the little horn of Daniel 7:8] will be in accordance with the work of Satan* displayed in all kinds of counterfeit miracles, signs and wonders [crediting the rapture as him destroying those who supposedly believed the lie that Jesus was God], and in every sort of evil [offering wealth in exchange for taking physical salvation for sin—known as the "mark of the beast"] that deceives those who are perishing.

2 Thessalonians 2:10: They perish because they refused to love the truth [Jesus is God] and so be saved.

2 Thessalonians 2:11–12: For this reason God sends them a powerful delusion [Satan appearing as God through the little horn of Daniel 7:8] so that they will believe the lie and so that all will be condemned who have not believed the truth but have delighted in wickedness.

When Satan appears as God, he will attempt to falsely copy God's method of salvation. He disguises his deadly mark of the beast as an offer of physical salvation. In this way, Satan appears to offer redemption in such a way that it won't appear to be a deadly mark, but instead, a gift of eternal life from God. To further cloud the issue, Satan will offer tremendous wealth to everyone who accepts his offer of salvation. However, since God has already offered us salvation through His Son, Jesus Christ, we should immediately discern that if someone comes to us claiming to be God and offering us salvation or forgiveness for sin, he is a beast and not God.

In order that the king of the North will appear as being the Man of Sin, Satan will have this man create an illusion. He will implement what everyone will believe is the mark of the beast. His so-called mark, using computer chips and bar codes or some such thing, is merely another strong delusion used to create fear and panic, especially in the church. Satan will use this ploy to divide the people of God.

Therefore, it is important, even as Christians, to understand how we are currently marked for salvation by God when we accept Jesus Christ as our personal Savior. We also need to fully understand the tactics Satan will use to convince the world that the king of the iron kingdom (king of the North) is the Man of Sin and how his false mark is used as an illusion to divide the people of God. Finally, we need to understand and comprehend the real mark of the beast and how Satan subtly disguises it as an offer of salvation in his bid to destroy the eternal destiny of anyone who accepts his offer, as well as destroy those who refuse. And in the course of this book, we will gain understanding in great detail of all these ploys of Satan.

THE WRITING ON THE WALL

Daniel 5 portrays a parable of the time when Satan, through his Man of Sin, or little horn of Daniel 7:8, comes to power and occupies the rebuilt temple in Jerusalem. This parable represents the "abomination that causes desolation" foretold by Jesus in Matthew 24:15. Amazingly, Daniel portrays this abomination that causes desolation as a great dinner reception. The reality of this parable is the fact that when Satan sits in the temple of God and proclaims to be God, he will pass it off as the wedding supper of the Lamb.

In response to the second coming of Jesus Christ, an angel instructed John to write in Revelation 19:9, "Blessed are those who are invited to the wedding supper of the Lamb!" Satan, in his bid to appear as the victorious Messiah, must duplicate this event. By doing so, Satan hopes people won't discern that what is truly taking place is the abomination that causes desolation. Just as Daniel shows Belshazzar desecrating the temple ornaments as an act of defiance, so Satan will desecrate the rebuilt temple of God, blaspheming God by proclaiming to be God. Second Thessalonians 2:3–4 confirms the delusion Satan creates when he sits on the Mount of Assembly, or in the temple in Jerusalem, and proclaims to be God in the flesh:

2 Thessalonians 2:3: Don't let anyone deceive you in any way, for that day [the day of the rapture] will not come until the rebellion occurs [Satan, through the little horn of Daniel 7:8, destroys the king of the North] and the man of lawlessness [or Satan, through the little horn of Daniel 7:8] is revealed [as being God], the man doomed to destruction [Jesus throws the Man of Sin into the lake of fire]. (Explanations in brackets are mine.)

2 Thessalonians 2:4: He [Satan, through the little horn of Daniel 7:8] will oppose [the king of the North] and will exalt himself over everything that is called God [Jesus] or is worshiped [for the Jews, God], so that he [Satan, through the little horn of Daniel 7:8] sets himself up in God's temple, proclaiming himself to be God [portraying his abomination that causes desolation as the wedding supper of the Lamb]. (Explanations in brackets are mine.)

God allows Satan to rule the world through the Man of Sin, or little horn of Daniel 7:8, for about three years before Jesus actually returns and throws him alive into the lake of fire. Jesus forewarns us about the time of Satan's rule in Matthew 24:21–22:

For then there will be great distress, unequaled from the beginning of the world until now—and never to be equaled again. If those days had not been cut short, no one would survive, but for the sake of the elect those days will be shortened.

In this passage, Jesus is not saying that it will be a time of distress for those who fall for Satan's delusion. For Satan's followers, it will be a time of tremendous peace and prosperity. In this passage, Jesus is speaking to the true believers of the church who are spit out to endure this time of testing, as well as to the Jews who will refuse to recognize and acknowledge the little horn of Daniel 7:8 as being God. For true believers, Jesus promises to shorten their time of exposure to this strong delusion. Later we'll see where Daniel was given the method for calculating the day of the rapture for all believers who are still alive when Satan possesses the little horn and portrays himself as being God. Daniel's portrayal of the writing on the wall is no more than a subtle message to those Christians who are still alive when this man reveals himself as being God that their time of trial is almost over.

THE LION'S DEN

Daniel 6 describes a time when he is thrown into a lion's den. Miraculously God shuts the mouth of the lion, thereby saving Daniel, a Jew whom God esteemed. This chapter is the last of Daniel's parables. He describes a time near the end of the age when Satan uses a certain end-time nation as a lion's den to destroy the people of God—Jews and those who refuse his twisted offer of salvation, otherwise known as the mark of the beast. We will see that this nation corresponds to the nation described in Revelation 17 and 18. Not only will we examine this in detail, but we will also see that this nation already exists today. It is the same nation Daniel saw in chapter 4 that had become bound by iron and bronze. That nation today is America.

THE END-TIME KINGDOMS

In chapter 7, Daniel begins to unfold the plot of this strong delusion by describing the main characters Satan will need to be successful in his bid to portray himself as God. These main characters are represented as nations that only the last generation will see materialize in the course of their lifetime. The formation of these nations and kingdoms precedes Satan appearing as the Messiah, a representation that copies the five kingdoms that preceded the first coming of Jesus Christ. We will discover that these four kingdoms of Daniel correspond precisely with the four riders on horses in Revelation.

TIMING IS ESSENTIAL

Daniel 8 and 9 provide the crucial details needed to understand how the end-time events described by John in Revelation take ten-years to complete. Daniel's account begins when a question is posed in Daniel 8:13:

> How long will it take for the vision to be fulfilled—the vision concerning the daily sacrifice [stopped by the king of the North], the rebellion that causes desolation [accomplished by Satan through the Man of Sin, or little horn, when he destroys the king of the North at what many will believe is the battle of Armageddon], and the surrender of the sanctuary [Satan sits in the temple and proclaims to be God] and of the host that will be trampled underfoot [those who are killed during the time of great distress for refusing to accept Satan's false mark of salvation]? (Explanations in brackets are mine.)

The understanding of the time required begins to be unraveled in Daniel 8:14 by showing us that we have to begin with the end in mind:

> It will take 2,300 evenings and mornings; then the sanctuary will be reconsecrated.

Combining the question with the answer tells us that from the time the king of the North stops the daily sacrifice from taking place on the Temple Mount, 2,300 days remain until Jesus returns and takes possession of the temple. That's 220 days short of seven years (which later I will show is very significant). Considering that 2,300 days is only 6.3 years, how can we surmise that the end-time period covering the king of the North's reign of terror and the Man of Sin's appearance and reign as the Messiah covers a period of ten-years? How do we get the other 3.6 years? The clue is given in Daniel 9:27:

He will confirm a covenant with many for one "seven." In the middle of the "seven" he will put an end to sacrifice and offering.

About three and one-half years after he confirms a covenant with many, the king of the North will stop the daily sacrifice from taking place on the Temple Mount. From that day, there remains 2,300 days, or about 6.3 years, until Jesus returns and reconsecrates the temple. Since 3.6 years go by from the time he confirms a covenant with many and then stops the sacrifice, we can now understand why Gabriel chose his words very carefully. The sacrifice is not stopped exactly in the middle of the first seven years of Daniel's ten-year end-time period. It's actually stopped at about three years and seven months. That gives us a total of approximately ten-years for the fulfillment of all end-time events described in Revelation.

The last seven years of this ten-year period start Daniel's seventieth week, or the tribulation period. This last seven-year span is split into two parts. The first half of this last seven-year period is the hour of trial, when the king of the North appears as supposedly being the Man of Sin. This is the period that Jesus proclaimed He was going to spit the church into. The last half of this seven-year period is the time of the great tribulation, when Satan deludes the world into believing he is God, through the little horn of Daniel 7:8.

The delusion of this entire prophecy is incredibly precise and very intricate. The first seven years of this ten-year end-time period will appear to most people as being the tribulation period, bringing to power the king of the North and Satan destroying him. There will be an enormous war, giving the appearance that Armageddon is being fought and the Messiah arriving. Satan's reign, although he appears as a victorious messiah, actually becomes a time of great distress for those who are left behind after the rapture. Figure 1-1 shows an overview of these prophecies.

Satan will accomplish three goals through this deceptive scheme:

- It will appear as if the Man of Sin (as portrayed by the king of the North) is destroyed when Satan poses as God (through the little horn of Daniel 7:8).

- He will be able to sit in God's temple in Jerusalem (on the Mount of Assembly) and proclaim to be like the Most High.
- He discredits Jesus' first coming as a mere delusion that he, now portraying himself as God, sent to mankind two thousand years ago. Doing this allows him to negate the fact that Jesus has yet to return.

Accomplishing these three delusions is critical in convincing the world that God is now supposedly dwelling with mankind here on earth—for the first and only time!

YEARS FOR END-TIME PERIOD

0 1 2 3 4 5 6 7 8 9 10

APPEARS AS IF IT IS DANIEL'S 70th WEEK

KING OF THE NORTH CONFIRMS COVENANT WITH MANY FOR ONE SEVEN (DAN. 9:27)

TEMPLE DESOLATIONS (DAN. 9:26)

2,300 DAYS (DAN. 8:13–14)

KING OF THE NORTH ABOLISHES SACRIFICE IN THE MIDDLE OF THE FIRST SEVEN YEARS (DAN. 9:27; 11:31–32) THE WORLD WILL BELIEVE HE IS THE MAN OF SIN

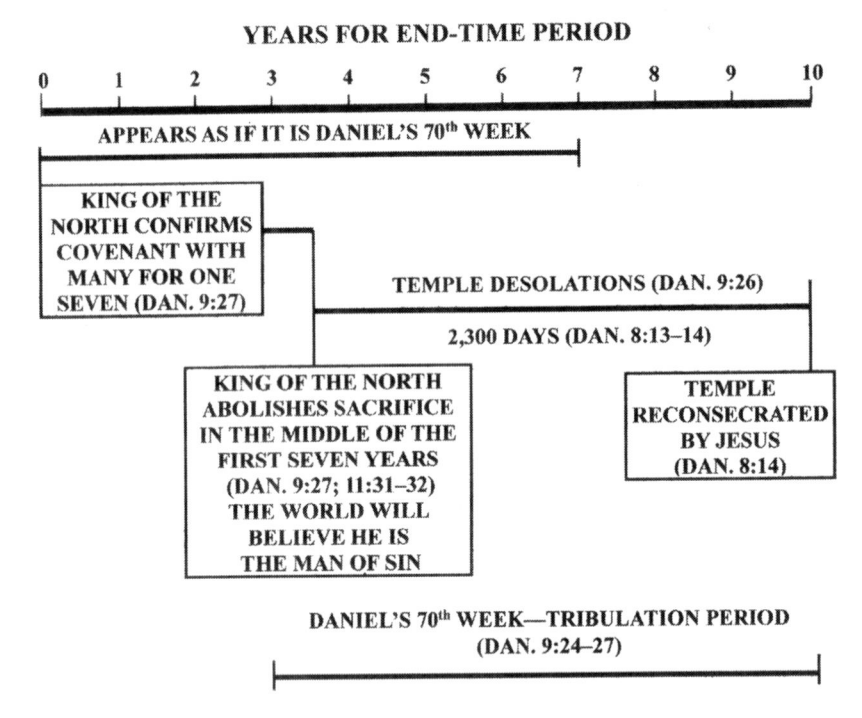

TEMPLE RECONSECRATED BY JESUS (DAN. 8:14)

DANIEL'S 70th WEEK—TRIBULATION PERIOD (DAN. 9:24–27)

FIGURE 1-1. DANIEL ESTABLISHES THE TEN-YEAR END-TIME PERIOD

CHAPTER 2

OPENING THE SEVEN SEALS

In John 16:33, we hear Jesus encourage His disciples: "I have told you these things, so that in me you may have peace. In this world you will have trouble. But take heart! I have overcome the world."

How fitting it was for John to record these words in his gospel of Jesus Christ. John was later chosen by Jesus to receive an escorted tour of heaven and our modern world and asked to write the end-time events.

How Jesus overcame the world from the cross is partly what John's book Revelation is all about. However, before Jesus returns to be King of Kings and Lord of Lords, we must discern the strong delusion that John records in Revelation—the message that Jesus gave to John concerning the time when Satan attempts to convince the world that he is God coming to redeem mankind.

Revelation covers the last ten-years preceding the second coming of Jesus Christ. Daniel established this time period. The seal judgments occur during the transition period, that period of time between the "last days" and the "beginning of sorrows." This period of time will be a time of wars and rumors of wars as the king of the North and the little horn of Daniel 7:8, henceforth called the king of the South, battle for world dominion. This time will ultimately bring to power the king of the North, the man Satan wants the world to believe is the Man of Sin.

The trumpet judgments occur during the hour of trial and ultimately bring to power the real Man of Sin, or the little horn of Daniel 7:8. The bowls of God's wrath occur at the very end of the great tribulation period when Jesus returns as King of Kings and Lord of Lords.

The last seven years of this ten-year period is Daniel's seventieth week, or the tribulation period. The first half of this tribulation period is known as the hour of trial (Rev. 3:10). The last half is known as great tribulation (Matt. 24:21). Figure 2-1 provides an overview of these different time periods.

Before Satan can attempt to appear to the world as God, he must precede himself with a person many will believe is the Man of Sin. Once Satan destroys this terrifying beast (noted by John in Revelation 13-1), Satan can appear as a victorious messiah (the man with the healed head wound as recorded by John in Rev. 13-2). In this chapter, we will study the rise of the terrifying beast, as recorded in Daniel 7:7, and known as the king of the North in Daniel 11:25-45.

A KINGDOM DIVIDED CANNOT STAND

Daniel 2:33: . . . its feet partly of iron and partly of baked clay.

Daniel 2:41–43: Just as you saw that the feet and toes were partly of baked clay and partly of iron, so this will be a divided kingdom; yet it will have some of the strength of iron in it, even as you saw iron mixed with clay. As the toes were partly iron and partly clay, so this kingdom will be partly strong and partly brittle. And just as you saw the iron mixed with baked clay, so the people will be a mixture and will not remain united, any more than iron mixes with clay.

A careful study of Daniel and Revelation reveals the rise of two different beasts during the end-times. The king of the North exalts himself. And the False Prophet exalts the Man of Sin, or little horn of Daniel 7:8. Why this difference?

Right now it is the Holy Spirit's responsibility to exalt God. He does this in many ways, too numerous to mention here. But Satan must imitate this same exaltation in order to have credibility and be able to quote Scripture. Satan will use the Word of God against the people of the world when he appears as the Messiah. Satan double-crosses the king of the North, specifically switching from a king of terror to a loving, kind, and caring king. This switch will lend credibility to Satan's claim that he is God.

YEARS FOR END-TIME PERIOD

```
0    1    2    3    4    5    6    7    8    9    10
```

APPEARS AS IF IT IS DANIEL'S 70th WEEK

KING OF THE NORTH CONFIRMS COVENANT WITH MANY FOR ONE SEVEN (DAN. 9:27)

TEMPLE DESOLATIONS (DAN. 9:26)

2,300 DAYS (DAN. 8:13–14)

KING OF THE NORTH ABOLISHES SACRIFICE IN THE MIDDLE OF THE FIRST SEVEN YEARS (DAN. 9:27; 11:31–32) THE WORLD WILL BELIEVE HE IS THE MAN OF SIN

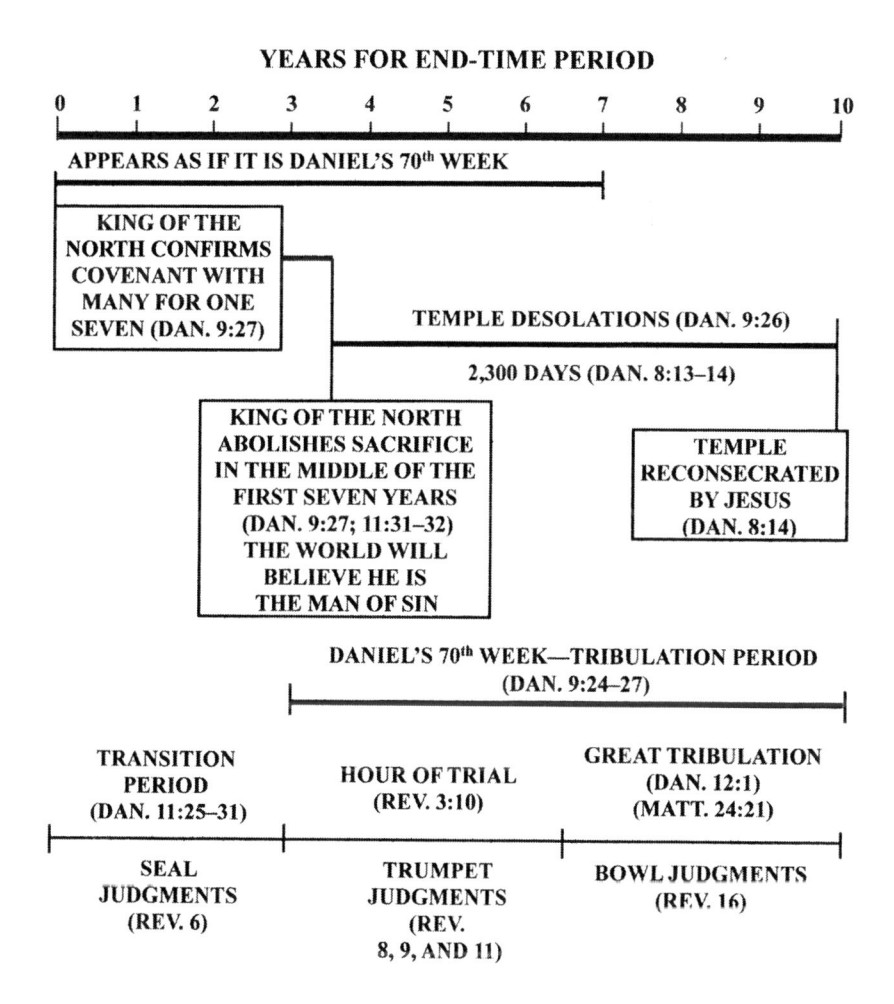

TEMPLE RECONSECRATED BY JESUS (DAN. 8:14)

DANIEL'S 70th WEEK—TRIBULATION PERIOD (DAN. 9:24–27)

TRANSITION PERIOD (DAN. 11:25–31)	HOUR OF TRIAL (REV. 3:10)	GREAT TRIBULATION (DAN. 12:1) (MATT. 24:21)
SEAL JUDGMENTS (REV. 6)	TRUMPET JUDGMENTS (REV. 8, 9, AND 11)	BOWL JUDGMENTS (REV. 16)

FIGURE 2-1. JOHN USES DANIEL'S ESTABLISHED TEN-YEAR END-TIME PERIOD TO CONSTRUCT REVELATION

The foundation for this strong delusion has been laid slowly during this last generation's lifetime. The king of the North's iron kingdom is the fourth end-time beast Daniel sees in chapter 7. It is arising from the current efforts to form a European Union. Although we've watched this alliance slowly merge, it will not hold together, even as an economic alliance. As Daniel confirms in chapter 11, the king of the North makes up the iron of this union of nations, and the king of the South becomes the clay that creates division in Europe.

We will see how Satan ensures the king of the North is successful over the king of the South and rises to become a terrifying beast. His acts of terror are designed to make the world believe he is the Man of Sin. However, we will see where his duration as a beast will last for only a little while. John received confirmation of this fact from an angel in Revelation 17:10.

PRINCE OF THE COVENANT

Daniel 7:7: After that, in my vision at night I looked, and there before me was a fourth beast —terrifying and frightening and very powerful. It had large iron teeth; it crushed and devoured its victims and trampled underfoot whatever was left. It was different from all the former beasts, and it had ten horns.

Daniel 7:19: Then I wanted to know the true meaning of the fourth beast, which was different from all the others and most terrifying, with its iron teeth and bronze claws—the beast that crushed and devoured its victims and trampled underfoot whatever was left.

Daniel 7:20: I also wanted to know about the ten horns on its head and about the other horn that came up, before which three of them fell—the horn that looked more imposing than the others and that had eyes and a mouth that spoke boastfully.

Daniel 7:23–24: He gave me this explanation: "The fourth beast is a fourth kingdom that will appear on earth. It will be different from all the other kingdoms and will devour the whole earth, trampling it down and crushing it. The ten horns are ten kings who will come from this kingdom. After them another king will arise, different from the earlier ones; he will subdue three kings."

After Daniel is shown that Europe divides, he's then given a clear picture of the king of the North rising to power. The king of the North will wreak havoc on the world scene for the first seven years of the ten-year end-time period. In chapter 11, Daniel describes the battles that occur between the king of the North and the king of the South and how the king of the North is successful over the king of the South.

However, Daniel 7:20 reveals that at the end of this seven-year period, there rises yet another king, described in Daniel 7:8 as a "little horn," who is the real Man of Sin. We will study more about the Man of Sin's rebellion and revelation in the next chapter. We begin our study of end-time events by focusing our attention on the king of the North (KON), who plays an evil role in Satan's plan to delude mankind.

KON CONFIRMS A COVENANT WITH MANY FOR ONE "SEVEN"

Daniel 9:26: The people of the ruler who will come will destroy the city and the sanctuary. The end will come like a flood: War will continue until the end, and desolations have been decreed. He will confirm a covenant with many for one "seven." In the middle of the "seven" he will put an end to sacrifice and offering. And on a wing of the temple, he will set up an abomination that causes desolation, until the end that is decreed is poured out on him.

Let's take the interpretation of this passage one line at a time. The ruler who will come is the king of the North, and the people are the ten nations that compose his kingdom. The king of the North will war against the king of the South immediately after the king of the South divides the current makeup of the European Union. War will continue for the first seven years of this ten-year end-time period.

Before this ten-year end-time period begins, the king of the North will confirm a covenant with many. In the middle of the first seven years of this ten-year end-time period, he will overrun the king of the South and push his armed forces into the Middle East. He will invade Israel and be the first king to desolate the rebuilt temple in Jerusalem. This is the first desolation. Daniel 9:26 proves there is more than one temple desolation. Daniel uses the plural form, *desolations*.

In chapter 2, Daniel envisioned five kingdoms rising to power preceding the first coming of Jesus Christ. In chapter 7, Daniel envisions five kingdoms preceding the second coming of Jesus Christ. Daniel describes each kingdom in such a way that they can be recognized only by the end-time generation. Daniel then gives a future end-time prophecy about each kingdom.

THE LION NATION

DANIEL 7:4: The first was like a lion, and it had the wings of an eagle. I watched until its wings were torn off and it was lifted from the ground so that it stood on two feet like a man, and the heart of a man was given to it.

America is recognized as the lion kingdom by virtue that Daniel represented us as having the wings of an eagle. Although America was originally founded on the concept that all citizens have the right to religious freedom, Daniel shows how America eventually takes away this right from the people, by relating that it is given a heart like a man. The reality of this prophecy is the fact that America will eventually force all citizens to worship the Man of Sin, believing he is God. Thus, the heart of a man, or the Man of Sin, is given to it.

America already has aligned itself militarily with the iron kingdom of Daniel 7:7, which will give birth to the king of the North. Although the United States is not one of his ten nations, we will continue to maintain a military alliance with the king of the North. We will maintain our own Constitution and religious freedom under the reign of the king of the North. But we will relinquish both when the Man of Sin destroys the king of the North and comes to dominate the world, appearing as the Messiah.

THE BEAR NATION

DANIEL 7:5: And there before me was a second beast, which looked like a bear. It was raised up on one of its sides, and it had three ribs in its mouth between its teeth. It was told, "Get up and eat your fill of flesh!"

In 1917, Russia came to be a prominent kingdom, the bear kingdom. Daniel sees it rise up and destroy many people. This is the Russian invasion of Israel as prophesied by Ezekiel in chapters 38 and 39. We will reveal all the great details surrounding this event later in this book.

THE LEOPARD KINGDOM

DANIEL 7:6: After that, I looked, and there before me was another beast, one that looked like a leopard. And on its back it had four wings like those of a bird. This beast had four heads, and it was given authority to rule.

Still to rise on the world scene is the king of the South and his leopard kingdom. It is not in existence as of this writing. But when it does come, it will create division in the current makeup of the European Union. Daniel 11:25–32 describes the battles between the king of the South (who heads this leopard kingdom) and the king of the North (who heads the iron kingdom of Daniel 7:7). Daniel describes this new alliance of nations as a leopard because of its mystique and because it rises on the world scene very quickly.

THE TERRIFYING BEAST

DANIEL 7:7: After that, in my vision at night I looked, and there before me was a fourth beast—terrifying and frightening and very powerful. It had large iron teeth; it crushed and devoured its victims and trampled underfoot whatever was left. It was different from all the former beasts, and it had ten horns.

DANIEL 7:8: While I was thinking about the horns, there before me was another horn, a little one, which came up among them; and three of the first horns were uprooted before it. This horn had eyes like the eyes of a man and a mouth that spoke boastfully.

All the former beasts—the lion, bear, and leopard kingdoms—will be affected by the fourth kingdom in Daniel 7:7, the iron kingdom of the king of the North. The sole purpose of the king of the North is to give the appearance that he is the Man of Sin. Satan will give this man the authority to temporarily rule the world—through terror. This way, he appears as supposedly being the devil to an unsuspecting world.

But Daniel doesn't stop with the rise of this king. Daniel confirms to us that there is still one more king—a "little horn"—who dominates the world scene after the king of the North. We will study more about this little horn, the real Man of Sin, in the next chapter.

In all, Daniel envisions five kingdoms: America, Russia, the king of the South's leopard kingdom, the iron kingdom of the king of the North, and the kingdom of the Man of Sin or little horn. All are end-time kingdoms that encircle their powers in and around the Mediterranean Sea. Daniel saw them coming out of the sea. Daniel's vision is verified in Revelation 13:1, when John accurately sees the king of the North come up out of the sea, having feet like a bear, the body of a leopard, and a mouth like a lion.

JOHN ENVISIONS THE SAME END-TIME KINGDOMS

In Revelation, John begins his tour of the end-times by verifying the accuracy of Daniel's visions of the first four end-time kingdoms. However, John visualizes these first four kingdoms as riders on horses.

THE RIDER ON THE WHITE HORSE

Revelation 6:1–2: I watched as the Lamb opened the first of the seven seals. Then I heard one of the four living creatures say in a voice like thunder, "Come!" I looked, and there before me was a white horse! Its rider held a bow, and he was given a crown, and he rode out as a conqueror bent on conquest.

The rider on this horse is the king of the South and his leopard kingdom. His kingdom is represented in Daniel 2:41 as the clay that separates itself from the iron kingdom. Just prior to this ten-year end-time period, the king of the South will quickly rise to power. He becomes enemy number one for the king of the North and the European Union. Although we've seen the rise of the lion and the bear kingdoms, as well as the slow formation of the iron kingdom, we have yet to see the rise of the king of the South's leopard kingdom.

Once the king of the South forms an alliance that separates Europe, he will spend the entire transition period fighting off the reunification efforts of the king of the North. Near the end of the transition period, the king of the North will finally be victorious in reuniting Europe—or so he will falsely believe.

John verifies the reunification of Europe by showing this beast, or the king of the North, coming out of the sea, with seven heads and ten horns. Daniel previously saw him as having only ten horns. Now John sees that he rules over the seven heads composing the king of the South's leopard kingdom, as well as the ten horns or nations that originally maintained its alliance with the king of the North.

THE RIDER ON THE RED HORSE

Revelation 6:3–4: When the Lamb opened the second seal, I heard the second living creature say, "Come!" Then another horse came out, a fiery red one. Its rider was given power to take peace from the earth and to make men slay each other. To him was given a large sword.

The rider on this horse is the king of the North. John further describes the civil war between the king of the North and the king of the South as told in Daniel 11:25:

> With a large army he [the king of the North] will stir up his strength and courage against the king of the South. The king of

the South will wage war with a large and very powerful army, but he will not be able to stand because of the plots devised against him. (Explanations in brackets are mine.)

Although the rider on the white horse, the king of the South, divides Europe, it is the rider on this red horse, the king of the North, who is given power to take peace from the earth. Daniel 11:25-45 shows the king of the North's continuous struggle for world dominion by reuniting Europe so he can establish himself as appearing to be the Man of Sin.

Daniel fully supports John's claim in Revelation 6:2 that the king of the South has a bow, but no arrows. In other words, John tells us the king of the South is not militarily strong like the king of the North. Although he holds a bow, there is no indication that he uses any arrows. This means that he'll have an army of ground forces, but he won't have an air force or missile fleet. In prophecy, the word *bow* represents an army. Arrows represent an air force or missile fleet.

Furthermore, it is the large sword that is given to the king of the North that results in his final victory in reuniting Europe. That large sword is American armed forces that are aligned with Europe.

THE RIDER ON THE BLACK HORSE

Revelation 6:5–6: When the Lamb opened the third seal, I heard the third living creature say, "Come!" I looked, and there before me was a black horse! Its rider was holding a pair of scales in his hand. Then I heard what sounded like a voice among the four living creatures, saying, "A quart of wheat for a day's wages, and three quarts of barley for a day's wages, and do not damage the oil and the wine!"

The rider on this horse represents America, the world's most prosperous and most powerful nation in the history of mankind. This horse correlates to the lion beast of Daniel 7:4. When civil war breaks out in Europe, America will experience triple-digit inflation. The European war will prove to be an economic disaster compared with the recent time of prosperity experienced by the United States.

While war is raging in Europe and tensions begin flaring up in the Middle East, the United States will issue a strong warning to other nations of the world to keep away from attempting to damage the world's oil supplies, truly the intoxicating wine, or source, of our twentieth- and twenty-first-century luxuries. Do not be deceived. Oil is America's primary interest in the Middle East. John reveals the true heart and soul of America: the protection of our luxurious lifestyle, based on the continuous supply of a single economic resource. In the span of a single generation, the oil America receives from the Middle East and through European refineries intoxicates the other kingdoms of the world (Rev. 17:2). As we learned in the early 1970s, America stops without a tremendous amount of oil flowing into its borders.

THE RIDER ON THE PALE HORSE

Revelation 6:7–8: When the Lamb opened the fourth seal, I heard the voice of the fourth living creature say, "Come!" I looked, and there before me was a pale horse! Its rider was named Death, and Hades was following close behind him. They were given power over a fourth of the earth to kill by sword, famine and plague, and by the wild beasts of the earth.

The rider on this horse is Russia, the bear beast of Daniel 7:5. John describes world conditions near the end of the transition period. With the civil war raging in Europe, the king of the North takes his first action against the holy covenant, as Daniel 11:28 confirms. He secretly convinces Russia to invade and loot Israel, a land of "unwalled villages," as prophesied in Ezekiel 38:11.

It's interesting to note that John sees Hades riding close behind Death. Hades, or hell, is the place where the souls of unbelievers are held pending the great white throne judgment. Just as Jesus predicted, the gospel will be preached around the world during the transition period. But many will still refuse to believe and accept Jesus Christ as their Lord and Savior. Many Third World countries forbid the preaching of Jesus Christ, thereby rejecting the gospel entirely. Some countries like Russia are predominantly atheistic.

Only recently have they been forced by the divine will of God to allow many Jews to leave and return to their homeland, Israel, and the gospel of Jesus Christ be preached.

However, in the near future, Russia will close its doors to the gospel and return to their hard-line communistic and atheistic ideologies. This will be one of the reasons they will attack and invade Israel. Unfortunately, this overwhelming Russian army will be destroyed on the mountains of Israel. Their ruin will contribute to the death of one-fourth of the earth's population. Many of those who die during the Russian invasion will not be saved because they have rejected the gospel of Jesus Christ. Many souls from this generation of unbelievers will find themselves in hell after they die (or pass away) because of their unbelief in Jesus. It's sad that John has to end his commentary on the four horsemen of the apocalypse with the fact that hell is a reality. Figure 2-2 shows the comparison between Daniel's beasts and the four horsemen of the apocalypse John saw in Revelation.

EXERCISING HIS AUTHORITY FOR FORTY-TWO MONTHS

Daniel 11:29–30: At the appointed time he will invade the South again, but this time the outcome will be different from what it was before. Ships of the western coastlands will oppose him, and he will lose heart. Then he will turn back and vent his fury against the holy covenant. He will return and show favor to those who forsake the holy covenant.

Daniel 11:36: The king will do as he pleases. He will exalt and magnify himself above every god and will say unheard-of things against the God of gods. He will be successful until the time of wrath is completed, for what has been determined must take place.

Daniel reveals to us the first action the king of the North takes against the covenant he confirmed with many concerning Israel three years earlier. The king of the North lures the Russians and Arabs into attacking Israel. In Revelation 12:13, John helps us understand that Satan is behind this diabolical scheme. The king of the North holds his talks with Russia in secret so as not to raise suspicion from

Opening The Seven Seals

END-TIME KINGDOMS

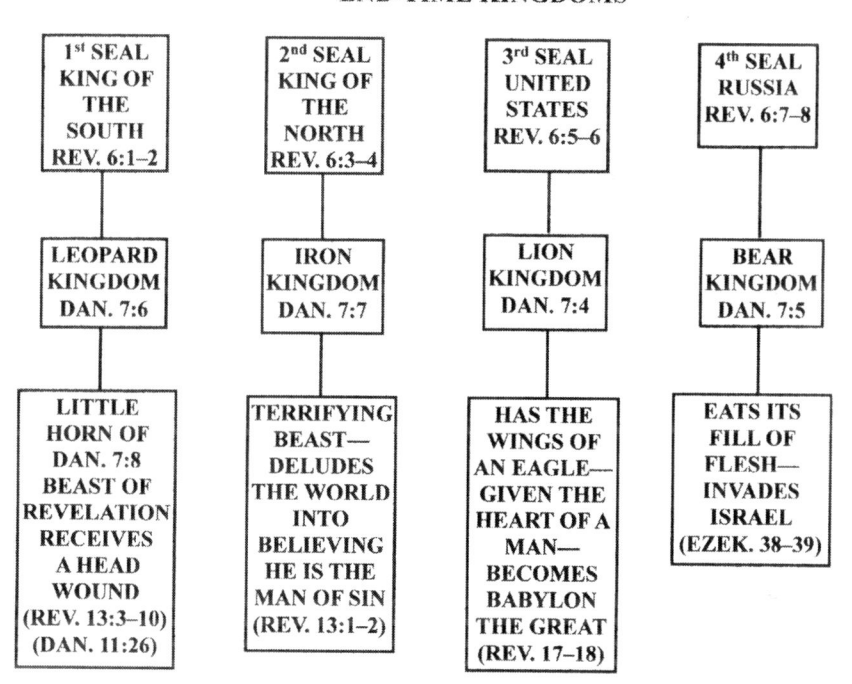

1st SEAL KING OF THE SOUTH REV. 6:1–2	2nd SEAL KING OF THE NORTH REV. 6:3–4	3rd SEAL UNITED STATES REV. 6:5–6	4th SEAL RUSSIA REV. 6:7–8
LEOPARD KINGDOM DAN. 7:6	IRON KINGDOM DAN. 7:7	LION KINGDOM DAN. 7:4	BEAR KINGDOM DAN. 7:5
LITTLE HORN OF DAN. 7:8 BEAST OF REVELATION RECEIVES A HEAD WOUND (REV. 13:3–10) (DAN. 11:26)	TERRIFYING BEAST— DELUDES THE WORLD INTO BELIEVING HE IS THE MAN OF SIN (REV. 13:1–2)	HAS THE WINGS OF AN EAGLE— GIVEN THE HEART OF A MAN— BECOMES BABYLON THE GREAT (REV. 17–18)	EATS ITS FILL OF FLESH— INVADES ISRAEL (EZEK. 38–39)

NOTE: DANIEL 7:8 REVEALS THE MAN OF SIN (LITTLE HORN) WHO RISES TO POWER AFTER THE IRON KINGDOM (TERRIFYING BEAST) IS DESTROYED.

FIGURE 2-2. SHOWING HOW THE FIRST FOUR SEAL JUDGMENTS LINE UP WITH THE KINGDOMS ENVISIONED BY DANIEL IN CHAPTER 7

the rest of the world. Then the king of the North returns to his own country to await Russia's impending invasion of Israel.

The forty-two-month reign of the king of the North begins when he secretly prompts Russia to invade Israel. His 3½-year reign of terror covers the time frame of the fourth seal through the sixth trumpet judgment of Revelation. The king of the North exercises his power during the hour of trial.

In Revelation 13:9–10, John does not hesitate to issue words of encouragement to the true believers of the Laodicea church generation who must endure the hour of trial:

> He who has an ear, let him hear. If anyone is to go into captivity, into captivity he will go. If anyone is to be killed with the sword, with the sword he will be killed. This calls for patient endurance and faithfulness on the part of the saints.

Hope exists for all Christians. God is in control of this time of trial. Although many will become prisoners of war and many will be killed by wars that occur during this time, we can be assured, if we have accepted Jesus Christ as our personal Savior, then we have a glorious future after our death.

LAST BELIEVERS OF THE PHILADELPHIA CHURCH ERA PASS AWAY

Matthew 24:34: I tell you the truth, this generation will certainly not pass away until all these things have happened.

Revelation 3:10: Since you have kept my command to endure patiently, I will also keep you from the hour of trial that is going to come upon the whole world to test those who live on the earth.

During this transition period, over one-fourth of the earth's population will die. It's a continuation of the last generation passing away as end-time prophecies are fulfilled. Before the hour of trial begins, the last true believers of the Philadelphia church era must also pass away, just as Jesus prophesied in Matthew 24:34. This fact will go completely unnoticed by the Laodicea church generation because elderly people (unbelievers) will still be alive after the true believers of the Philadelphia church pass away.

It is through death that Jesus keeps these true believers from the hour of trial, a time He said would come upon the rest of the world. Many of them will pass away from diseases that have recently come upon the elderly citizens of this church era. Currently, they are diseases for which no cure can be found in spite of our medical technology. However, we will shortly find out that the very last believers from this church era are kept from the hour of trial as a result of the Russian invasion of Israel.

THE HOUR OF TRIAL BEGINS

Revelation 3:16: So, because you are lukewarm—neither hot nor cold—I am about to spit you out of my mouth.

Revelation 13:10: This calls for patient endurance and faithfulness on the part of the saints.

Nearly one-half of mankind that remains after the transition period will die as a result of the hour of trial. This is another fulfillment of Jesus' prophecy in Matthew 24:34. Although John never uses the word *church* in chapters 4 through 19, he refers to the true believers by using the term *saints*. After the Russian invasion, unbelievers still alive from the Philadelphia church era, as well as believers and unbelievers from the Laodicea church era, will be spit out to endure the upcoming hour of trial because the motives of their hearts are not pure. As we will see, even the saints from the Laodicea church era must pass away in one form or another.

THE BEAR AWAKES

Daniel 7:5: And there before me was a second beast, which looked like a bear. It was raised up on one of its sides, and it had three ribs in its mouth between its teeth. It was told, "Get up and eat your fill of flesh!"

Ezekiel 38:2–3: Son of man, set your face against Gog, of the land of Magog, the chief prince of Meshech and Tubal; prophesy against him and say: "This is what the Sovereign Lord says: 'I am against you, O Gog, chief prince of Meshech and Tubal.'"

Ezekiel 38:10: On that day *thoughts* will come into your mind and you will devise an evil scheme. (Emphasis is mine.)

Ezekiel 38:11: You will say, "I will invade a land of unwalled villages; I will attack a peaceful and unsuspecting people—all of them living without walls and without gates and bars. I will plunder and loot and turn my hand against the resettled ruins and the people gathered from the nations, rich in livestock and goods, living at the center of the land."

Matthew 24:6–8: You will hear of wars and rumors of wars, but see to it that you are not alarmed. Such things must happen, but the end is still to come. Nation will rise against nation, and kingdom against kingdom. There will be famines and earthquakes in various places. All these are the beginning of birth pains.

Daniel sees the bear kingdom raised up on one side, with three ribs in its mouth. Most people would concentrate on trying to explain why one side of the bear is raised up. I believe we need to explain the side that has suffered loss and why it is no longer as strong as it portrays itself.

Russia suffered tremendous defeats during the Cold War and in Afghanistan throughout the 1980s and early 1990s. Communism suffered tremendous blows in Poland and East Germany, giving way to more democratic ideals. Although the Soviet Union itself is still a force to be reckoned with, it suffered a tremendous breakup in 1991. Additionally, Russia lost a large portion of its population when it allowed many Russian Orthodox Jews to return to their homeland of Israel. This mass exodus was prophesied in Jeremiah 31:8.

The side that is raised up represents the fact that Russia still holds a place of prominence and military might in the world. In chapters 38 and 39 of Ezekiel, we clearly see where Russia will lead an invasion against Israel. They also will serve as an arms provider to the nations that unite to carry out this invasion.

It is amazing how Daniel accurately describes Russia today. Russia will gladly attack Israel in an effort to show its citizens and the world that they are still a world power. Also, the Russian people will have a tremendous hatred for the Jews. They will be experiencing severe famine brought on by the civil war in Europe. The Russian leader will take note of the fact that Israel is not experiencing famine and inflation like the other nations of the world. He will fail to discern that God specifically designed it that way.

Even though the world will be alarmed over this Russian invasion, Jesus calmly tells believers to not be alarmed. He tells us that the end, meaning His actual return, is still to come. According to Daniel's prophecies, His return occurs seven years after this Russian invasion.

Daniel 11:30 helps us understand that it is the king of the North whose heart is set against the holy covenant confirmed by many three years prior to this Russian invasion. Additionally, Ezekiel helps us understand that it is the king of the North who secretly plants the thoughts of this invasion into the Russian leader's mind. When his secret meeting with the Russian leader is over, the king of the North returns to his own country and awaits the impending invasion.

AN OVERWHELMING ARMY UNITES

Ezekiel 38:5–6: Persia, Cush and Put will be with them, all with shields and helmets, also Gomer with all its troops, and Beth Togarmah from the far north with all its troops—the many nations with you.

Ezekiel 38:8–9: After many days you will be called to arms. In future years you will invade a land that has recovered from war, whose people were gathered from many nations to the mountains of Israel, which had long been desolate. They had been brought out from the nations, and now all of them live in safety. You and all your troops and the many nations with you will go up, advancing like a storm; you will be like a cloud covering the land.

Revelation 12:15–16: Then from his mouth the serpent spewed water like a river, to overtake the woman and sweep her away with the torrent.

Satan will unite the Russians with the Arab world in an attempt to annihilate the nation of Israel. The modern nations that unite are Russia (Gog), Iran/Iraq/Afghanistan (Persia), Ethiopia (Cush) and Sudan, Libya (Put), Austria, Eastern Europe (Gomer), southeastern Europe (Beth Togarmah), and various other republics still allied with Russia.

CONVENING THE UNITED NATIONS

Ezekiel 38:13: Sheba and Dedan and the merchants of Tarshish and all her villages will say to you, "Have you come to plunder? Have you gathered your hordes to loot, to carry off silver and gold, to take away livestock and goods and to seize much plunder?"

Matthew 24:6-8: You will hear of wars and rumors of wars [the Russian invasion of Israel], but see to it that you are not alarmed. Such things must happen, but the end [the return of Jesus] is still to come. Nation will rise against nation [Russia invades Israel], and kingdom against kingdom [the king of the North will continue to war against the king of the South]. There will be famines [in Russia and the Arab world] and earthquakes in various places [God puts the Russian invasion down by sending a great earthquake to the land of Israel]. All these are the beginning of birth pains [the beginning of the tribulation period, or last seven years preceding the return of Jesus Christ]. (Explanations in brackets are mine.)

As soon as Russia invades Israel, the United Nations will immediately convene here in America. This fact is revealed in Ezekiel 38:13, where we see that the nations of the world collectively assemble and issue a rebuke to the Russian diplomat. The king of the North, as represented by Tarshish, will act as if he had no prior knowledge of this attack.

In Matthew 24:6–8, Jesus begins His dissertation of the end-time events with the Russian invasion of Israel, indicating it is the sign that begins the final seven-year countdown to His return. He describes the "beginning of sorrows," or "birth pains," as being a time of wars (KON versus KOS) and rumors of wars as the whole world comes to a standstill over news reports of the Russian-Arab invasion of Israel. Additionally, Jesus includes the fact that the Russian-Arab invasion comes as a result of famine experienced throughout Russia and the Arab nations, as well as in many European nations. Jesus finishes by showing that the greatest sign of all will be the devastating earthquake that God will send upon the land of Israel to annihilate the Russian-Arab forces.

THE SEA OF GLASS ASKS, "HOW LONG, O LORD?"

Revelation 6:9–11: When he opened the fifth seal, I saw under the altar the souls of those who had been slain because of the word of God and the testimony they had maintained. They called out in a loud voice, "How long, Sovereign Lord, holy and true, until you judge the inhabitants of the earth and avenge our blood?" Then each of them was given a white robe, and they were told to wait a little longer, until the number of their fellow servants and brothers who were to be killed as they had been was completed.

These souls represent the souls of all the church-age saints who died from the time Jesus was on the cross until the last believer of the Philadelphia church era passes away. These souls are located in paradise, where the dead in Jesus Christ are held pending the rapture. John first saw these souls when he arrived in heaven. In Revelation 4:6, John sees these souls as a sea of glass.

In Revelation 6:10, when the seventieth week of Daniel begins, these souls rise up and ask the sovereign Lord how long will it be until He judges the inhabitants of the earth and avenges their blood, meaning their physical deaths. The answer to that question is seven years. Jesus will return to earth in seven years and destroy the armed forces gathered at Armageddon under the rule of the Man of Sin.

Here at the fifth seal, instead of being raised from under the altar of God to in front of the throne of God, these souls are given white robes to wear and told to wait in paradise, which John saw in Revelation 4:6 as a sea of glass. By giving these souls white robes, Christ assures them they are covered by His righteousness. After giving them white robes to wear, God makes war against the Russian-Arab alliance.

144,000 JEWISH EVANGELISTS ARE SEALED

Revelation 7:1–8: After this I saw four angels standing at the four corners of the earth, holding back the four winds of the earth to prevent any wind from blowing on the land or on the sea or on any tree. Then I saw another angel coming up from the east, having the seal of the living God. He called out in a loud voice to the four angels who had been given power to harm the land and the sea: "Do not harm the land or the sea or the trees until we put a seal on the foreheads of the servants of our God." Then I heard the number of those who were sealed: 144,000 from all the tribes of Israel.

Ezekiel 9:2–4: And I saw six men coming from the direction of the upper gate, which faces north, each with a deadly weapon in his hand. With them was a man clothed in linen who had a writing kit at his side. They came in and stood beside the bronze altar. Now the glory of the God of Israel went up from above the cherubim, where it had been, and moved to the threshold of the temple. Then the Lord called to the man clothed in linen who had the writing kit at his side and said to him, "Go throughout the city of Jerusalem and put a mark on the foreheads of those who grieve and lament over all the detestable things that are done in it."

Ezekiel 9:11: Then the man in linen with the writing kit at his side brought back word, saying, "I have done as you commanded."

The 144,000 Jewish-Christian evangelists are sealed during the Russian invasion of Israel. They must be in place before the king of the North invades Israel himself, which, according to Daniel 11:29–31, is the second action he takes against the holy covenant.

Since the 144,000 serve as a witness for Jesus Christ to the Jews during the hour of trial, which begins immediately following the destruction of the Russian army, the evangelists must be sealed during the Russian invasion. These evangelists will prove to be a never-ending source of contention for the king of the North because they will preach the gospel of Jesus Christ to the world. The king of the North will not be able to harm them or stop them.

THE GREAT MULTITUDE IN WHITE ROBES

Revelation 7:9: After this I looked and there before me was a great multitude that no one could count, from every nation, tribe, people and language, standing before the throne and in front of the Lamb. They were wearing white robes and were holding palm branches in their hands.

Revelation 7:14: These are they who have come out of the great tribulation.

There has been much confusion over this great multitude wearing white robes and holding palm branches, coming out of great tribulation. The confusion has surrounded the fact that the previous group is in paradise, those who were given white robes. Now John is given a future vision at the beginning of Daniel's seventieth week of the saints who will come out of the great tribulation. Remember that Daniel's seventieth week is the tribulation period, or the last seven years preceding the return of Jesus Christ. This seven-year period is divided into two segments: the hour of trial and the great tribulation.

In this passage, John is once again using the concept of juxtaposition. At the beginning of the tribulation period, John shows us the souls that come out of the great tribulation, or the last half of the tribulation period, or the last three years of Daniel's ten-year end-time period. Therefore, Revelation 7:9–17 is no more than a future vision of what John will later write about and actually see take place in Revelation 15:2–4:

> And I saw what looked like a sea of glass [the dead in Christ] mixed with fire [the last souls from the church age who are killed

I Will Make Myself Like The Most High!

during the hour of trial when the king of the North reigns, up to and including the rapture] and, standing beside the sea, those who had been victorious over the beast and his image and over the number of his name [the king of the South, or real Man of Sin, or little horn of Daniel 7:8]. (Explanations in brackets are mine.)

Between Revelation 6:9–11 and Revelation 7:9–17 is a seven-year time span covering the details of the seventieth week of Daniel, or the plot behind God sending the world a strong delusion. An elder tells John they come out of the great tribulation. From where John is currently writing, this is a future event. After receiving this future vision, John proceeds to tell the events of the last seven years preceding the return of Jesus, beginning with the Russian-Arab invasion of Israel. The events from Revelation 7:17 to 15:2 will explain how these saints become a part of the great multitude that eventually comes out of great tribulation. Then John tells us in Revelation 15:5 through Revelation 19:21 how Satan, through the little horn of Daniel 7:8, appears to fulfill the prophecies of a returning messiah, setting himself up to appear as God.

Figure 2-3 shows John's use of juxtaposition in Revelation 7:9–17, as well as the layout and construction of Revelation.

Between Revelation 6:9–11 and Revelation 7:9–17 is a seven-year time span covering the details of the seventieth week of Daniel, or the plot behind God sending the world a strong delusion. An elder tells John they come out of the great tribulation. From where John is currently writing, this is a future event. After receiving this future vision, John proceeds to tell the events of the last seven years preceding the return of Jesus, beginning with the Russian-Arab invasion of Israel. The events from Revelation 7:17 to 15:2 will explain how these saints become a part of the great multitude that eventually comes out of great tribulation. Then John tells us in Revelation 15:5 through Revelation 19:21 how Satan, through the little horn of Daniel 7:8, appears to fulfill the prophecies of a returning messiah, setting himself up to appear as God.

Figure 2-3 shows John's use of juxtaposition in Revelation 7:9–17, as well as the layout and construction of Revelation.

Opening The Seven Seals

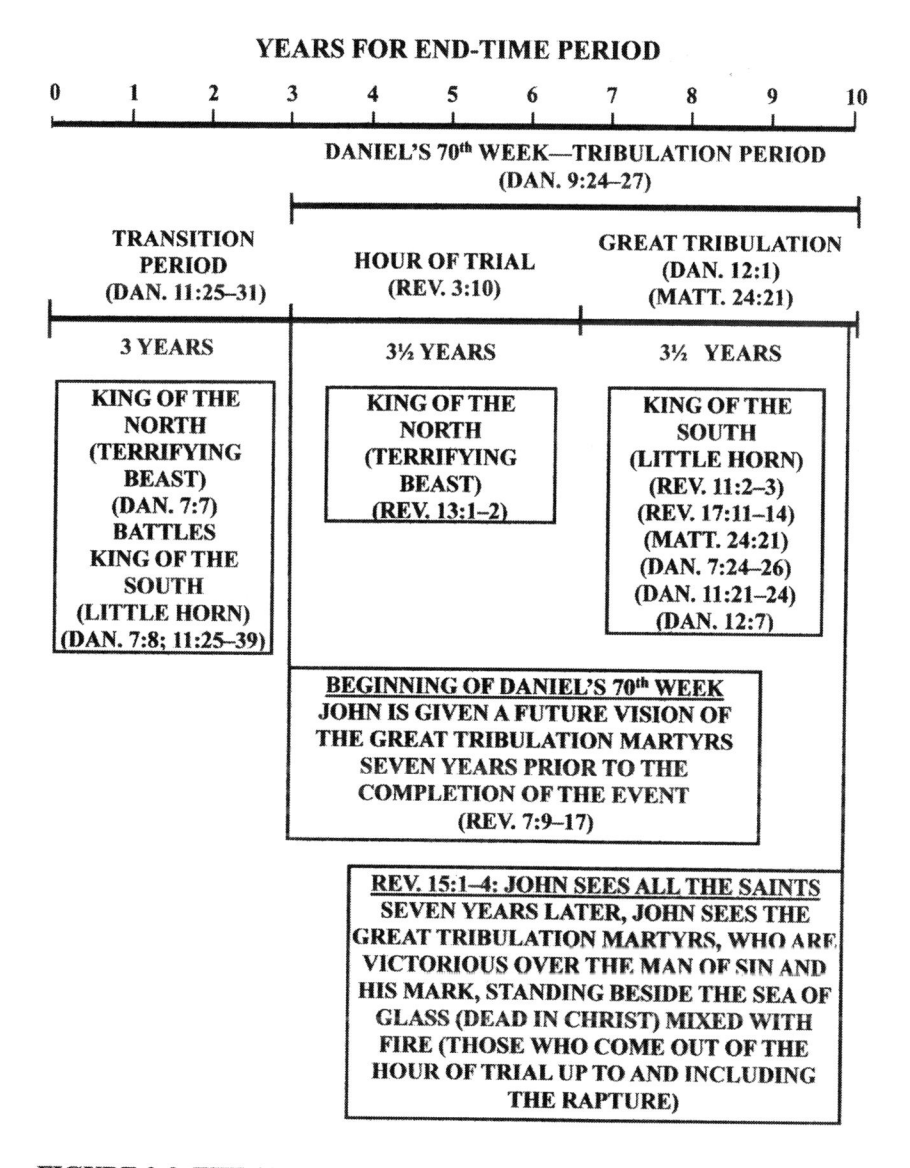

YEARS FOR END-TIME PERIOD

0　1　2　3　4　5　6　7　8　9　10

DANIEL'S 70th WEEK—TRIBULATION PERIOD
(DAN. 9:24–27)

TRANSITION PERIOD (DAN. 11:25–31)	HOUR OF TRIAL (REV. 3:10)	GREAT TRIBULATION (DAN. 12:1) (MATT. 24:21)
3 YEARS	3½ YEARS	3½ YEARS
KING OF THE NORTH (TERRIFYING BEAST) (DAN. 7:7) BATTLES KING OF THE SOUTH (LITTLE HORN) (DAN. 7:8; 11:25–39)	KING OF THE NORTH (TERRIFYING BEAST) (REV. 13:1–2)	KING OF THE SOUTH (LITTLE HORN) (REV. 11:2–3) (REV. 17:11–14) (MATT. 24:21) (DAN. 7:24–26) (DAN. 11:21–24) (DAN. 12:7)

<u>**BEGINNING OF DANIEL'S 70th WEEK**</u>
JOHN IS GIVEN A FUTURE VISION OF THE GREAT TRIBULATION MARTYRS SEVEN YEARS PRIOR TO THE COMPLETION OF THE EVENT (REV. 7:9–17)

<u>**REV. 15:1–4: JOHN SEES ALL THE SAINTS**</u> **SEVEN YEARS LATER, JOHN SEES THE GREAT TRIBULATION MARTYRS, WHO ARE VICTORIOUS OVER THE MAN OF SIN AND HIS MARK, STANDING BESIDE THE SEA OF GLASS (DEAD IN CHRIST) MIXED WITH FIRE (THOSE WHO COME OUT OF THE HOUR OF TRIAL UP TO AND INCLUDING THE RAPTURE)**

FIGURE 2-3. THE STRUCTURE OF REVELATION AND JOHN'S USE OF JUXTAPOSITION IN REVELATION 7:9–17

THE BOW IS STRUCK FROM HIS LEFT HAND

Revelation 12:16: But the earth helped the woman by opening its mouth and swallowing the river that the dragon had spewed out of his mouth.

Ezekiel 38:19: In my zeal and fiery wrath I declare that at that time there shall be a great earthquake in the land of Israel. The fish of the sea, the birds of the air, the beasts of the field, every creature that moves along the ground, and all the people on the face of the earth will tremble at my presence. The mountains will be overturned, the cliffs will crumble and every wall will fall to the ground.

Ezekiel 39:3–5: Then I will strike your bow from your left hand and make your arrows drop from your right hand. On the mountains of Israel you will fall, you and all your troops and the nations with you. I will give you as food to all kinds of carrion birds and to the wild animals. You will fall in the open field, for I have spoken, declares the Sovereign Lord.

    Figure 2-4 lays out the events which occur during the Russian invasion of Israel. Notice in Ezekiel 39:3, God states His destruction of Russia occurs in two stages. First, God strikes the bow from Russia's left hand. Then God makes the Russian leader's arrows drop from his right hand. We will first look at how God strikes the bow from Russia's left hand.

    Within ten days of Russia's invasion of Israel, its destruction will be history past. But those ten days will be extremely stressful for the world. Within a few days of the invasion, God Himself will send a devastating earthquake to the land of Israel, striking the Russian leader's bow from his left hand—or completely destroying the Russian-Arab ground forces. The earthquake will cause such tremendous confusion to this invading army that the Russian forces will turn on each other. The chemical agents they intended to use on the Jews will instead completely annihilate themselves.

    Because of its precise timing and location, this earthquake is the sign Jesus had us focus on in Matthew 24:7, where He states we would see earthquakes in various or "divers" places (American Standard Version of the Bible—meaning the most unlikely places), indicating it was the beginning of the end. When Russia is destroyed in the land of Israel by almighty God, all the members of the United Nations—and all the people of the world—will stand completely amazed at the devastating and miraculous defeat of the Russian army in the very place where, seven years later, the people are gathered for the battle of Armageddon.

The defeat of Israel's enemies will fulfill the words of God in Ezekiel 38:23: "And so I will show my greatness and my holiness, and I will make myself known in the sight of many nations. Then they will know that I am the Lord."

These words ring true as we look at our modern world. All the nations of the world will receive the news at the very same time because they are all gathered in one location, the United Nations building located in New York. For a brief moment, they will all acknowledge the God of Israel. As the people celebrate this Russian catastrophe, their faces will soon turn to horror as the next news flash is announced to the United Nations: the fact that the Russians have launched a full-scale nuclear strike against the United States of America.

THE WORLD'S GREATEST PRAYER MEETING

Revelation 6:15–17: Then the kings of the earth, the princes, the generals, the rich, the mighty, and every slave and every free man hid in caves and among the rocks of the mountains. They called to the mountains and the rocks, "Fall on us and hide us from the face of him who sits on the throne and from the wrath of the Lamb! For the great day of their wrath has come, and who can stand?"

Today we know the United Nations would convene at the onset of this invasion. If the United Nations had not become a reality during this last generation's lifetime, all that John sees and writes about in Revelation 6:15–17 would not be possible. John shows the great gathering of the world's presidents, prime ministers, their generals, and important heads of state, as well as wealthy statesmen (free men). He

I Will Make Myself Like The Most High!

YEARS FOR END-TIME PERIOD

```
0    1    2    3    4    5    6    7    8    9    10
```

APPEARS AS IF IT IS THE TRIBULATION PERIOD

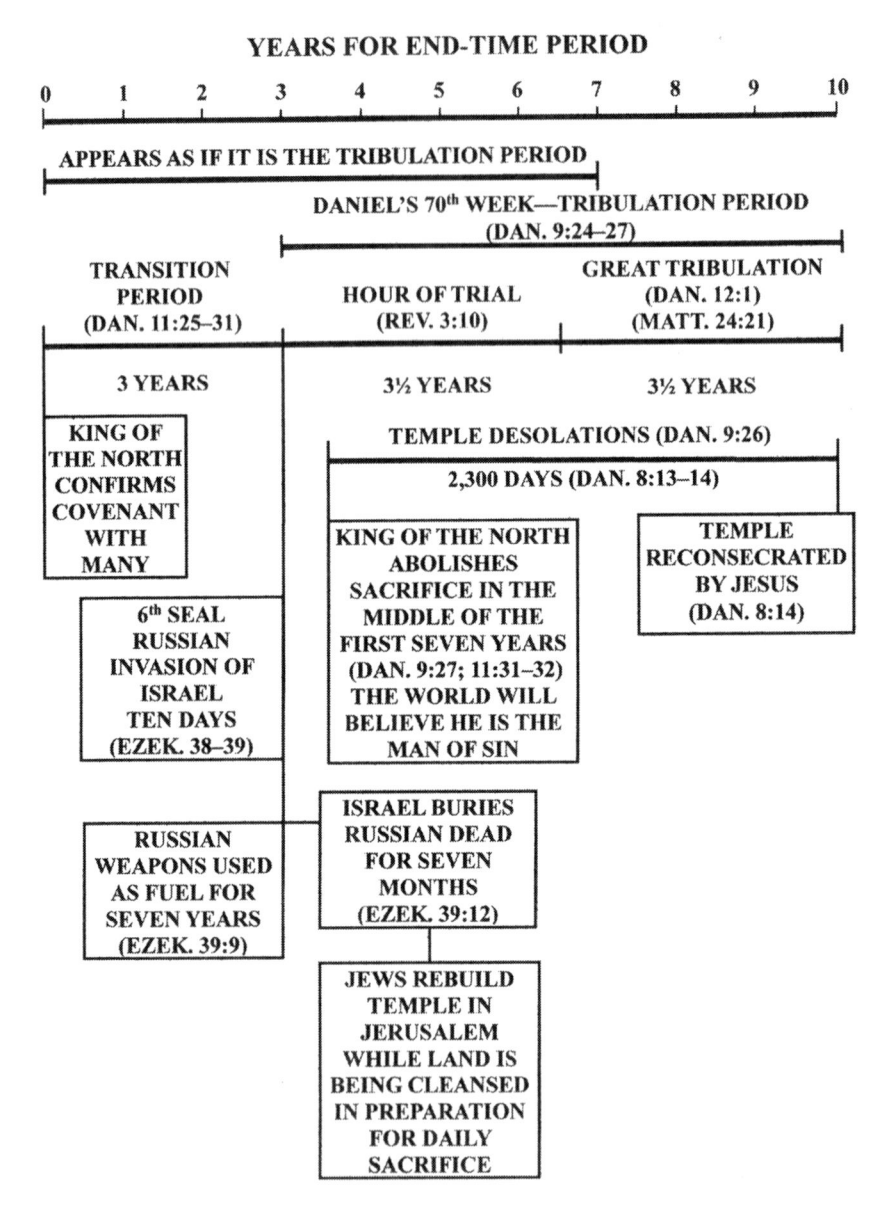

DANIEL'S 70th WEEK—TRIBULATION PERIOD (DAN. 9:24–27)

TRANSITION PERIOD (DAN. 11:25–31)	HOUR OF TRIAL (REV. 3:10)	GREAT TRIBULATION (DAN. 12:1) (MATT. 24:21)
3 YEARS	3½ YEARS	3½ YEARS

TEMPLE DESOLATIONS (DAN. 9:26)

2,300 DAYS (DAN. 8:13–14)

KING OF THE NORTH CONFIRMS COVENANT WITH MANY

KING OF THE NORTH ABOLISHES SACRIFICE IN THE MIDDLE OF THE FIRST SEVEN YEARS (DAN. 9:27; 11:31–32) THE WORLD WILL BELIEVE HE IS THE MAN OF SIN

TEMPLE RECONSECRATED BY JESUS (DAN. 8:14)

6th SEAL RUSSIAN INVASION OF ISRAEL TEN DAYS (EZEK. 38–39)

RUSSIAN WEAPONS USED AS FUEL FOR SEVEN YEARS (EZEK. 39:9)

ISRAEL BURIES RUSSIAN DEAD FOR SEVEN MONTHS (EZEK. 39:12)

JEWS REBUILD TEMPLE IN JERUSALEM WHILE LAND IS BEING CLEANSED IN PREPARATION FOR DAILY SACRIFICE

FIGURE 2-4. HOW THE RUSSIAN INVASION BEGINS DANIEL'S SEVENTIETH WEEK—THE TRIBULATION PERIOD

tells of employees of the government, their aides and advisors, who are considered by John as slaves because they work for someone else. But subtly John goes one step beyond their great gathering. He tells us these people are located in "caves," using the plural form.

We need to discern why heroic generals would be hiding in caves. Examine our modern military structure and the answer is evident. John is describing the fact that these generals are in US underground military-command centers. In first-century language, John can only describe our modern sophisticated underground command centers as "caves." Therefore, not only is John describing the assembly of the United Nations, but he is also describing the high-level alert status of the entire United States Department of Defense.

Instead of accepting defeat, Russia becomes embittered because of its humiliating loss of military might. As a last-ditch effort to save face, they launch a full-scale nuclear strike against the United States. With about twenty minutes until detonation, mass panic and fear will break out all over America. As the president is whisked away by helicopter to his war room, many people will fall to their knees and pray while others seek a place to hide. In their despair, some will exclaim to the rocks that line the walls of these facilities, "Fall on us and hide us from the face of him who sits on the throne and from the wrath of the Lamb! For the great day of their wrath has come, and who can stand?"

After witnessing the God of heaven totally destroy the ground forces of Russia, we can understand why they mistake this full-scale nuclear strike as a continuation of God's fiery wrath. John demonstrates how the church is still very much alive by having the true believers give credence to God and acknowledge the Lamb, Jesus Christ.

Although they believe they are on the brink of nuclear annihilation, we are about to see that they have completely misinterpreted the meaning behind this event. They are not witnessing the wrath of God. They are experiencing a last-ditch effort by Satan to annihilate a nation that God has continuously used as a golden cup (Rev. 17:4) in His hand during these last days.

After the Russian invasion, there's still about seven years remaining before Jesus returns. The truth is, God is not done using

America as a gold cup. Therefore, we are about to see another miraculous intervention by God as the United States is saved from nuclear holocaust. Because of superior military technology that God has bestowed upon America, the Russians are about to experience their second humiliating defeat.

MAKING WAR WITH THOSE WHO HOLD TO THE TESTIMONY OF JESUS

Revelation 12:17: Then the dragon was enraged at the woman and went off to make war against the rest of her offspring—those who obey God's commandments and hold to the testimony of Jesus. And the dragon stood on the shore of the sea.

Satan becomes enraged at the United States when almighty God annihilates Russia on the mountains of Israel. Israel's offspring is the church of Jesus Christ. It is the church that maintains the testimony of Jesus. And the bulk of Christianity has found its home in America because of religious freedom granted in its Constitution. Here at the very beginning of the hour of trial, Satan attempts to destroy the entire church by destroying America. But as we're about to see, Satan's plan to destroy America will come to ruin.

THE BEGINNING OF BIRTH PAINS

Matthew 24:6–8: You will hear of wars and rumors of wars, but see to it that you are not alarmed. Such things must happen, but the end is still to come. Nation will rise against nation, and kingdom against kingdom. There will be famines and earthquakes in various places. All these are the beginning of birth pains.

The world leaders at this time will feel they are witnessing the wrath of God and the end of the world. But we read in Matthew 24:6–8 that Jesus foretold all that has happened up to this point, and yet the end, or His return, is still far off—seven years to be exact.

Although these people have been told they will be secure in these command centers, they would rather have the rocks fall on them and be killed than face the possibility of surviving a nuclear exchange of this magnitude. As far as they know, all their families and friends who are outside these cavelike command centers are about to be completely annihilated. Their reaction to this total nuclear strike is purely human. That's why John sees them asking, "Who can stand?" They believe the wrath of God has finally been unleashed, and from all appearances, it is a logical and appropriate human conclusion.

Just the announcement of this nuclear strike will fulfill the words of Jesus' prophecy in Luke 21:25–26: "There will be signs in the sun, moon and stars. On the earth, nations will be in anguish and perplexity at the roaring and tossing of the sea. Men will faint from terror, apprehensive of what is coming on the world, for the heavenly bodies will be shaken."

When the American public is informed that Russia has launched an unprovoked full-scale nuclear attack with only twenty to thirty minutes until detonation, mass hysteria will break out all over the country. Many will literally faint from the news. Many elderly people will experience heart attacks and die. There will be nothing but confusion in our cities from working mothers and fathers attempting to get to their children and family members. As people in hospitals literally abandon their jobs, many elderly people will pass away. Traffic jams will bring police and medical-action teams to a complete state of helplessness and chaos. For a short while, the leaders of the nations will hold their breath and pray like they've never prayed before as they wait to be consumed.

But since the end-time events still carry on for another seven years, it is apparent that the United States is not annihilated. What could possibly keep us from nuclear annihilation? The clue is found in Jesus' prophecy from Luke 21:26: "for the heavenly bodies will be shaken." Note that Jesus didn't say anything about the earth being shaken or destroyed. He said the heavenly bodies would be shaken. Keep this prophecy in mind as we search for other clues as to how America is spared from nuclear disaster.

THE ARROWS DROP FROM HIS RIGHT HAND

Revelation 6:12–14: I watched as he opened the sixth seal. There was a great earthquake. The sun turned black like sackcloth made of goat hair, the whole moon turned blood red, and the stars in the sky fell to earth, as late figs drop from a fig tree when shaken by a strong wind. The sky receded like a scroll, rolling up, and every mountain and island was removed from its place.

Ezekiel 39:3: I will strike your bow [army] from your left hand and make your arrows [missiles] drop from your right hand. (Explanations in brackets are mine.)

John begins describing this time of anguish and perplexity by telling about the great earthquake God will send upon the land of Israel in order to annihilate the Russian forces. He then describes the nuclear exchange between Russia and the United States. In a brilliant display of words, John paints a poetic picture of how America is spared from destruction by the nuclear missiles, comparing the Russian missiles to late figs that drop from a fig tree. All this destruction in the atmosphere turns the sun into sackcloth, and the moon blood red. The missiles, seen by John as stars, just fall from the sky.

In Revelation 17 and 18, John shows us that America, Babylon the Great, is alive and well seven years after this full-scale launch. Seven years after this nuclear launch, America is busy with world trade and very prosperous. We can easily conclude that America is not destroyed by this seal judgment. Somehow, as the people pray to God, they are miraculously spared from this tragedy.

Ezekiel 39:3 provides another clue as to why we are not destroyed: the Russian missiles are rendered useless. Ezekiel shows this by writing poetically that God will make the missiles drop from the Russian leader's right hand.

John tells the same story as Ezekiel, showing how the Russian missiles fall like late figs. Late figs are considered as being dead. In Ezekiel 39:3, God verifies this fact, informing us that He will ensure that the Russian arrows, or missiles, fall from Russia's right hand, rendering them useless. Short of God Himself catching the Russian missiles in His own hand, what could possibly happen to so many missiles at the same time that would render all of them useless and they would fall to the ground as dead?

The Russian missiles will be destroyed by our space-based anti-missile defense system known as the Strategic Defense Initiative (SDI). Just as late figs are considered as dead, the Russian missiles will fall from the Russian leader's right hand and be completely destroyed in space by the laser technology of SDI. Thus, in accordance with Jesus' prophecy, they will appear as heavenly bodies being shaken, their breakup appearing as stars falling from the sky, or just as late figs drop from a fig tree when shaken by a strong wind.

The Pentagon learned during the Gulf War that our best ground-launched missile interceptors cannot do what SDI can do to prevent the United States from being devastated by a nuclear attack. We learned this lesson when we had a hard time trying to knock down SCUD missiles in Israel. In Jeremiah 51:58, God calls SDI a "high gate." In Revelation 16:19 and 17:18, John refers to America as being Babylon the Great, or a great city. Therefore, SDI becomes the high gate above the great city of America.

From Luke 21:25–26, we can discern that the mere rumors, or reporting of this nuclear launch, and the resulting mass hysteria and confusion are how Jesus fulfills His promise of keeping the last believers of the Philadelphia church era from the hour of trial. The elderly will be a good portion of those who suddenly faint, or pass away from fear, shock, or abandonment in nursing homes and hospitals as people flee from their jobs in an effort to be reunited with their children and families.

I can't begin to describe the panic and chaos that will come upon the American population. But I can tell you that the best action anyone can take when the sky begins to fall around us is to stand still. Jesus tells us not to be alarmed. We should remember the time when Moses and the Israelites were pinned between the Red Sea and Pharaoh's army. Exodus 14:13 shows us that Moses told the people, "Do not be afraid. Stand firm and you will see the deliverance the Lord will bring you today."

Unfortunately, many will not heed this advice, and the public at large will go mad. The result will be the death of many people because of the chaos. By the time the world calms down, the believers from the Philadelphia church era will all be gone. The remainder from that generation who are still living—all the unsaved from the Philadelphia church era, as well as the saved and unsaved from the Laodicea church era—will find themselves spit out to endure the hour of trial. The hour of trial covers the next 3½ years when the king of the North deludes the world into believing he is the Man of Sin.

GOD SENDS FIRE ON MAGOG

Ezekiel 39:6: I will send fire on Magog and on those who live in safety in the coastlands, and they will know that I am the Lord.

Although America is spared from this holocaust, John writes in Revelation 6:12–14 that he still saw the sky recede like a scroll, the sun turn like sackcloth, and the moon turn blood red, with mountains and islands being removed from their places. The reason for this is found in Ezekiel 39:6, where God sends fire on the coastlands of Magog, which is the land of Russia.

The Russian leader will soon realize he made another grave mistake. To his horror, America will launch a limited counterattack that will result in a nuclear detonation on the coastlands of Russia. That's why John still saw the sky recede like a scroll, "rolling up, and every mountain and island was removed from its place." Russia finally succumbs to defeat. And now there will be much work to be done in the land of Israel. The biological and chemical agents that helped destroy the invading forces will have contaminated the land. Thus Ezekiel shows how America helps Israel cleanse the land. This cleansing will take seven months.

THE WEAPONS ARE USED AS FUEL
FOR THE NEXT SEVEN YEARS

Ezekiel 39:9: Then those who live in the towns of Israel will go out and use the weapons for fuel and burn them up—the small and large shields, the bows and arrows, the war clubs and spears. For seven years they will use them for fuel.

We can now understand Jesus' words in Matthew 24:6–8. The Russian invasion of Israel and Russia's subsequent destruction at the hands of God serves as the sign for the beginning of the tribulation period—known as Daniel's seventieth week—or the last seven years preceding the return of Jesus to earth. The heavenly bodies will appear to be shaken when the missiles explode in space and are turned into harmless trash. And yet seven years still remain for God to send the world a strong delusion and have Jesus return to reconsecrate the temple in Jerusalem. See Figure 2-5 for details.

THE DEAD ARE BURIED FOR SEVEN MONTHS

Ezekiel 39:12: For seven months the house of Israel will be burying them in order to cleanse the land.

After Russia finally succumbs to defeat, Israel will spend the next seven months burying the dead remains of the Russian-Arab alliance near the Dead Sea, according to Ezekiel 39:11. This time of burial is needed to cleanse the land so Israel can start sacrifices on the Temple Mount. Therefore, the building of the temple in Jerusalem will coincide with the burial process, since the Muslim threat will no longer exist. It may well be that the earthquake used to destroy the invading forces will also destroy the Dome of the Rock, now standing on the Temple Mount. No one need hasten the rebuilding of the temple. Their labor is in vain. God will ensure it is rebuilt on time, in accordance with Scripture.

WORSHIPING A GOD OF FORTRESSES

Daniel 11:38: Instead of them, he [the king of the North] will honor a god of fortresses [the United States of America]; a god unknown to his fathers [Europe and ancient Rome] he will honor with gold

I Will Make Myself Like The Most High!

DAYS FOR RUSSIAN INVASION OF ISRAEL

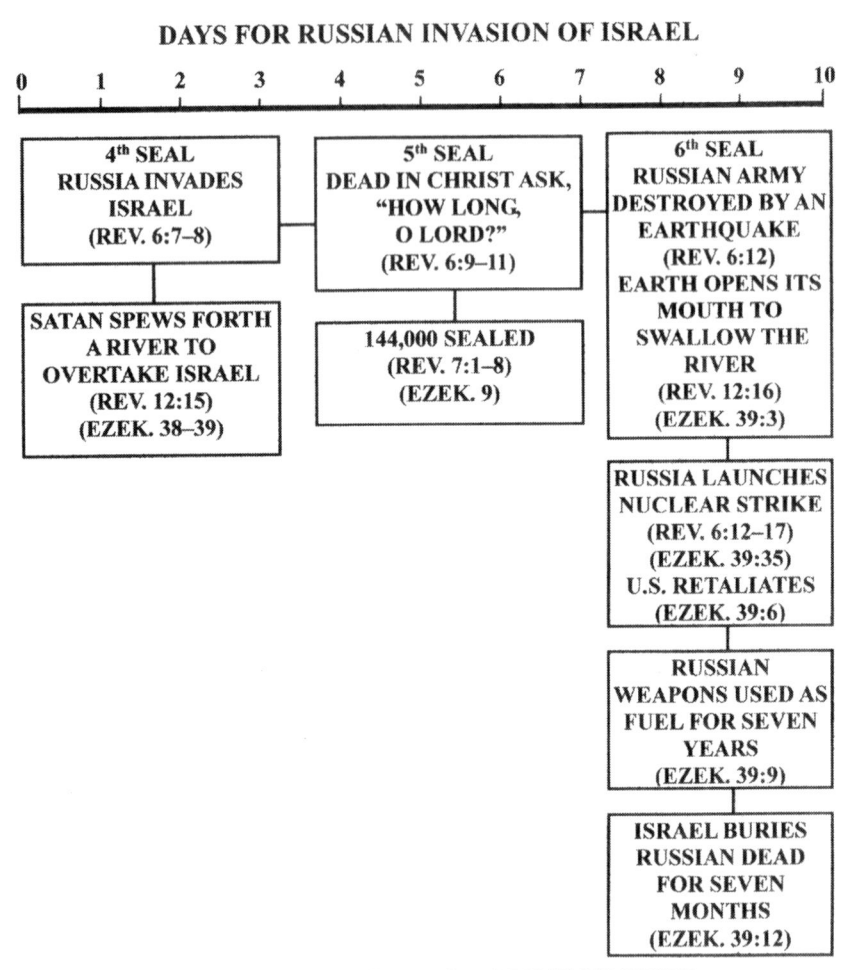

```
0    1    2    3    4    5    6    7    8    9    10
```

4th SEAL RUSSIA INVADES ISRAEL (REV. 6:7–8)	5th SEAL DEAD IN CHRIST ASK, "HOW LONG, O LORD?" (REV. 6:9–11)	6th SEAL RUSSIAN ARMY DESTROYED BY AN EARTHQUAKE (REV. 6:12) EARTH OPENS ITS MOUTH TO SWALLOW THE RIVER (REV. 12:16) (EZEK. 39:3)
SATAN SPEWS FORTH A RIVER TO OVERTAKE ISRAEL (REV. 12:15) (EZEK. 38–39)	144,000 SEALED (REV. 7:1–8) (EZEK. 9)	

RUSSIA LAUNCHES NUCLEAR STRIKE (REV. 6:12–17) (EZEK. 39:35) U.S. RETALIATES (EZEK. 39:6)
RUSSIAN WEAPONS USED AS FUEL FOR SEVEN YEARS (EZEK. 39:9)
ISRAEL BURIES RUSSIAN DEAD FOR SEVEN MONTHS (EZEK. 39:12)

FIGURE 2-5. EZEKIEL'S PROPHECIES LINE UP WITH REVELATION AND DANIEL

and silver, with precious stones and costly gifts. (Explanations in brackets are mine).

Once SDI is seen to work, the king of the North, empowered by Satan, will begin to pour massive amounts of money into continued research and development. Daniel saw the time when this great buildup in space defenses would take place. Unlike our European forefathers, the king of the North will come to rely heavily on our technology of warfare and space defense, a god unknown to his European forefathers. It's apparent today that America remains militarily committed to Europe through NATO. With SDI, America becomes that "god of fortresses" Daniel envisioned thousands of years ago.

FLYING ON THE WINGS OF A GREAT EAGLE

Revelation 12:6: The woman fled into the desert to a place prepared for her by God, where she might be taken care of for 1,260 days.

John tells what happens shortly after the Russian invasion: many Israelis are evacuated to a place in the desert. Where is this desert? John provides two clues where this desert is located. In Revelation 17:3, John states he was carried away to the desert, Babylon the Great. We will see in great detail that Babylon the Great is America. This claim is further supported by John in Revelation 12:14: "The woman was given the two wings of a great eagle, so that she might fly to the place prepared for her in the desert, where she would be taken care of for a time, times and half a time, out of the serpent's reach."

The serpent is a reference to Satan controlling the actions of the king of the North, who Satan wants the world to believe is the Man of Sin. Daniel 7:4 states how the lion beast, America, started out as having the wings of an eagle. By the divine will of God, America will maintain its own Constitution under the king of the North's rule and also maintain religious freedom for evacuated Jews and Christians.

SATAN CREATES A LION'S DEN

Revelation 12:17: Then the dragon was enraged at the woman and went off to make war against the rest of her offspring—those who obey God's commandments and hold to the testimony of Jesus. And the dragon stood on the shore of the sea.

Daniel 7:4: The first was like a lion, and it had the wings of an eagle. I watched until its wings were torn off and it was lifted from the ground so that it stood on two feet like a man, and the heart of a man was given to it.

Satan, a master of deception, devises yet another evil scheme. His motto is "If you can't beat them by brute force, destroy them through deception." His plan is to create a strong delusion that will make America abandon its godly heritage. Daniel helps us understand that Satan is successful with his diabolical scheme. America eventually abandons its religious freedom and persecutes the people of God, including those Jews who were evacuated to her shores during the reign of the king of the North. The switch in America's loyalties from God Almighty to Satan is accomplished through the delusion of the little horn of Daniel 7:8.

Satan begins to silently make war against the Christians of this country and the Jews by having America serve as a place of refuge for evacuated Israelis. By the time the little horn poses as God, America will be unsuspectingly used as a lion's den for Jews and those who hold fast the name of Jesus. This is how Satan accomplishes his goal of destroying the saints of God.

Daniel verifies Satan's master plan to use America as a lion's den by visualizing America as a lion beast in Daniel 7:4. Although Daniel first sees America as a lion having the wings of an eagle, he informs us that the time is coming when the wings of liberty, which represent religious freedom, will be torn off. In those days, America takes on the heart of a man. This man is the Man of Sin, or the little horn of Daniel 7:8 posing as God. The people of America become convinced he is God, and those who refuse his offer of salvation are enemies of God. They willingly persecute the Jews and those who refuse his offer of salvation. Those who are persecuted become the prophetic reality of Daniel in the lion's den.

We'll look closer at how America becomes a lion's den when we study the Man of Sin, who comes to world power during the last three years of this ten-year end-time period. Suffice it to say that at this point in time, Satan wreaks havoc on the world through the king of the North, the man Satan wants everyone to believe is the devil in the flesh.

THE BEAST OUT OF THE SEA OVERRUNS A MIGHTY FORTRESS

Daniel 11:39: He [king of the North] will attack the mightiest fortresses [king of the South] with the help of a foreign god [this is the United States backed up with SDI and other stealth technology] and will greatly honor those who acknowledge him. (Explanations in brackets are mine.)

Daniel 11:31–32: His armed forces will rise up to desecrate the temple fortress and will abolish the daily sacrifice. Then they will set up the abomination that causes desolation. With flattery he will corrupt those who have violated the covenant, but the people who know their God will firmly resist him.

In reality, there will never be a sacrifice offered on the Temple Mount. When the temple is finished, coinciding with seven months of cleansing the land, the king of the North will move to stop the first sacrifice from taking place. Just when war seems to be a foregone conclusion because of the disastrous Russian invasion, enter the king of the North and his three-year campaign of terror in an effort to make the world believe he is the Man of Sin.

He begins this hour of trial by overpowering the king of the South. At the same time, he moves his armed forces into the Middle East, stopping the sacrifice from taking place. This occurs near the middle of the first seven years of this ten-year period, just as Gabriel foretold in Daniel 9:27. The king of the North is the first person to invade Israel and desolate the rebuilt temple. Remember, Daniel

9:26 informs us there will be desolations, meaning there will be more than one. His use of the plural form means this is only the first desolation. The second desolation comes when the real Man of Sin, or little horn of Daniel 7:8, rebels against the king of the North, destroys him, and sits in the temple, deluding the world into believing that he is God.

THE SACRIFICE IS ABOLISHED IN THE MIDDLE OF THE SEVEN

Daniel 9:26: The people of the ruler who will come will destroy the city and the sanctuary. The end will come like a flood: War will continue until the end, and desolations have been decreed.

Daniel 9:27: In the middle of the "seven" he will put an end to sacrifice and offering.

Daniel 9:27 is a double prophecy. Both the king of the North and the Man of Sin, or little horn of Daniel 7:8, fulfill it. But it will be fulfilled in two different ways at two different times. In the process of bringing the real Man of Sin to power and destroying the king of the North, Satan will destroy two-thirds of mankind during the remaining hour of trial. When it is all said and done, Israel will nearly be annihilated.

THE FIRST DESOLATION OF THE TEMPLE

Daniel 9:27: In the middle of the "seven" he will put an end to sacrifice and offering. And on a wing of the temple he will set up an abomination that causes desolation, until the end that is decreed is poured out on him.

Daniel 11:31–32: His armed forces will rise up to desecrate the temple fortress and will abolish the daily sacrifice. Then they will set up the abomination that causes desolation. With flattery he will corrupt those who have violated the covenant, but the people who know their God will firmly resist him.

The king of the North desolates the rebuilt temple in Jerusalem just after the beginning of the hour of trial—in the middle of the first seven years of this ten-year period—just as Gabriel told Daniel in 9:27. Daniel 8:14 informs us that Jesus will return and reconsecrate the temple 2,300 days later.

2,300 DAYS REMAIN UNTIL JESUS RECONSECRATES THE TEMPLE

Daniel 8:13–14: Then I heard a holy one speaking, and another holy one said to him, "How long will it take for the vision to be fulfilled—the vision concerning the daily sacrifice, the rebellion that causes desolation, and the surrender of the sanctuary and of the host that will be trampled underfoot?" He said to me, "It will take 2,300 evenings and mornings; then the sanctuary will be reconsecrated."

During the next 2,300 days, the king of the North will complete his reign of terror during the hour of trial. Near the end of the hour of trial, the little horn of Daniel 7:8 will rebel against the king of the North and challenge him for world dominion. Through mystery and intrigue, the little horn will be successful in his bid to overcome the king of the North and appear to the world as God coming to redeem mankind from evil. Because of the plots devised against him, the king of the North will be destroyed in what Satan wants most people to believe is the notorious battle of Armageddon. However, this world war will just be another part of the diabolical scheme Satan devises to bring his real Man of Sin to world power. This devastating war serves as a critical part of the overall strong delusion that God is sending to the world before Jesus returns and takes His rightful place as King of Kings and Lord of Lords. Figure 2-6 depicts how the seal judgments of Revelation fit into the outline of Daniel's 2,300-day prophecy.

SILENCE IN HEAVEN FOR ABOUT HALF AN HOUR

Revelation 8:1–5: When he opened the seventh seal, there was silence in heaven for about half an hour. And I saw the seven angels

I Will Make Myself Like The Most High!

YEARS FOR END-TIME PERIOD

```
0    1    2    3    4    5    6    7    8    9    10
|----------------------------------------------|
     APPEARS AS TRIBULATION PERIOD
          |----------------------------------------|
          DANIEL'S 70th WEEK—TRIBULATION PERIOD
                      (DAN. 9:24–27)
```

TRANSITION PERIOD (DAN. 11:25–31)	HOUR OF TRIAL (REV. 3:10)	GREAT TRIBULATION (DAN. 12:1) (MATT. 24:21)
3 YEARS	3½ YEARS	3½ YEARS

TEMPLE DESOLATIONS (DAN. 9:26)

2,300 DAYS (DAN. 8:13–14)

KING OF THE NORTH CONFIRMS COVENANT WITH MANY (DAN. 9:27)

KING OF THE NORTH ABOLISHES SACRIFICE (DAN. 9:27; 11:31–32)

1,290 DAYS AFTER SACRIFICE IS ABOLISHED, THE MAN OF SIN (KING OF THE SOUTH) COMMITS ABOMINATION THAT CAUSES DESOLATION (DAN. 12:11) (MATT. 24:15) SATAN PORTRAYS HIMSELF AS GOD THROUGH THE LITTLE HORN OF DANIEL 7:8

JESUS RETURNS (DAN. 8:14)

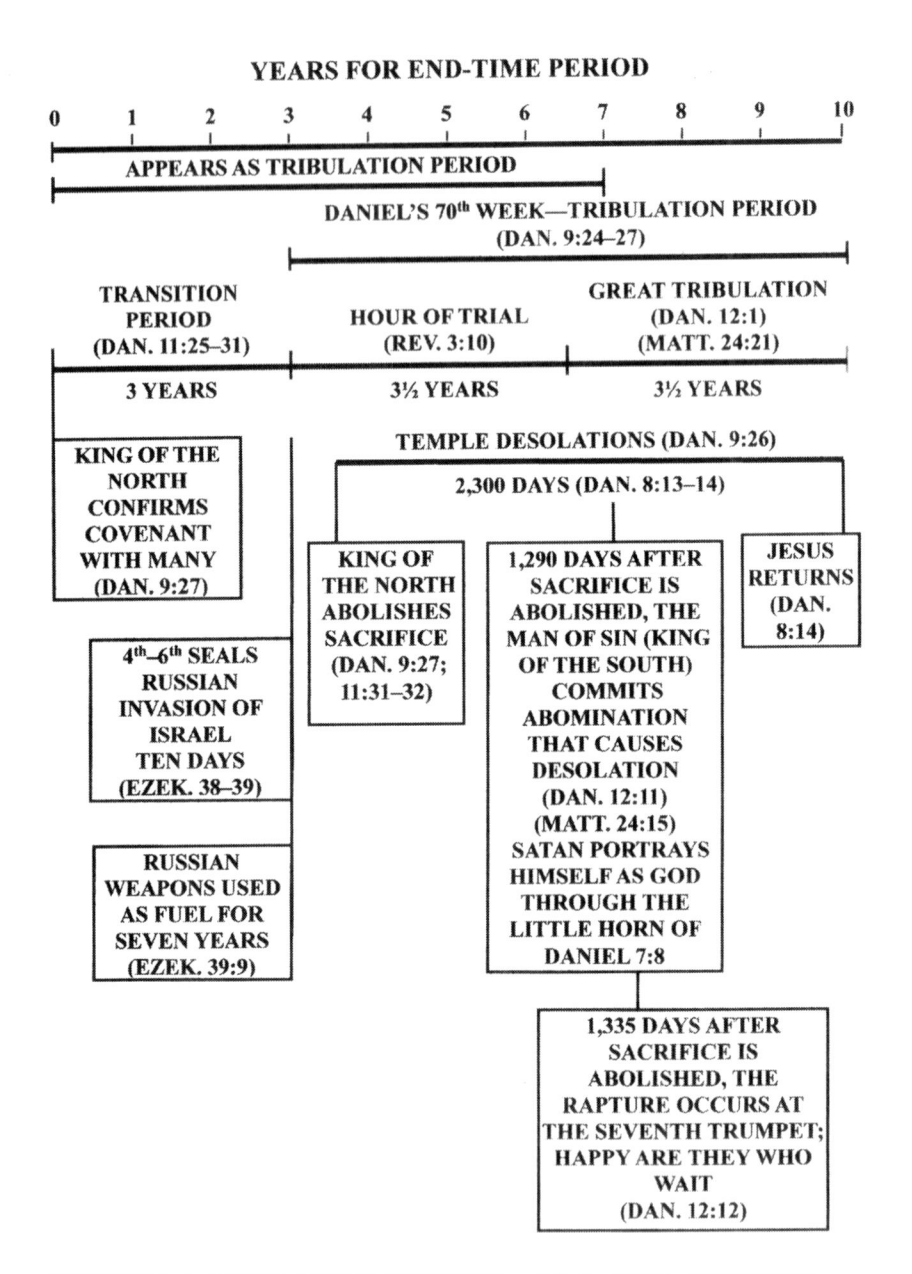

4th–6th SEALS RUSSIAN INVASION OF ISRAEL TEN DAYS (EZEK. 38–39)

RUSSIAN WEAPONS USED AS FUEL FOR SEVEN YEARS (EZEK. 39:9)

1,335 DAYS AFTER SACRIFICE IS ABOLISHED, THE RAPTURE OCCURS AT THE SEVENTH TRUMPET; HAPPY ARE THEY WHO WAIT (DAN. 12:12)

FIGURE 2-6. REVELATION, EZEKIEL, AND DANIEL COINCIDE WITH DANIEL'S 2,300-, 1,290-, AND 1,335-DAY PROPHECIES

who stand before God, and to them were given seven trumpets. Another angel, who had a golden censer, came and stood at the altar. He was given much incense to offer, with the prayers of all the saints, on the golden altar before the throne. The smoke of the incense, together with the prayers of the saints, went up before God from the angel's hand. Then the angel took the censer, filled it with fire from the altar, and hurled it on the earth; and there came peals of thunder, rumblings, flashes of lightning and an earthquake.

We must first realize that the prayers of the saints show us that the believers of the Laodicea church era are on the earth. This is the time Jesus told the Laodicea church generation in Revelation 3:18 to "buy from me gold refined in the fire, so you can become rich." This claim is supported in Daniel 11:33–35. I have added explanations in brackets for further clarification of Scripture:

Daniel 11:33: Those who are wise [those of the Laodicea church who are saved] will instruct many [those who are not saved], though for a time they will fall by the sword or be burned or captured or plundered [during the hour of trial].

Daniel 11:34: When they fall, they will receive a little help, and many who are not sincere will join them.

Daniel 11:35: Some of the wise will stumble [those who are going to be saved after the rapture will enter the time of great tribulation, yet refuse to worship Satan posing as God], so that they may be refined, purified and made spotless until the time of the end [great tribulation], for it will still come at the appointed time [after the Man of Sin rebels, the king of the North is destroyed, and the Man of Sin, or little horn of Daniel 7:8, appears as being God]. (Explanations in brackets are mine.)

It is during the hour of trial that many believers from the Laodicea church era offer up prayers of salvation, and thus their prayers go up before God. Their prayers during this time will ultimately lead to the rapture for all prepared believers still alive at the blowing of the seventh trumpet.

It is also important to grasp the meaning of this one-half hour of silence in heaven and establish its time duration here on earth, and how it fits into Daniel's 2,300-day time line.

In Revelation 3:10, Jesus promised to keep the believers of the Philadelphia church era from the "hour" of trial, which is about 3½ years.

Revelation 13:5 informs us that the king of the North exercises his authority for forty-two months, or 3½ years, during the hour of trial.

Revelation 17:12 reveals that the ten kings set up by the eighth king, or Man of Sin, during the great tribulation period will receive authority as kings, along with the Man of Sin for "one hour," which again comes out to about 3½ years.

Daniel 7:25 and 12:7 also inform us that the Man of Sin will rule the world for a "time, times and half a time," or 3½ years.

Through deductive reasoning, we can conclude that 3½ years is considered as one hour on God's prophetic timetable. Thus the half hour of silence is one-half of a 3½-year period, or approximately twenty-one months.

Satan sets the stage for the next phase of this strong delusion during this time. He begins by making the king of the North appear as a devil, or beast, so that he can eventually have this madman destroyed by his Man of Sin. When the king of the North is defeated on the plains of Megiddo, it will appear as if it is the notorious battle of Armageddon. The king of the North will be challenged for his right to rule the world, and a great rebellion will be mounted against him. An angel represents this conflict by taking the censor, filling it with fire from the altar, and hurling it onto the earth.

THE KING WHO EXALTS HIMSELF

Daniel 11:36–37: The king will do as he pleases. He will exalt and magnify himself above every god and will say unheard of things against the God of gods. He will be successful until the time of wrath is completed, for what has been determined must take place. He will show no regard for the gods of his fathers or for the one desired by women, nor will he regard any god, but will exalt himself above them all.

Revelation 13:12: And I saw a beast coming out of the sea. He had ten horns and seven heads, with ten crowns on his horns, and on each head a blasphemous name. The beast I saw resembled a leopard, but had feet like those of a bear and a mouth like that of a lion. The dragon gave the beast his power and his throne and great authority.

The king of the North uses outright force to demand worship, and he severely persecutes those who will not worship him. This way he appears as a beast. In the king of the North's process of coming to world power, John shows that he is composed of the seven heads of the leopard kingdom led by the king of the South. John shows this by describing the king of the North as having the body of a leopard, which represents the king of the South's kingdom; the feet of a bear, representing the defeat of Russia; and the mouth of a lion, representing the American military alliance. Figure 2-7 shows how the king of the North deludes the world into believing he is the Man of Sin.

THE NEW ECONOMIC MARK

Revelation 13:16: He also forced everyone, small and great, rich and poor, free and slave, to receive a mark on his right hand or on his forehead, so that no one could buy or sell unless he had the mark, which is the name of the beast or the number of his name.

This is another double prophecy. Satan will have the king of the North imitate the fulfillment of this scripture. The so-called mark that is implemented by the king of the North will be the implantation of a computer chip under the skin of the forehead or the hand. This mark of the king of the North will be implemented purely for economic security reasons. This computerized security program is not the real mark of the beast. But of course Satan will delude mankind in such a way that the church will deem this security measure as the condemning mark of the beast.

This delusion is part of Satan making war against those who hold to the testimony of Jesus. His goal is to divide the church. If

YEARS FOR END-TIME PERIOD

```
3        4        5        6        7        8        9        10
|--------|--------|--------|--------|--------|--------|--------|
```

DANIEL'S 70th WEEK—TRIBULATION PERIOD (DAN. 9:24-27)

HOUR OF TRIAL	GREAT TRIBULATION
(REV. 3:10)	(DAN. 12:1)
3½ YEARS	(MATT. 24:21)
	3½ YEARS

SILENCE IN HEAVEN FOR ONE-HALF HOUR, OR 21 MONTHS 7th SEAL (REV. 8:1)

220 DAYS

TEMPLE DESOLATIONS (DAN. 9:26)
2,300 DAYS (DAN. 8:13–14)

ISRAEL BURIES RUSSIAN DEAD FOR SEVEN MONTHS TO CLEANSE THE LAND IN PREPARATION FOR THE DAILY SACRIFICE (EZEK. 39:12)

- THE KING OF THE NORTH ABOLISHES SACRIFICE IN THE MIDDLE OF THE FIRST SEVEN YEARS (DAN. 9:27) (DAN. 11:31–32)
- KING OF THE NORTH WORSHIPS A GOD OF FORTRESSES, OR AMERICA AND ITS SPACE DEFENSE TECHNOLOGY (DAN. 11:31–32, 39)
- KING OF THE NORTH EXALTS HIMSELF (DAN. 11:36–37) (REV. 13:1–2)
- KING OF THE NORTH IMPLEMENTS FALSE MARK, OR ECONOMIC COVENANT WITH MANY—THIS DELUSION APPEARS TO FULFILL REV. 13:16 (THE MARK OF THE BEAST)

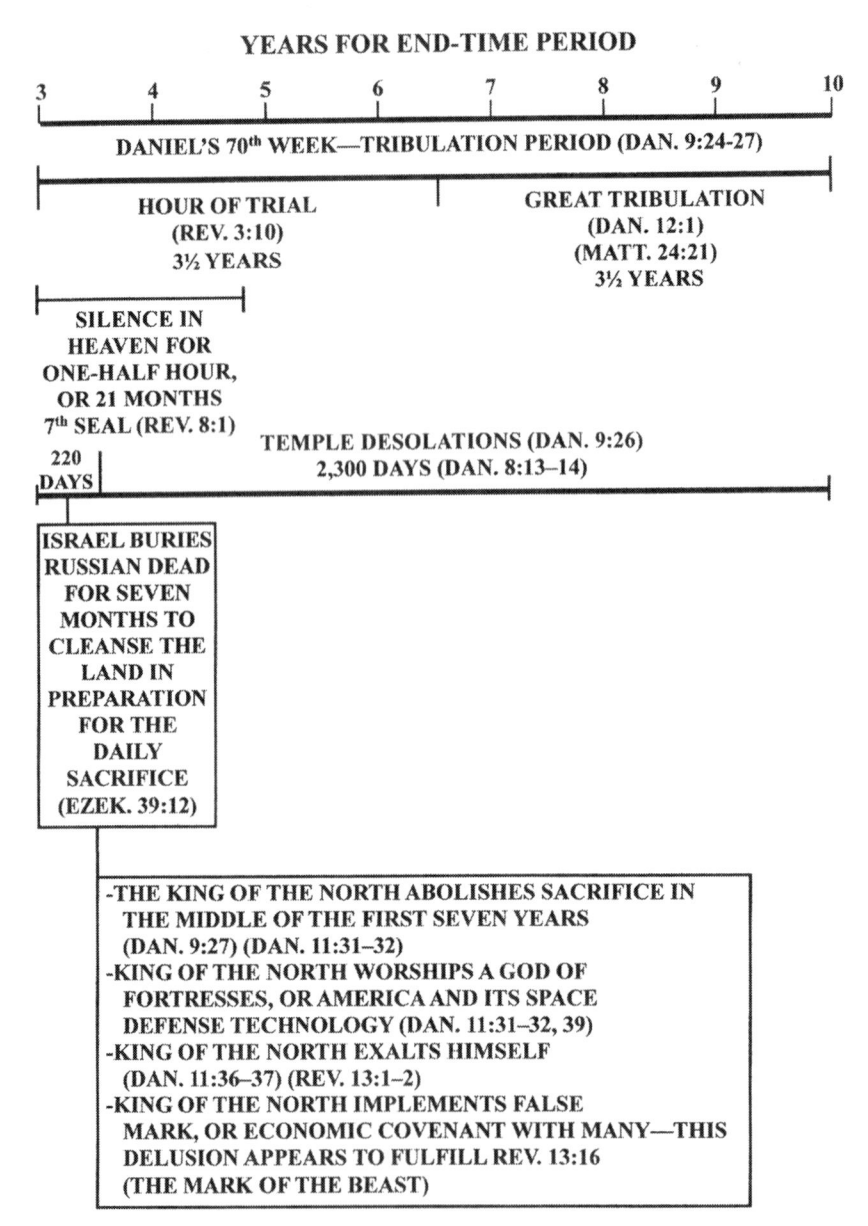

FIGURE 2-7. THE KING OF THE NORTH DELUDES THE WORLD INTO BELIEVING HE IS THE MAN OF SIN

successful, Satan will ensure that the debate over this so-called mark results in the true believers of Jesus being persecuted.

THE MAN OF SIN CONFIRMS A COVENANT WITH MANY

Daniel 9:27: He will confirm a covenant with many for one "seven."

Satan will delude the leaders within the church into falsely reasoning they are halfway through the end-time period. When the king of the North abolishes the sacrifice and implements his new economic- security program near the middle of the first seven years of this ten-year end-time period, the church will decide that half of the tribulation period is over. But they are really only one-third of the way through this deceptive time. They are actually at the very beginning of the tribulation period, which is the last seven years of this ten-year period.

Many will overlook the fact that the Man of Sin will be present when the king of the North abolishes the sacrifice and implements this economic security program. His presence will also fulfill Gabriel's prophecy to Daniel, when he confirms the implementation of this new economic covenant that is now made between many kings of the world and the king of the North. Gabriel carefully chose the word *confirm* so both men could fulfill this prophecy, but in different ways.

A little over 3½ years prior to this time, we see where the king of the North confirmed a covenant with many, meaning he didn't *make* it, but only *agreed* to a covenant that was made by someone else. Likewise, when the king of the North comes to dominate the world and stops the sacrifice from taking place on the Temple Mount, the Man of Sin will be present and agree, or *confirm*, the implementation of this economic security program. This is how both men fulfill Gabriel's prophecy to Daniel in two different ways at two different times.

This computer accounting system is the covenant that the Man of Sin *confirms* with many. But it is actually the king of the North who devises, or *makes*, this covenant so that it appears as if he is implementing the mark of the beast. Satan has the king of the North *confirm a peace covenant* with many for one "seven." He has the real Man of Sin *confirm an economic covenant* with many for one "seven." Notice that Gabriel was very careful in never stating the type of covenant that is confirmed. We have to remember that with the king of the North, Satan is attempting to duplicate every prophecy that applies to the Man of Sin. That's how he continuously deludes the Laodicea church.

THE RISE OF FALSE APOSTLES

2 Peter 2:1–3: But there were also false prophets among the people, just as there will be false teachers among you. They will secretly introduce destructive heresies, even denying the sovereign Lord who bought them—bringing swift destruction on themselves. Many will follow their shameful ways and will bring the way of truth into disrepute. In their greed these teachers will exploit you with stories they have made up. Their condemnation has long been hanging over them, and their destruction has not been sleeping.

2 Peter 2:14: They seduce the unstable.

2 Corinthians 11:13–14: For such men are false apostles, deceitful workmen, masquerading as apostles of Christ. And no wonder, for Satan himself masquerades as an angel of light. It is not surprising, then, if his servants masquerade as servants of righteousness.

Colossians 2:8: See to it that no one takes you captive through hollow and deceptive philosophy, which depends on human tradition and the basic principles of this world rather than on Christ.

1 Timothy 4:1: The Spirit clearly says that in later times some will abandon the faith and follow deceiving spirits and things taught by demons.

2 Timothy 4:3–4: For the time will come when men will not put up with sound doctrine. Instead, to suit their own desires, they will gather around them a great number of teachers to say what their itching ears want to hear. They will turn their ears away from the truth and turn aside to myths.

Hosea 4:14: A people without understanding will come to ruin.

The true mark of the beast that results in the loss of eternal life for the soul comes after the Man of Sin rebels against the king of the North, causing the sixth trumpet war. This war will be mistaken by most as the battle of Armageddon. The Man of Sin will then be revealed (thus, the book of Revelation) to the true believers of Jesus Christ who are still alive from the Laodicea church era. Shortly thereafter, they will be raptured at the sounding of the seventh trumpet.

During the hour of trial, under the reign of the king of the North, Satan simply sets the church up for a grand delusion by which the church itself persecutes the real believers of God. In other words, the religious hypocrites within the Laodicea church, who are not really saved but are masquerading as angels of light, will persecute anyone in the church who takes the computer chip. The religious hypocrites will falsely claim it is the mark of the beast, believing the king of the North is the Man of Sin.

In accordance with Revelation 12:17, this is how Satan makes war against those who hold to the testimony of Jesus. He divides the church on this issue in an effort to destroy the real believers within the Laodicea church who have been spit out to face the hour of trial.

FOLLOWING THE INSTRUCTIONS OF THE WISE

Daniel 11:33–35: Those who are wise will instruct many, though for a time they will fall by the sword or be burned or captured or plundered. When they fall, they will receive a little help, and many who are not sincere will join them. Some of the wise will stumble, so that they may be refined, purified and made spotless until the time of the end, for it will still come at the appointed time.

Here we find where the 144,000 properly instruct the true believers of God during the time that the king of the North implements this new financial economic program using computer chips and codes. The taking of this computer chip will allow people to provide for their families—without condemnation. Since the Man of Sin has yet to come, this economic system will not condemn any soul to hell. It's merely used as a delusional tactic, or weapon, against the people of God by Satan. The implementation of this economic program is strictly used to incite fear and panic inside the church.

By taking the computer chip, Christians will be prone to persecution by the very church they have been attending for years. The church, proclaiming to be the so-called army of God in a fallen world, will condemn any member of their congregation who participates in this program. The church will claim that those who take the chip must be of the devil and are worshiping the person that the church falsely assumes is the beast of Revelation.

Ironically, it was the religious leaders of Jesus' day—all of the Sanhedrin, the Pharisees, and the Sadducees—who, incited by Satan, persecuted Jesus and eventually crucified Him on the cross. Here again, Satan incites religious persecution.

Those "wise" people (in this case, meaning those who eventually come out of the great tribulation), who stumble over the truth behind this program, stand to be deluded during this time of religious debate, confusion, and persecution. By not discerning the truth, they stand to be further deluded when the Man of Sin makes his appearance as supposedly being the Messiah. But they will come to realize the truth when he is fully revealed as the beast of Revelation and not the Messiah. They will become the martyrs of the great tribulation period as they refuse to take his deadly mark, which will appear as a physical offer of salvation, sweetened deceitfully with a promise of untold riches if they accept his offer. One mark is a delusion used to confuse the church and does not result in the worship of anyone; the real mark results in the worship of the Man of Sin as God.

SUFFERING RELIGIOUS PERSECUTION

Matthew 24:9–14: Then you will be handed over to be persecuted and put to death, and you will be hated by all nations because of me. At that time many will turn away from the faith and will betray and hate each other, and many false prophets will appear and deceive many people. Because of the increase of wickedness, the love of most will grow cold, but he who stands firm to the end will be saved. And this gospel of the kingdom will be preached in the whole world as a testimony to all nations, and then the end will come.

This scripture is also a double prophecy. It is fulfilled under the king of the North as well as the Man of Sin. Jesus tells us that it is the hypocritical church that is infected with Satan's false prophets appearing as workers of righteousness. Satan knows the institutionalized church will immediately reject this method of financial accounting under the king of the North. The church will claim it must be the notorious mark of the beast. Bookstores are filled with numerous books claiming this is the method Satan will use to implement the mark. These false prophets are already in place!

Unfortunately, the church has allowed itself to be deceptively drawn to many hollow philosophies, theories, human traditions, and heresies concerning end-time events. Many false teachers have brought the truth of end-time events into disrepute during these last days, specifically setting the stage for all these grand delusions. These false prophets, masquerading as angels of light, will attempt to discredit the teaching of the 144,000, claiming they are the false prophets Jesus and His apostles predicted would come at the time of the end to deceive many. True believers who take the lead of the 144,000 will find themselves being persecuted and flogged by those refusing to accept the truth concerning the use of computer chips as a form of information and economic and identity control, and their misinterpreting this action as being the mark of the beast.

FLOGGED IN THE SYNAGOGUES

Mark 13:9–13: You must be on your guard. You will be handed over to the local councils and flogged in the synagogues. On account of me you will stand before governors and kings as witnesses to them. And the gospel must first be preached to all nations. Whenever you are arrested and brought to trial, do not worry beforehand about what to say. Just say whatever is given you at the time, for it is not you speaking, but the Holy Spirit. Brother will betray brother to death, and a father his child. Children will rebel against their parents and have them put to death. All men will hate you because of me, but he who stands firm to the end will be saved.

Jesus is clearly talking about persecution within the institutionalized church, meaning the religious community as a whole. The false teachers are within the church, deceiving many. Many people within the church will turn away from the faith by not accepting the teaching of the 144,000 Jewish-Christian evangelists, even though John confirms their faithfulness in Revelation 14:5: "No lie was found in their mouths; they are blameless."

First John 4:1 tells us, "Dear friends, do not believe every spirit, but test the spirits to see whether they are from God, because many false prophets have gone out into the world." What is one method by which people can test the spirit of these false prophets? Use 1 John 2:9 as a measuring line: "Anyone who claims to be in the light but hates his brother is still in the darkness."

The 144,000 will not be attempting to physically harm any person who does not agree with them. However, inside the church, Jesus said these false prophets will harm others physically and incite hate amongst their congregations. Listen to 2 Corinthians 11:20: "In fact, you even put up with anyone who enslaves you or exploits you or takes advantage of you or pushes himself forward or slaps you in the face."

These actions are not the doctrines Jesus taught His followers. They have no part in true Christianity. Physical harm or violence in the name of Christ is against the teachings of true Christianity. The Great Commission that Jesus gave to His disciples never included the harming of people who refuse to abide by God's commandments. Our mission is only to preach the gospel, allowing the Holy Spirit of God to work in people's lives. Our mission is not to harm, destroy, boycott, or kill those who decide to live differently.

Rejecting this computer chip naturally makes sense to their human reasoning and false teaching. But accepting it goes completely along with God's methods of demonstrating faith. It didn't make any human sense for Abraham to sacrifice his promised son. It didn't make any sense for Nahum to dip in the Jordan River seven times. It didn't make any sense for Joshua to march around Jericho seven times. It made no sense for Noah to build an ark. It made no sense for Lot to leave Sodom.

On and on it goes with God's methods of demonstrating faith. It will require great faith for believers to accept this computer chip. It will be no different than accepting Social Security numbers and ATM cards — even when the entire religious community is claiming that it appears to be the mark of the Man of Sin. It will be a legitimate economic security program that only masquerades as the mark of the beast.

The personal acceptance of this legitimate economic security measure has serious repercussions for true believers, and Jesus is telling us what we can expect: persecution by the religious community. But if we understand the truth and accept Jesus as our personal Savior, repent of our sins, and publicly confess Him as Lord before men, to the glory of God the Father, we are saved. If we have done that and discern the truth of end-time events, and then we take the microchip implant, Jesus tells us in Mark 13:9 what we can expect on the first Sunday we walk into our local church.

WITNESSING TO THE HYPOCRITES

Luke 21:12–19: But before all this, they will lay hands on you and persecute you. They will deliver you to synagogues and prisons, and you will be brought before kings and governors, and all on account of my name. This will result in your being witnesses to them. But make up your mind not to worry beforehand how you will defend yourselves. For I will give you words and wisdom that none of your adversaries will be able to resist or contradict. You will be betrayed even by parents, brothers, relatives and friends, and they will put some of you to death. All men will hate you because of me. But not a hair of your head will perish. By standing firm you will gain life.

When true believers in Jesus Christ take this so-called mark, they will be persecuted. As they stand up in church and try to explain the truth behind this economic security measure and the true meaning of the king of the North, the religious hypocrites and the false teachers inside the church will turn against them and persecute them inside the church. They will believe they are doing God a favor by beating and possibly killing any person who enters the doors of the church and tries to preach the truth about taking the computer chip. Satan successfully implements this so-called mark to divide the church.

Jesus taught a house divided cannot stand. Satan will use this truth to create a tremendous division between the true believers and the hypocrites in the church. His work has already started in our churches today. The false prophets will lead their flocks into error. The hypocrites who refuse this economic security measure will in turn gladly accept the deadly mark of the Man of Sin, believing he is the true Messiah when the king of the North is destroyed.

With the church slowly becoming more militant and political, it lends complete credibility to Daniel's, John's, and Jesus' prophecies. It is estimated that fifty million believers of Jesus Christ lost their lives as a result of the religious rules and regulations of the church during the tenth through fourteenth centuries. It was Peter who wrongly wanted to start the church by force the night of the Last Supper. But Jesus would have no part of it. It was the politically correct religious community that put the Lord Jesus, as well as the first-century apostles and members of the church, to death. There is nothing more cruel and devastating to mankind on the face of this earth than religious persecution—falsely believing you're doing God a favor by killing those who don't agree with your religious beliefs.

In this passage, it is easy to envision being ostracized by your own local church. Churches will engage in many types of persecution: striking you, flogging you, plundering your house and possessions, burning you at the stake, or imprisoning you. This will happen when they believe your actions are evil, illegal, or against their teaching. That is exactly the direction Satan is taking the church. Fear and ignorance will rule the day!

Through prosperity and affluence, the church is operating under the false pretense that because they are rich, they are more favored by God. They are falsely using their wealth as a measure of being more favored by God than others. They believe that because they are richly blessed, they must be saved. But in Revelation 3:17, Jesus tells the hypocritical Laodicea church generation that it is truly "wretched, pitiful, poor, blind and naked."

To use these words, along with the fact that Jesus portrays Himself as having to stand outside His own church and knock on the door, indicates that the church is on the verge of going to hell! These words describe the state of lost sinners, not true believers. Thus the end-time church is full of hypocrites. And that's why Jesus spits it out to endure the hour of trial: in hopes that most will come to a full knowledge of the truth when their wealth and prosperity are threatened and taken away. By the grace of God, evidently even in its wretched state, Jesus still sees some redeeming qualities in this church.

Jesus predicted the church's betrayal of faith in John 16:1–2: "All this I have told you so that you will not go astray. They will put you out of the synagogue; in fact, a time is coming when anyone who kills you will think he is offering a service to God." James 5:6 supports Jesus' prediction, warning the hypocritical church, "You have condemned and murdered innocent men, who were not opposing you."

The bottom line for the true believer is this: Follow the directions of the 144,000 Jewish-Christian evangelists. Follow their lead—not the institutionalized, hypocritical, worldly church. We can take courage in the words of Solomon in Proverbs 14:32: "When calamity comes, the wicked are brought down, but even in death the righteous have a refuge." Jesus encourages us to stand firm. Religious persecution is always of the devil, even if it is carried out in the name of Jesus or God.

As we'll see in a later chapter, the Man of Sin's mark will be completely different from what is implemented under the king of the North. It will symbolize a completely different meaning and will be tied to worship. Satan will sweeten the taking of the deadly mark with an offer of tremendous wealth for those who will take it and worship him as God. That's why Peter tells us these false prophets exploit people within the church because of their greed. Through greed, they are falsely leading people down a path where they will accept the deadly mark in exchange for untold worldly riches. Figure 2-8 shows how the church confuses the king of the

North's economic program as being the mark of the beast, and how the real Man of Sin later implements the real mark.

RESERVING THE UNRIGHTEOUS FOR JUDGMENT

2 Peter 2:9: The Lord knows how to rescue godly men from trials and to hold the unrighteous for the day of judgment, while continuing their punishment.

Here Peter tells us that the Lord knows how to rescue His true believers out of the hour of trial, even though it results in death. It continues to fulfill Jesus' prophecy that this generation will pass away in one form or another. Meanwhile, He holds the synagogue of Satan (Rev. 3:9) for the day of judgment. Later they will be deluded into believing the Man of Sin is the Messiah.

MIXING THE SEA OF GLASS WITH FIRE

Revelation 15:2: And I saw what looked like a sea of glass mixed with fire.

When John first got to heaven, he saw only a sea of glass (Rev. 4:6). Here John sees it mixed with fire, adding the souls of those who are persecuted during the hour of trial.

ACCOMMODATING THE STRONG DELUSION

Daniel and Revelation were specifically written to accommodate Satan's ability to pull off these deceptive schemes. Another form of unique authorship that only God could devise is the fact that both Daniel and John are full of double prophecies, prophecies that can be fulfilled in different ways by more than one person. Because God is in control of all end-time events, He has ensured Scripture achieves three goals:

(1) All prophecies concerning the Man of Sin are completed by the king of the North in a way that makes everyone believe

YEARS FOR END-TIME PERIOD

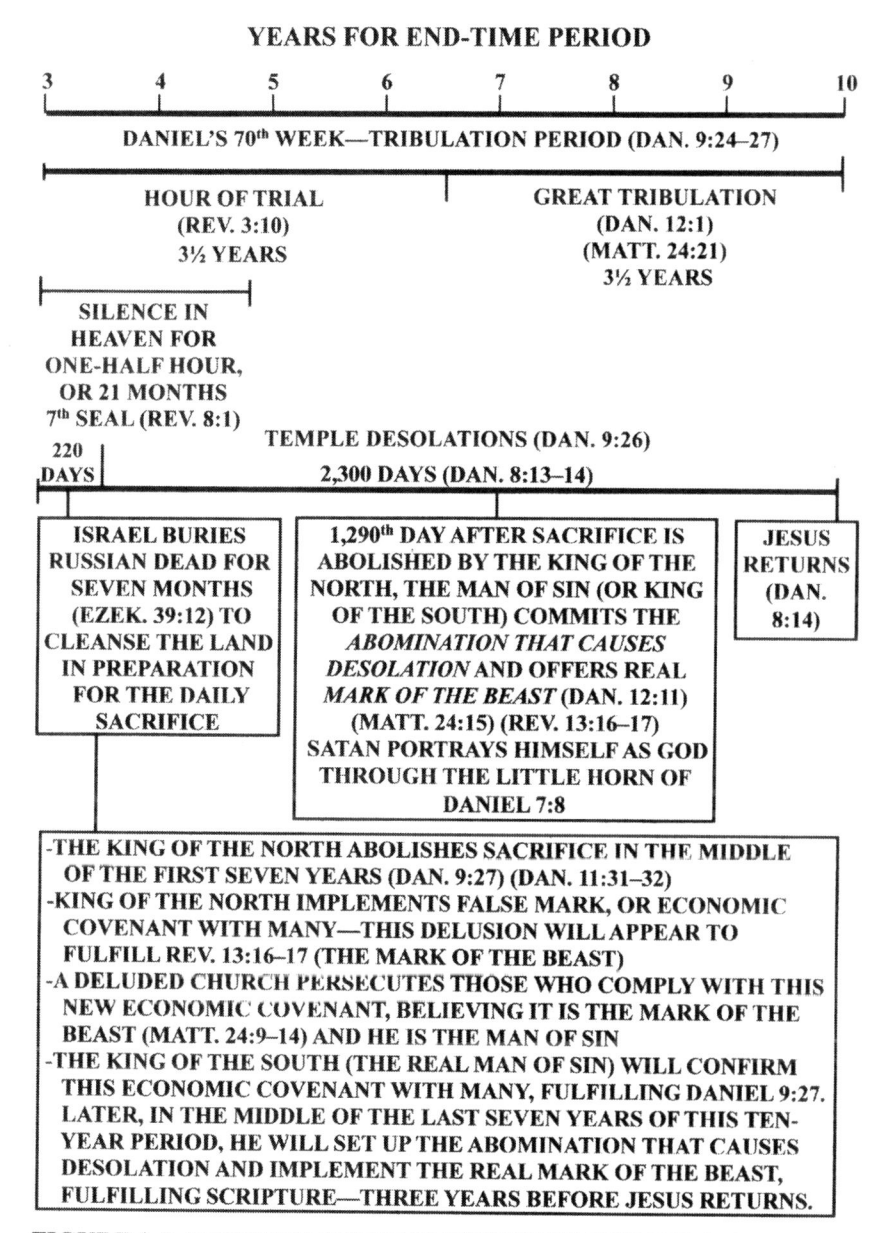

```
3     4     5     6     7     8     9     10
|-----|-----|-----|-----|-----|-----|-----|
```

DANIEL'S 70th WEEK—TRIBULATION PERIOD (DAN. 9:24–27)

| HOUR OF TRIAL (REV. 3:10) 3½ YEARS | GREAT TRIBULATION (DAN. 12:1) (MATT. 24:21) 3½ YEARS |

SILENCE IN HEAVEN FOR ONE-HALF HOUR, OR 21 MONTHS 7th SEAL (REV. 8:1)

220 DAYS | TEMPLE DESOLATIONS (DAN. 9:26)
2,300 DAYS (DAN. 8:13–14)

| ISRAEL BURIES RUSSIAN DEAD FOR SEVEN MONTHS (EZEK. 39:12) TO CLEANSE THE LAND IN PREPARATION FOR THE DAILY SACRIFICE | 1,290th DAY AFTER SACRIFICE IS ABOLISHED BY THE KING OF THE NORTH, THE MAN OF SIN (OR KING OF THE SOUTH) COMMITS THE *ABOMINATION THAT CAUSES DESOLATION* AND OFFERS REAL *MARK OF THE BEAST* (DAN. 12:11) (MATT. 24:15) (REV. 13:16–17) SATAN PORTRAYS HIMSELF AS GOD THROUGH THE LITTLE HORN OF DANIEL 7:8 | JESUS RETURNS (DAN. 8:14) |

- THE KING OF THE NORTH ABOLISHES SACRIFICE IN THE MIDDLE OF THE FIRST SEVEN YEARS (DAN. 9:27) (DAN. 11:31–32)
- KING OF THE NORTH IMPLEMENTS FALSE MARK, OR ECONOMIC COVENANT WITH MANY—THIS DELUSION WILL APPEAR TO FULFILL REV. 13:16–17 (THE MARK OF THE BEAST)
- A DELUDED CHURCH PERSECUTES THOSE WHO COMPLY WITH THIS NEW ECONOMIC COVENANT, BELIEVING IT IS THE MARK OF THE BEAST (MATT. 24:9–14) AND HE IS THE MAN OF SIN
- THE KING OF THE SOUTH (THE REAL MAN OF SIN) WILL CONFIRM THIS ECONOMIC COVENANT WITH MANY, FULFILLING DANIEL 9:27. LATER, IN THE MIDDLE OF THE LAST SEVEN YEARS OF THIS TEN-YEAR PERIOD, HE WILL SET UP THE ABOMINATION THAT CAUSES DESOLATION AND IMPLEMENT THE REAL MARK OF THE BEAST, FULFILLING SCRIPTURE—THREE YEARS BEFORE JESUS RETURNS.

FIGURE 2-8. WHY THE CHURCH CONFUSES THE KING OF THE NORTH'S ECONOMIC PROGRAM AS BEING THE MARK OF THE BEAST

the king of the North is the Man of Sin.
(2) Naturally, all prophecies relating to the Man of Sin are completed by him. But they will be fulfilled in such a way that people won't see him as the Man of Sin. Instead, most will believe he is a loving, forgiving, and victorious messiah.
(3) All prophecies concerning the second coming of Jesus are completed by the Man of Sin as well as prophecies of Jesus' first coming. Satan can then discredit Jesus and negate His second coming, thereby deluding the people of God (the church). This is why Jesus said even the elect could be fooled, if it were possible.

Satan's goal of deluding the church is to convince the people of God to accept his offer of salvation instead of waiting for the rapture, which will occur shortly after the Man of Sin poses as God.

Both Daniel and John specifically wrote their prophecies to accommodate God allowing Satan to complete these three ultimate delusions. No wonder Daniel 8:23 states the Man of Sin, or little horn of Daniel 7:8, is a master of intrigue. And we will now proceed to unveil the delusions of this Man of Sin.

CHAPTER 3

THE GREAT REBELLION

The trumpet judgments begin to describe the great rebellion created and masterminded by the Man of Sin. In order for the Man of Sin to be brought to power, there are several delusions Satan must create in an effort to make people believe he is the Messiah:

(1) The great rebellion actually involves the Man of Sin rebelling against the king of the North. During the course of this rebellion, the city of Rome will be destroyed, giving the appearance that the throne of the beast, sometimes referred to as Babylon the Great by many false prophets, is destroyed. This illusion is created in an effort to keep America from recognizing itself as being Babylon the Great.

(2) The kingdom of the king of the North must be destroyed. The world must be convinced that the king of the North is the Man of Sin so that Satan can appear as a victorious messiah through the king of the South, who is the little horn of Daniel 7:8.

(3) All the world's armed forces must be enticed to converge on Israel. This illusion must be created so that it appears as though Armageddon is a reality when the king of the North is destroyed. It has to appear as if all Bible prophecy is fulfilled when the little horn appears and claims to be God.

(4) Satan must silently and deceptively make war against those who hold to the testimony of Jesus Christ by convincing the

people of America to destroy the people of God. He won't have to say that he hates Christians or Jews. All he has to do is convince the world to worship him as God, thereby putting to death anyone who will not worship him.

Satan's goal is to give the appearance or delusion that the entire book of Revelation has been fulfilled in his coming. The strongest delusion this church generation has accepted is that the bowl judgments coincide with the trumpet judgments. But as we will see, there is a three-year time span between the blowing of the seventh trumpet and the pouring out of God's bowls of wrath when Jesus returns and destroys the Man of Sin.

Satan hopes to convince the world that he is the Messiah coming to earth to redeem mankind for the first and only time. To do this, he must destroy the king of the North, who everyone will believe is the Man of Sin. Additionally, he must convince people that Jesus was a strong delusion that he, posing as God, sent to mankind two thousand years ago. If his plan is successful, then he will be able to convince the remaining population that the new millennium, the one-thousand-year reign of God with mankind on earth, has become a reality.

Once the world is convinced he is God, Satan will then move to offer tremendous wealth to everyone who accepts his offer of salvation. Keep in mind, Jesus came the first time to offer salvation and forgiveness for sin. Jesus is the atoning sacrifice for the sins of the world. Therefore, if Satan successfully discredits Jesus and convinces the world that he is God in the flesh, then he must offer some form of salvation for sin. The Bible is clear that God must redeem mankind from sin. Satan must appear to do just that—offer redemption. Later in this book, we will clearly see that this is the path he uses to destroy many through peace (see Dan. 8:23-25).

INSTANT REPLAY

The first four trumpet judgments, similar to the seal judgments, set the stage for the Man of Sin to rise to power. They affect all the nations of the world. The fifth trumpet brings about a call for justice, just as the fifth seal did. Once Satan has the world's population longing for a messiah, he then makes his move to destroy the person everybody believes is the Man of Sin—the king of the North—bringing about the sixth trumpet war.

This devastating war is staged to appear as the much prophesied battle of Armageddon. Just as the sixth seal war—the Russian invasion of Israel—brought about the rise of the king of the North, the sixth trumpet war will bring about the rise of the Man of Sin.

Just as the seventh seal covered the time the false beast (king of the North) reigned, so the seventh trumpet covers the period of time the Man of Sin rules the world. Figure 3-1 compares the similarities of the seal judgments and trumpet judgments. The trumpet judgments occur with ever-increasing intensity as the Man of Sin mounts his rebellion against the king of the North and challenges his right for world dominion.

Figure 3-1 depicts how the seal and trumpet judgments are designed to fulfill a seven-year period of time, the first seven years of this ten-year period. It is Satan's desire to create the illusion that the first seven years of this ten-year period is the tribulation period, or Daniel's seventieth week. This first seven-year period ends with the destruction of the king of the North in the very place where Armageddon is to occur when Jesus returns. The king of the South initiates this war so that it gives the appearance of the little horn as supposedly being the Messiah, or God in the flesh. In reality, it is the last seven years of this ten-year period that is the tribulation period—the first half being the hour of trial when the terrifying beast, or king of the North, rules, and the last half being the time of great tribulation when the little horn, or Man of Sin, rules the world, appearing as God.

FIRE MIXED WITH BLOOD

Revelation 8:7: The first angel sounded his trumpet, and there came hail and fire mixed with blood, and it was hurled down upon the earth. A third of the earth was burned up, a third of the trees were burned up, and all the green grass was burned up.

YEARS FOR END-TIME PERIOD

```
0         1         2         3         4         5
|---------|---------|---------|---------|---------|
```

| 1st THROUGH 4th SEALS -EUROPEAN CIVIL WAR -KING OF THE NORTH WARS AGAINST THE KING OF THE SOUTH | 5th SEAL -DEAD IN CHRIST ASK, "HOW LONG, O LORD?" (REV. 6:9–11) -THEY LONG TO BE WITH JESUS BUT ARE TOLD TO WAIT (REV. 6:11) | 6th SEAL -RUSSIAN INVASION OF ISRAEL (APPEARS AS ARMAGEDDON) -144,000 SEALED (REV. 7:3–8) -JOHN IS GIVEN A VISION OF THE GREAT TRIBULATION MARTYRS (REV. 7:9–17) | 7th SEAL -KING OF THE NORTH RULES (DELUDES THE WORLD INTO BELIEVING HE IS THE MAN OF SIN) (REV. 13:1–2) -HE MUST BE TAKEN OUT OF THE WAY BEFORE THE REAL MAN OF SIN RISES TO POWER (2 THESS. 2:6–12) |

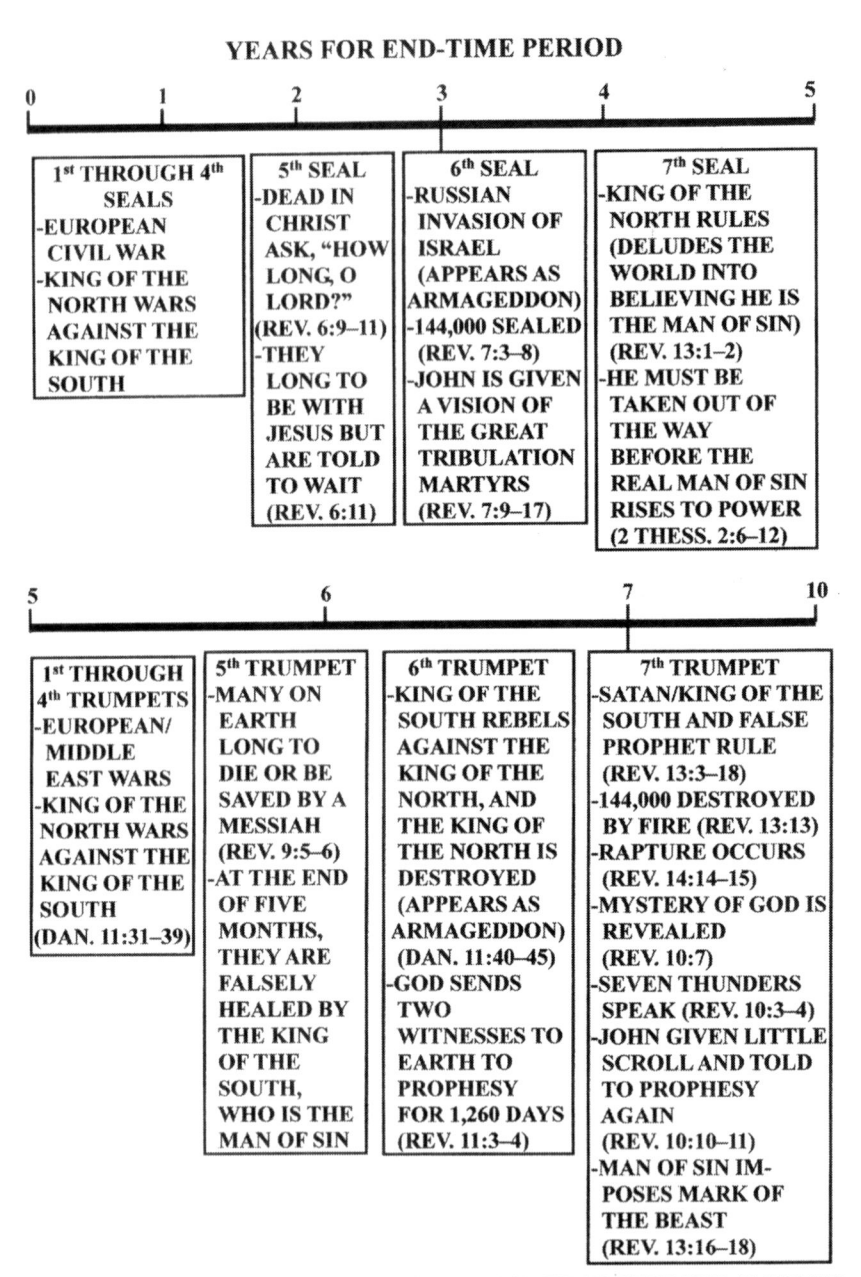

```
5                   6                   7              10
|-------------------|-------------------|--------------|
```

| 1st THROUGH 4th TRUMPETS -EUROPEAN/ MIDDLE EAST WARS -KING OF THE NORTH WARS AGAINST THE KING OF THE SOUTH (DAN. 11:31–39) | 5th TRUMPET -MANY ON EARTH LONG TO DIE OR BE SAVED BY A MESSIAH (REV. 9:5–6) -AT THE END OF FIVE MONTHS, THEY ARE FALSELY HEALED BY THE KING OF THE SOUTH, WHO IS THE MAN OF SIN | 6th TRUMPET -KING OF THE SOUTH REBELS AGAINST THE KING OF THE NORTH, AND THE KING OF THE NORTH IS DESTROYED (APPEARS AS ARMAGEDDON) (DAN. 11:40–45) -GOD SENDS TWO WITNESSES TO EARTH TO PROPHESY FOR 1,260 DAYS (REV. 11:3–4) | 7th TRUMPET -SATAN/KING OF THE SOUTH AND FALSE PROPHET RULE (REV. 13:3–18) -144,000 DESTROYED BY FIRE (REV. 13:13) -RAPTURE OCCURS (REV. 14:14–15) -MYSTERY OF GOD IS REVEALED (REV. 10:7) -SEVEN THUNDERS SPEAK (REV. 10:3–4) -JOHN GIVEN LITTLE SCROLL AND TOLD TO PROPHESY AGAIN (REV. 10:10–11) -MAN OF SIN IM- POSES MARK OF THE BEAST (REV. 13:16–18) |

FIGURE 3-1. COMPARING THE SEAL AND TRUMPET JUDGMENTS

John is not talking about a third of the earth as we know it today. In John's day, he knew nothing about North or South America. John was only aware of the Middle East, Asia Minor, parts of Russia, Africa, and Europe. John is telling his readers about the final conflict of the king of the North in the Middle East.

Daniel 11:40–45 provides a brief synopsis of how the king of the North storms through many countries, causing massive destruction. During his struggle to gain world dominion, the king of the North will invade many countries. The effects of war will bring on the burning of a third of the earth. This may mean the countries of Africa, Europe, Russia, and the Middle East. America will basically be able to keep these wars off its own continent because of its military and technological superiority.

As we're about to see in the next few trumpet judgments, America not only maintains its "wings," or right of religious freedom for all citizens, but actually becomes a safe haven for many Jews. However, its military technology will wreak much havoc on the rest of the world. America will do all this damage in the name of two causes: (1) protecting its interests in Middle East oil and (2) providing peace and safety to its citizens.

OH! YOU DESTROYING MOUNTAIN

Revelation 8:8–9: The second angel sounded his trumpet, and something like a huge mountain, all ablaze, was thrown into the sea. A third of the sea turned into blood, a third of the living creatures in the sea died, and a third of the ships were destroyed.

In this passage, John is not speaking about the oceans of the world. At this stage in his tour of the future, John is speaking about the Mediterranean Sea. John is describing the final conflict revolving around Europe and the Middle East. The Mediterranean Sea is strategically important, as it provides a means of transporting the oil of the Middle East to Europe. Whoever controls this sea can control the flow of oil to the world.

This is an attempt to destroy the king of the North. A nuclear strike will be made against the city of Rome to destroy his religious power base. It will be devastating. Rome will literally be sunk into the sea. This will cause the other cities outlining the Mediterranean Sea's coastlines to be shaken and somewhat destroyed, appearing to fulfill Bible prophecies concerning the coming of the Messiah.

Satan deludes the world into believing that Babylon the Great is Rome in order to mask the truth of Babylon the Great being America. His goal during these trumpet judgments is to make it appear as if Revelation 17 and 18 are fulfilled at this time—so that he may appear as the Messiah!

ANCIENT BABYLON REBELS

Revelation 8:10-11: The third angel sounded his trumpet, and a great star, blazing like a torch, fell from the sky on a third of the rivers and on the springs of water—the name of the star is Wormwood. A third of the waters turned bitter, and many people died from the waters that had become bitter.

This is another nuclear strike that comes against Europe and the king of the North. Detonating it high in the atmosphere will cause radiation fallout over much of Europe.

LITTLE HORN UPROOTS THREE EUROPEAN KINGS

Revelation 8:12: The fourth angel sounded his trumpet, and a third of the sun was struck, a third of the moon, and a third of the stars, so that a third of them turned dark. A third of the day was without light, and also a third of the night.

John is not talking about one-third of the earth. This is John's poetic way of telling how one-third of the iron kingdom is uprooted by the little horn of Daniel 7:8. John is describing another nuclear strike against northern Europe. Not only does radioactive debris fall on a third of the water supplies in Europe, but also one-third of this geographic region is affected from debris and radioactive dust.

The subtle message John relays in these first four trumpet judgments is that they affect one-third of the iron kingdom. If the

European Union is composed of ten European nations, then one-third of the iron kingdom is destroyed during this time of rebellion. We find in Daniel 7:8 and 8:4 where the little horn uproots three of these nations. John shows how one-third of the iron kingdom is uprooted and destroyed by having Satan incite rebellion against the kingdom of the king of the North.

THE KING OF THE JUNGLE ROARS

Revelation 8:13: As I watched, I heard an eagle that was flying in midair call out in a loud voice: "Woe! Woe! Woe to the inhabitants of the earth, because of the trumpet blasts about to be sounded by the other three angels!"

America stands outside the conflict at this point, since we are only aligned militarily with Europe through NATO. We are still a sovereign nation and unwilling to give up our Constitution or right of religious freedom during the time of the king of the North's rule. We will never be a member of the European Union. We are aligned militarily with Europe only to protect our interests around the world. John is telling us that America—seen by Daniel as a lion nation—will issue a strong warning to radical Middle Eastern countries. The flying eagle represents America, proclaiming its national sovereignty and superior air power to the world. As a god of fortresses, America says there will be devastating consequences to what has happened in Europe.

DRINKING FROM THE CUP OF GOD'S WRATH

Revelation 17:4: She held a golden cup in her hand.

Jeremiah 25:38: Like a lion he will leave his lair, and their land will become desolate because of the sword of the oppressor and because of the Lord's fierce anger.

Jeremiah 25:29: See, I am beginning to bring disaster on the city that bears my name, and will you indeed go unpunished? You will not go unpunished, for I am calling down a sword upon all who live on the earth, declares the Lord Almighty.

We've already learned that Old Testament prophets saw America as a lion nation. Daniel sees America becoming bound to Europe, or ensnared by the king of the North. Here John shows how America temporarily departs from this entrapment (lair) and stands alone to wreak havoc on these rebelling countries.

On a human level, America's anger is raised because the war in Europe has severed our oil supply. Oil from the Middle East is routed through Europe to reach America. Thus John sees us issuing a strict warning concerning the devastating consequences of their actions. It's our policy to first negotiate, then annihilate a threat. However, because we fall for this diabolical scheme, America actually brings about its own demise.

OPENING THE ABYSS

Revelation 9:1–2: The fifth angel sounded his trumpet, and I saw a star that had fallen from the sky to the earth. The star was given the key to the shaft of the Abyss. When he opened the Abyss, smoke rose from it like the smoke from a gigantic furnace. The sun and the sky were darkened by the smoke from the Abyss.

The star who is given the key to the shaft of the Abyss is Satan. The first move he makes in his bid to appear as a messiah is to incite America against ancient Babylon, or Iraq and Iran. Figure 3-2 shows the period of time when the Man of Sin begins his reign on earth. The king of the North actually began his forty-two-month reign by inciting Russia against Israel at the fourth seal judgment. So now, in like manner, the Man of Sin's time of terror begins at the fifth trumpet judgment when he pits America, Babylon the Great, against Iran and Iraq, ancient Babylon.

Although John shows us spiritually that Satan is that star that has been given the key to the shaft of the bottomless pit, or the Abyss, John shows us the physical reality of how this Abyss is opened. It begins with Iraq and Iran's defiance against America's stern warning.

The Great Rebellion

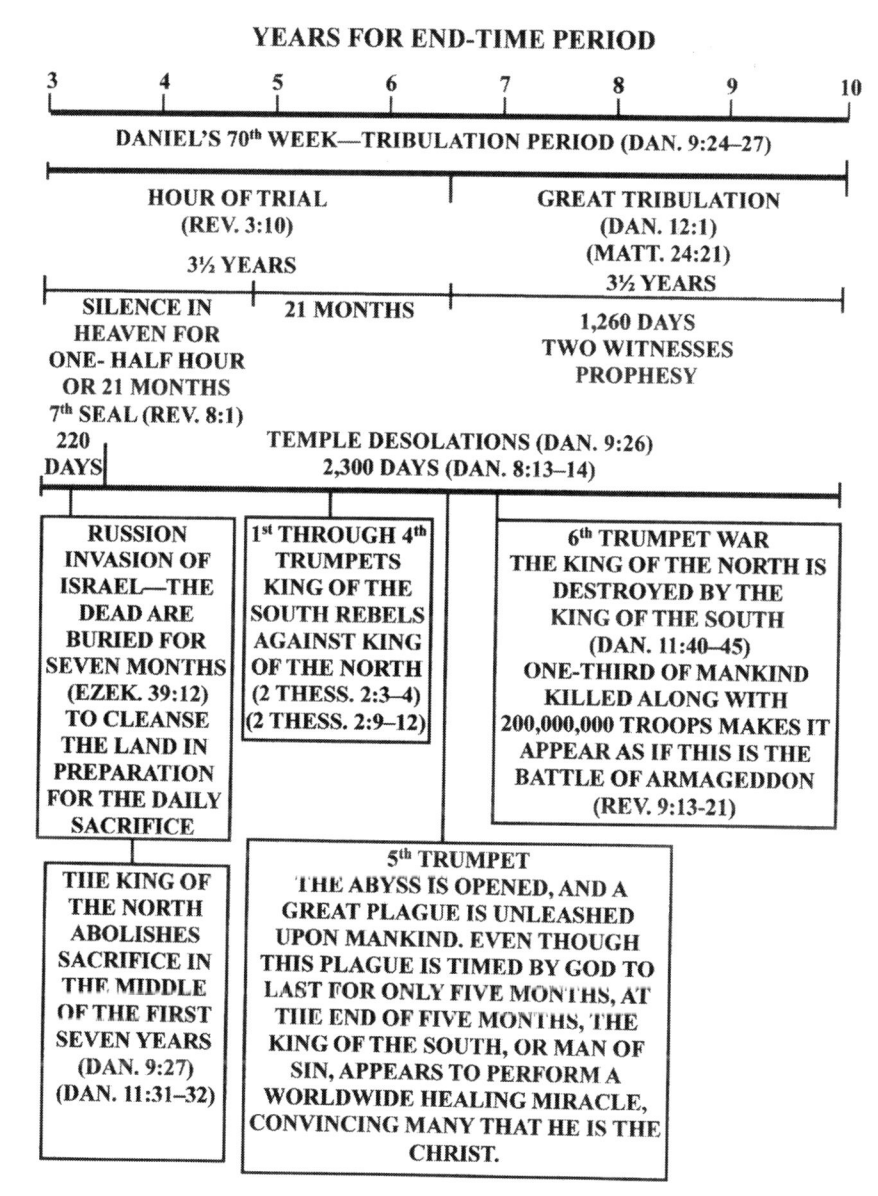

YEARS FOR END-TIME PERIOD

```
3        4        5        6        7        8        9        10
|--------|--------|--------|--------|--------|--------|--------|
```

DANIEL'S 70th WEEK—TRIBULATION PERIOD (DAN. 9:24–27)

HOUR OF TRIAL (REV. 3:10) 3½ YEARS	GREAT TRIBULATION (DAN. 12:1) (MATT. 24:21) 3½ YEARS
SILENCE IN HEAVEN FOR ONE-HALF HOUR OR 21 MONTHS 7th SEAL (REV. 8:1)	21 MONTHS	1,260 DAYS TWO WITNESSES PROPHESY

220 DAYS | TEMPLE DESOLATIONS (DAN. 9:26)
2,300 DAYS (DAN. 8:13–14)

| RUSSIAN INVASION OF ISRAEL—THE DEAD ARE BURIED FOR SEVEN MONTHS (EZEK. 39:12) TO CLEANSE THE LAND IN PREPARATION FOR THE DAILY SACRIFICE | 1st THROUGH 4th TRUMPETS KING OF THE SOUTH REBELS AGAINST KING OF THE NORTH (2 THESS. 2:3–4) (2 THESS. 2:9–12) | 6th TRUMPET WAR THE KING OF THE NORTH IS DESTROYED BY THE KING OF THE SOUTH (DAN. 11:40–45) ONE-THIRD OF MANKIND KILLED ALONG WITH 200,000,000 TROOPS MAKES IT APPEAR AS IF THIS IS THE BATTLE OF ARMAGEDDON (REV. 9:13-21) |

| THE KING OF THE NORTH ABOLISHES SACRIFICE IN THE MIDDLE OF THE FIRST SEVEN YEARS (DAN. 9:27) (DAN. 11:31–32) | 5th TRUMPET THE ABYSS IS OPENED, AND A GREAT PLAGUE IS UNLEASHED UPON MANKIND. EVEN THOUGH THIS PLAGUE IS TIMED BY GOD TO LAST FOR ONLY FIVE MONTHS, AT THE END OF FIVE MONTHS, THE KING OF THE SOUTH, OR MAN OF SIN, APPEARS TO PERFORM A WORLDWIDE HEALING MIRACLE, CONVINCING MANY THAT HE IS THE CHRIST. |

FIGURE 3-2. THE MAN OF SIN BEGINS HIS REBELLION (2 THESSALONIANS 2:3–12)

I Will Make Myself Like The Most High!

Any time John writes that a star falls from the sky, he is describing an instrument of warfare having the capacity of a missile launch of some form. This missile comes out of Iran/Iraq into Kuwait, literally opening what is called the Abyss, once known as the Garden of Eden!

Let's give this geographical location the historical significance it deserves. Kuwait sits over the original location of the gate to the Garden of Eden. Within the ancient Garden of Eden, or what is now the Abyss, are millions of demons that have been locked up because of God's judgment on them. They have been reserved until the end-times to be let loose with their deceitful and destructive powers. The significance of this location, during this last generation's lifetime, is how God has brought mankind full circle to the Garden of Eden. Only during this last generation has it played its most important role: serving as the wine of America's luxury. It is our dependence on oil that makes America Babylon the Great.

Looking at the area historically, the Abyss was first opened when America began drilling oil wells in the 1970s, unsuspectingly letting some of the demons loose. This brought about a dramatic increase in knowledge—worldly knowledge—coupled with the rise of false prophets claiming to have knowledge of end-time events described in Daniel and Revelation. In short, these evil spirits were let loose to lay the foundation for Satan to eventually appear to mankind as a messiah. Thus many within the church have falsely been taught that Revelation covers only a seven-year period, when in fact it covers a ten-year period of time.

Concerning worldly knowledge, we went from bulky handheld calculators and typewriters to computers and microprocessors. Then, in 1991, the Abyss was opened again. As a result of the Gulf War, and from the madness of Saddam Hussein, American oil wells were set on fire. It took several months for American engineers and firefighters to put out the fires from these oil wells.

Strangely enough, since 1991, we've seen even more dramatic changes in the world. We've seen the most prosperous time in the history of mankind—sweepstakes, lotteries, gambling, wasteful government spending, overtaxation, prosperous world stock markets, and a worldwide increase in American mass-marketing ploys. The

The Great Rebellion

Dow has jumped several thousand points since the Gulf War. There has been a tremendous increase in world terrorism, lawlessness, and injustice. The burning of Kuwait oil wells was strictly controlled for the releasing of end-time demonic activity, both inside and outside the church.

Now this passage describes what happens to the world when a missile is launched into this area. Millions of demonic angels are let loose to wreak havoc on mankind. We can see that the Abyss is not some mystical place or myth. It is a literal dungeon for demons, located in the area where the original Garden of Eden was located. It is divinely located underneath American oil wells!

Kuwait is the land of Ur, where Abraham lived with his father and wife before God had him move to the area of Israel. We also see in Genesis where the Garden of Eden was located in this land, occupying the area of Kuwait and Iraq and Iran. The Euphrates River ran through the Garden of Eden. It is no wonder that Babylon, shown to Daniel as being the first world empire, was located along the Euphrates River. However, the ancient city of Babylon, even though it did undergo some reconstruction by Saddam Hussein, is not the Babylon the Great that John later writes about in Revelation 17 and 18.

Ancient Babylon does not sit "on many waters," as recorded by John. Nor do all the merchants of the world trade with Iran and Iraq today. Amazingly enough, just as John prophesied over two thousand years ago, America sits on many waters, has become adorned in luxury during these last days, and has a crucial interest in the Middle East and Europe—oil. As a result of our dependence on that resource, America has been able to intoxicate the world with its vast trade programs. Additionally, as a result of liberal freedom, John pictured America in Revelation 18-2 as a home for many false prophets, "a home for demons and a haunt for every evil spirit, a haunt for every unclean and detestable bird."

Here John is not talking about cults alone. He's talking about evil spirits, or false prophets within the churches of America, who are masquerading as workers of righteousness, misleading many people about the truths behind end-time events.

Therefore, as an added twist to this drama, ancient Babylon is about to be destroyed by the nation that Jeremiah 51:33 calls the "daughter of Babylon," or that nation John describes as "Babylon the Great," namely, America! Daniel envisioned America as a tree in chapter 3. In these last days, America has bound itself to Europe through NATO and has literally touched the heavens with its space program and air superiority. Additionally, it has become a nation, or tree, of refuge for all nationalities, depicted by Daniel as birds perching on its branches. It is the nation God uses during the end-times as a golden cup in His hand to bring certain destruction upon the world, just as ancient Babylon was used by God in its day.

This time, however, it is Iran and Iraq that are about to be completely annihilated, never to be inhabited again. Even though it is deemed as warranted judgment by the people of the world, Satan will use the destruction of ancient Babylon—and Rome—to delude people into believing that Revelation 17 and 18 are being fulfilled in their destruction. This is done so that America doesn't see itself as Babylon the Great. As portrayed in Revelation 17:5, this is the great mystery behind Babylon the Great—the fact that it cannot recognize itself as being Babylon the Great! Instead, Satan's plan is to delude America into believing it is God's most favored nation when he portrays himself as God through the little horn of Daniel 7:8.

THE HISTORY OF BABYLON THE GREAT

Ancient Babylon sits directly over the original Garden of Eden. It is also located along the fourth river on the earth today that was also flowing in the Garden of Eden, the Euphrates River, as recorded in Genesis 2:14. In Genesis 2:9, we find where God planted a fertile garden in Eden, and that's why this land is rich in oil, or fossil fuel, today. Strangely enough, in the middle of the garden were the Tree of Life and the Tree of Knowledge of Good and Evil. It was in this very location where the devil tempted Adam and Eve to commit the first sin against God.

Years later, the people of earth vowed to build a tower to God on this very spot. The result brought God's judgment, and He caused confusion in the common language of the day. This is the account

The Great Rebellion

of the Tower of Babel. Mankind has been confused about itself and with each other's differences ever since.

But in these last days, America has struggled to bring all the cultural differences together into one melting pot. We have labored to eliminate the confusion that God brought upon mankind in the days of ancient Babylon. Amazingly, just as ancient Babylon attempted to prove the existence of God by building a tower to God, America has searched the outer reaches of space in its quest to know its creator. Using the finest instruments of our technology, the world still refuses to be convinced that God truly exists. Therefore, we are still devising ways that will take us to the outermost regions of the universe, hoping to concretely know the source of mankind's existence, even though God tells us that our labor is in vain.

Centuries after the Tower of Babel, a young Jewish captive named Daniel received visions of future world empires in this very location. He was given visions of Jesus' first and second advents. Daniel's visions also included the time when Satan would possess the Man of Sin and convince America, in its never-ending search for physical proof there is a God that *he* is God.

Today God is still using the resources of the Garden of Eden to bring mankind full circle to where its existence began. America has divinely become dependent upon this part of the world in fulfillment of Bible prophecy. Jesus showed Daniel and John how this would happen. Since God knows the end from the beginning, it should be proof enough that Jesus is God. But regardless of this fact, Satan continues to plague mankind over God's existence and who God is. Just as Satan was behind the building of the Tower of Babel, he is behind America's ability to reach the heavens through our space programs, ever searching the source of our existence. God has shown us the source of our existence—Jesus Christ. But because the world constantly shows contempt for God through lack of faith and doubt over who God is (Jesus), He's purposely brought mankind full circle back to the Garden of Eden, historically, prophetically, and spiritually speaking, and has made the world ripe for judgment.

Scripture is littered with the significant role America plays in the fulfillment of end-time prophecy. All the Old Testament prophets were given visions of America's existence. Isaiah 47:1 calls us the

"Virgin Daughter of Babylon." Jeremiah 50:42 calls us the "Daughter of Babylon." In Revelation 17:5 John calls us "Babylon the Great." The mystery that bridges America to ancient Babylon—noted by John in Revelation 17:7—has one simple common denominator—oil that is located under the ancient land of Babylon.

Because America has become dependent upon oil from this region of the world, no previous generation would discern that this nation would become Babylon the Great, the Mother of Prostitutes, promoting all the abominations of the earth. Oil has linked America to trade with all the other nations of the world. Because of our technology in this industry, all the leaders of the world now speak a common language once again, English. This comparison to ancient Babylon could only be discerned during this generation, bringing us full circle as a result of America being raised up in these last days.

John hears the fifth trumpet blow, then sees the evil demons that have been locked in the bottomless pit for centuries, awaiting the day and hour that they could be let loose upon mankind. This is exactly what happens as the fifth trumpet is blown. Kuwait, or the ancient land of the Garden of Eden, is once again opened, as evidenced by John seeing the "black smoke rising as if from a gigantic furnace."

Saddam Hussein knew the best way to hurt America was to destroy our oil interests in the Middle East. This is why he left Kuwait burning in 1991. Unknowingly, by divine providence, he ever so slightly opened the Abyss, allowing evil spirits to escape their dark dungeon and bring about the fulfillment of end-time Scripture. Now here at the fifth trumpet, the Abyss is opened full measure, letting loose the most vicious demonic plague to ever strike mankind. The Gulf War syndrome will look small in comparison.

The Gulf War syndrome is a small example of a plague of demons that was let loose in 1991. But here at the fifth trumpet, they are let loose to unleash their pent-up torture upon all of mankind. John describes the five months of torture this demonic plague wreaks upon all those who do not have the mark of God on their forehead.

In Revelation 9:5–6, John writes, "They [the demons] were not given power to kill them [people], but only to torture them for five months. And the agony they suffered was like that of the sting of a scorpion when it strikes a man. During those days men will seek death, but will not find it; they will long to die, but death will elude them."

A GREAT PLAGUE OF LOCUSTS

Jeremiah 51:14: The Lord Almighty has sworn by himself: I will surely fill you with men, as with a swarm of locusts, and they will shout in triumph over you.

Isaiah 33:4: Your plunder, O nations, is harvested as by young locusts; like a swarm of locusts men pounce on it.

Revelation 9:7–11: The locusts looked like horses prepared for battle. On their heads they wore something like crowns of gold, and their faces resembled human faces. Their hair was like women's hair, and their teeth were like lions' teeth. They had breastplates like breastplates of iron, and the sound of their wings was like the thundering of many horses and chariots rushing into battle. They had tails and stings like scorpions, and in their tails they had power to torment people for five months. They had as king over them the angel of the Abyss, whose name in Hebrew is Abaddon, and in Greek, Apollyon.

In 1991, we could hear the beginning shouts of triumph from American forces as they liberated Kuwait. When Iran/Iraq rebels against the warnings of America, John poetically describes how infuriated America will become against their outright defiance, when John records in Revelation 13:4: "Who is like the beast? Who can make war against him?" Jeremiah 51:14 clearly shows us God's intent to fill the ancient land of Babylon with an overwhelming army, described as a swarm of locusts. Revelation 9:7–11 is John's poetic description of the American Department of Defense in its modern form today:

(1) *Crowns of gold* is how John sees that this army is supernaturally manipulated by Satan, who, according to John in Revelation 12:3, has seven heads and ten horns and seven crowns on his heads.

(2) *Faces resembling human faces* clearly depicts that this swarm of locusts is a human army—just as God announced in Jeremiah 51:14—that runs headfirst into a spiritual swarm of demons.

(3) *Hair like women's hair* clearly depicts the makeup of our current armed forces, the world's only force in which women are allowed to participate in combat.

(4) *Teeth like lions' teeth* is John's way of relying on Daniel's prophetic vision of America being a lion nation according to Daniel 7:4.

(5) *Breastplates of iron* comes from the prophetic vision of Daniel 5:23, showing that America first becomes bound to the iron kingdom of the king of the North.

(6) *The sound of their wings* is a prophetic vision Daniel had that America, as a lion kingdom, was symbolized as having the great wings of an eagle, indicating that we maintain air superiority around the world.

(7) *Tails and stings like scorpions* obviously describes our superior arsenal of weapons, in which we have heavily invested during these last days.

(8) The Greek name *Apollyon* means "destroyer," a clear indication that these armed forces, as well as the spiritual swarm of locusts, are now being manipulated by the Man of Sin. This conflict will be the beginning of America loosening its bonds with the king of the North and slowly becoming bound to the bronze kingdom of the Man of Sin as envisioned in Daniel 4:23.

THE TWO WITNESSES BEGIN TO PROPHESY

Revelation 11:2–3: They will trample on the holy city for 42 months. And I will give power to my two witnesses, and they will prophesy for 1,260 days, clothed in sackcloth.

Here at the end of the hour of trial, God sends two witnesses to earth. They prophesy outside the holy temple in the city of Jerusalem. The Russian invasion begins this final seven years leading to the

The Great Rebellion

return of Jesus Christ. Therefore, the temple is rebuilt after the Russian invasion of Israel, during the seven months Israel is busy burying the dead.

The two witnesses will witness about Jesus during the great tribulation period. They serve as a constant thorn in the Man of Sin's side as he attempts to convince the world that he is God. He will not have the power to kill them until just before the actual return of Jesus with His saints. Although John follows these two witnesses to the time of the end, I'm going to come back to them later when we approach the return of Jesus to earth with His saints.

The 144,000 Jewish-Christian evangelists were sealed and in place before the king of the North desolated the temple and stopped the sacrifice from taking place. Likewise, these two witnesses must take their place at the temple before the Man of Sin commits the abomination that causes desolation, passing it off as the wedding supper of the Lamb. Whereas the fifth seal brought the sealing of the 144,000 Jewish-Christian evangelists, the fifth trumpet reigns in the period of time for these two witnesses to prophesy.

THE DEMONIC SWARM OF LOCUSTS

Revelation 9:3–6: And out of the smoke locusts came down upon the earth and were given power like that of scorpions of the earth. They were told not to harm the grass of the earth or any plant or tree, but only those people who did not have the seal of God on their foreheads. They were not given power to kill them, but only to torture them for five months. And the agony they suffered was like that of the sting of a scorpion when it strikes a man. During those days men will seek death, but will not find it; they will long to die, but death will elude them.

Revelation 9:10–11: They had tails and stings like scorpions, and in their tails they had power to torment people for five months. They had as king over them the angel of the Abyss, whose name in Hebrew is Abaddon, and in Greek, Apollyon.

In these last days, America has been blessed with a rich knowledge of medical technology. Time and again, we have overcome plague after plague that Satan has brought against mankind. However, as Americans enter this region and return home, the results of this plague are horrendous. And it is catching, as John indicates by stating that the whole world is subjected to its effects. So horrible will be this plague that people will want to die. But John makes it clear that people will not die. Satan now sets the stage for the world to cry out for a miracle cure. Any person who can cure them would surely be worshiped as God. And this is exactly where Satan wants America.

When the Man of Sin steps forward and claims that he is God, America of course will ask for a sign. When the demonic torture is stopped, it will pave the way for America to take on the heart of a man—the real Man of Sin, or the little horn of Daniel 7:8—posing as the Messiah! When America is convinced that the Man of Sin is God in the flesh, they will weep and mourn that they have missed his existence all along. The Man of Sin, of course, will use this opportunity to incite the entire world against the king of the North, who they now are convinced must evidently be the evil Man of Sin. It's the ultimate double-cross, for the king of the North and for the great harlot—America.

THE LITTLE HORN'S GREAT REBELLION

Revelation 9:13–19: The sixth angel sounded his trumpet, and I heard a voice coming from the horns of the golden altar that is before God. It said to the sixth angel who had the trumpet, "Release the four angels who are bound at the great river Euphrates." And the four angels who had been kept ready for this very hour and day and month and year were released to kill a third of mankind. The number of the mounted troops was two hundred million. I heard their number.

The horses and riders I saw in my vision looked like this: Their breastplates were fiery red, dark blue, and yellow as sulfur. The heads of the horses resembled the heads of lions, and out of their mouths came fire, smoke and sulfur. A third of mankind was killed by the three plagues of fire, smoke and sulfur that came out of their mouths. The power of the horses was in their mouths and in their tails; for their tails were like snakes, having heads with which they inflict injury.

Daniel 8:23–24: In the latter part of their reign, when rebels have become completely wicked, a stern-faced king [the Man of Sin or little horn of Daniel 7:8], a master of intrigue [2 Thessalonians 2:9 states the Man of Sin will come to power under the influence of using all kinds of counterfeit miracles, signs and wonders, and in every sort of evil that deceives those who are perishing], will arise. He will become very strong, but not by his own power [he's Satan incarnate posing as God]. He will cause astounding devastation [the sixth trumpet war appears as Armageddon] and will succeed in whatever he does [convince the world he's God]. He will destroy the mighty men [the king of the North and his empire] and the holy people [the people of God]. (Explanations in brackets are mine.)

Daniel 8:12: Because of rebellion [because of the Man of Sin rebelling against the king of the North], the host of the saints [144,000 Jewish-Christian evangelists] and the daily sacrifice [originally stopped by the king of the North] were given over to it [the Man of Sin, or king of the South, or the little horn of Daniel 7:8]. (Explanations in brackets are mine.)

2 Thessalonians 2:3: Don't let anyone deceive you in any way, for that day [the day of the rapture] will not come, until the rebellion occurs and the man of lawlessness [Satan, through the little horn of Daniel 7:8] is revealed [as supposedly being God], the man doomed to destruction [destroyed by Jesus]. (Explanations in brackets are mine.)

Daniel 11:21–23: He [the king of the North] will be succeeded by a contemptible person [the little horn of Daniel 7:8] who has not been given the honor of royalty. He will invade the kingdom when its people feel secure, and he will seize it through intrigue [convincing America he is God through a healing miracle]. Then an overwhelming army will be swept away before him [the sixth trumpet war appears as if it is Armageddon]; both it and a prince of the covenant [king of the North] will be destroyed. After coming to an agreement with him [that he is the Messiah], he will act deceitfully, and with only a few people [the False Prophet and the ten new kings he establishes] he will rise to power. (Explanations in brackets are mine.)

This is the war of rebellion that brings the Man of Sin to world power, appearing as a messiah (see Figure 3-2). This is the end for the king of the North. This war will appear to be the last great battle for mankind, Armageddon. Even though this will be mankind's most devastating war to date, it is a war that Satan stages in an effort to make the Man of Sin appear as the Messiah. In an effort to delude people into believing the Man of Sin is God, this war must be staged in the very location Jesus will come three years after this war ends. Satan must attempt to make people believe that all Bible prophecies concerning the return of Jesus have been fulfilled through the Man of Sin.

After the king of the North invades the Middle East, Daniel 11:44-45 tells us that he will meet his end in Israel: "But reports from the east and north will alarm him, and he will set out in a great rage to destroy and annihilate many. He will pitch his royal tents between the seas at the beautiful holy mountain. Yet he will come to his end, and no one will help him."

Let's begin by comparing these scriptures with modern-day geography. Once again we are taken to the place of the ancient Garden of Eden. Four angels bound long ago near the Euphrates River are let loose to kill one-third of mankind. This is accomplished through a world war in the Middle East and in the land of Iran, Iraq, Kuwait, and Israel. One to two billion people die as a result of this war and its devastating effects. As in all wars, this includes Christians and non-Christians alike. It is part of the doctrine of this generation passing away, just as Jesus explained in Matthew 24:34. This war begins near the very end of the hour of trial, as the Man of Sin

The Great Rebellion

reveals himself as God to an undiscerning world. The entire world will appear to have gone mad, except for one man—the Man of Sin.

Daniel 8:23 states the Man of Sin will be a master of intrigue. He will have to deal with so many religious factions and kingdoms that come against each other in one single location. They all join together to annihilate each other for many different reasons and for many different causes.

Daniel 11:44-45 indicates the ultimate showdown of all the world's forces will come when the king of the North pitches his royal tents near the beautiful holy mountain. That mountain, of course, is the Mount of Olives. His forces will be gathered in the Valley of Jehoshaphat, called Megiddo today, or known as Armageddon in Hebrew. Thus Daniel writes that the king of the North brings all the world's forces into the land of Israel, outside the city of Jerusalem where there is a bowl-shaped valley. As we've already seen, this is where Russia met its end. This is where the king of the North will meet his end also. Ultimately, this is where the Man of Sin will meet his end when Jesus returns.

This valley is the great winepress of God. This is where the great Jordan River stretches for a distance of two hundred miles. This is the spot where evil had its ultimate beginning and will meet its ultimate end. Through intrigue, the Man of Sin convinces all the nations of the world to rebel and converge on this location against the remaining forces of the king of the North, who many will believe is the one and only Antichrist.

THE WRATH OF APOLLYON

Revelation 9:11: They had as king over them the angel of the Abyss, whose name in Hebrew is Abaddon, and in Greek, Apollyon.

Isaiah 54:16: And it is I who have created the destroyer to work havoc.

Instead of this battle bringing in the kingdom of Jesus, it brings in the kingdom of the Man of Sin. Although the fifth trumpet war between Iraq/Iran and America will appear as the great rebellion, it is actually the sixth trumpet war, incited by the Man of Sin against the king of the North and all the nations of the world that fulfills the prophecies of the great rebellion. This is the strong delusion that God sends the world as spoken of in 2 Thessalonians 2:3–4.

CREATING THE STRONG DELUSION

Since this great battle brings in the kingdom of the Man of Sin posing as God, it will appear as if the bowl judgments of Revelation 16 are fulfilled in this great battle. This is how people become deluded into believing that the king of the North is the notorious beast and the Man of Sin is the Messiah.

The mistake made by all previous generations is their attempt to overlay the trumpet judgments with the bowl judgments. This places all the events of Revelation in a seven-year time frame. It doesn't work according to Daniel's prophetic ten-year time frame for the end-times. The following paragraphs relate how this strong delusion can appear to occur when the trumpet judgments are improperly overlaid with the bowls of God's wrath.

The plague that sweeps the world when the Abyss is opened will appear to be the completion of the first bowl of wrath described in Revelation 16:2, where "ugly and painful sores broke out on the people who had the mark of the beast and worshiped his image." He wants people to be convinced that whoever took the false beast's microchip are surely receiving the punishment of God.

The four angels that are released at the great river Euphrates will appear to be the completion of the third and sixth bowls of wrath as stated in Revelation 16:4: ". . . on the rivers and springs of water, and they became blood;" and Revelation 16:12–14: ". . . on the great river Euphrates, and its water was dried up to prepare the way for the kings from the East."

With the second trumpet judgment of Revelation 8:8–9, John shows us that a mountain all ablaze is thrown into the sea. The sea is turned into blood. A third of the living creatures in the sea are killed, and a third of the ships on the Mediterranean Sea are destroyed. This will appear to be the fulfillment of the second bowl of wrath

The Great Rebellion

described in Revelation 16:3: ". . . on the sea, and it turned into blood like that of a dead man, and every living thing in the sea died."

Revelation 8:12, where a third of the sun is struck, will appear to fulfill the fourth bowl of wrath described in Revelation 16:8–9: ". . . on the sun, and the sun was given power to scorch people with fire."

In the first trumpet judgment, we see hail and fire mixed with blood are hurled down upon the earth. This burns up a third of the trees and all the green grass. In the fifth trumpet judgment, we see where the sun and sky are darkened by the smoke from the Abyss. These two judgments will appear to be the completion of the fifth bowl of wrath, Revelation 16:10: ". . . on the throne of the beast, and his kingdom was plunged into darkness."

Since this war is fought in northern Israel, the sixth trumpet judgment will appear to fulfill Revelation 16:16: "Then they gathered the kings together to the place that in Hebrew is called Armageddon."

The seat of religion for the king of the North will be situated in Rome. Therefore, many false prophets today are teaching that Revelation 17 and 18 are prophecies concerning the destruction of the city of Rome, which is known for sitting on seven hills. They teach that the woman Babylon the Great represents the false religion of the Beast, who leads the European Union. Therefore, under this false scenario created by Satan, the destruction of Rome will appear to be the fulfillment of the seventh bowl of wrath described in Revelation 16:17–21.

What previous generations have failed to discern is that Satan portrays himself as God through the little horn of Daniel 7:8. But Satan is Apollyon, the destroyer of God's people and all of mankind. It is Satan who empowers the Man of Sin by the will of God. This entire delusion is created so that when the kingdom of the king of the North is destroyed, people will believe the strong delusion that the Man of Sin is God and America is his most favored nation—seen as a harlot in Revelation by John.

The false prophets of Satan are falsely teaching today that there is only one beast, the king of the North; that either Rome or ancient Babylon (Iran/Iraq) is Babylon the Great; and that Revelation covers only seven years and is the story of how God reveals Himself to the world. As you have seen from this book, all of their teaching is completely false, designed strictly to lead people to believe that when the king of the North is destroyed, the person who comes after him must evidently be the Christ.

The truth is, the man who comes after what appears to be the battle of Armageddon will be the strong delusion that God sends to an unbelieving world that has rejected His true and only Son, Jesus.

Jesus won't return to fulfill the prophecies concerning the bowls of wrath for about another three years. Before we study His return, we'll study the path America takes in becoming bound to the Man of Sin.

ACCOMMODATING THE MAN OF SIN

Revelation 9:20–21: The rest of mankind that were not killed by these plagues still did not repent of the work of their hands; they did not stop worshiping demons, and idols of gold, silver, bronze, stone and wood—idols that cannot see or hear or walk. Nor did they repent of their murders, their magic arts, their sexual immorality or their thefts.

John is actually ending this segment with a note of bewilderment—or an intriguing analysis. If the sixth trumpet war was Armageddon and the Messiah now reigns, why is it people are still involved in idolatry? Why are the people still sinning? If righteousness reigns, why is everybody's heart so bent on evil?

The sad reality of John's vision is the fact that the sixth trumpet war did not bring in the Messiah. Instead, it brought to power the Man of Sin posing as the Messiah. Just as Daniel interpreted the true message of the writing on the wall (Daniel 5), what we have here is the fact that Satan's days of posing as God have been numbered.

Essentially, previous generations have completely left out the time period that allows for God's strong delusion of Satan portraying God. The details of this strong delusion have been in the Bible all along. God divinely sealed its understanding from previous generations. God meant for this strong delusion to be understood by only one generation—the last generation—the only generation that would have a need to know.

CHAPTER 4

SATAN'S REVELATION: "I AM THE CHRIST!"

In this chapter we will study the revealing of the Man of Sin (Satan) appearing as being God, as recorded by Daniel, John, and Jesus. So strong will be the delusion of Satan posing as God that Jesus said even the remaining members of the Laodicea church era could be duped into believing the Man of Sin is the Messiah. Chapters 10, 12, 13, 14, and 17 of Revelation reveal the true Man of Sin. They depict the actions he takes during the short period of time he has been granted to establish himself as the Messiah.

In Revelation 9:20, John expresses his confusion over the fact that sin is still rampant in a world where supposedly the Messiah reigns. In answer to John's bewilderment, an angel provides John the answer behind the mystery of this perplexing problem. John is presented with a little scroll that contains the mystery of the Man of Sin posing as the Messiah. We will continue by looking at chapter 10 of Revelation.

THE SEVEN THUNDERS SPOKE

Revelation 10:2–4: He was holding a little scroll, which lay open in his hand. He planted his right foot on the sea and his left foot on the land, and he gave a loud shout like the roar of a lion. When he shouted, the voices of the seven thunders spoke. And when the seven thunders spoke, I was about to write; but I heard a voice from heaven say, "Seal up what the seven thunders have said and do not write it down."

Revelation 10:10–11: I took the little scroll from the angel's hand and ate it. It tasted as sweet as honey in my mouth, but when I had eaten it, my stomach turned sour. Then I was told, "You must prophesy again about many peoples, nations, languages and kings."

The angel's scroll lay open for John to read. Because of the horror that was about to be revealed to John, the seven thunders spoke. Just as Jesus previously told Daniel to seal up the understanding of his book until the time of the end, so the understanding of the message by the seven thunders was to remain sealed—until the last generation's lifetime. In reality, the seven thunders simply stated that it was Satan posing as the Messiah.

Although this dark message is within the context of Scripture, John does not relay the message in a direct way. Before John begins to prophesy again, he begins to realize that up until now he has only written about the trumpet judgments of God, even though they appeared as God's wrath. Amazingly enough, the seven thunders reveal to John that the true wrath of God is still to come upon an unbelieving world over the next three years before the real Messiah, Jesus, returns to earth. Thus John must prophesy again about the reign of the Man of Sin, and how Satan is successful at deluding many peoples, nations, languages, and kings.

DAYS BEFORE THE SEVENTH TRUMPET SOUNDS

Revelation 10:6–7: There will be no more delay! But in the days when the seventh angel is about to sound his trumpet, the mystery of God will be accomplished, just as he announced to his servants the prophets.

The mystery—just as God told the prophets Jeremiah, Isaiah, Daniel and John—is the sending of a strong delusion to the entire world. Understanding what was written on the little scroll and discerning the wisdom of the seven thunders will bring end-time events into clear focus. Instead of Jesus coming back at the end of the sixth trumpet war, which appears as Armageddon, God sends the world a strong delusion. This delusion is the Man of Sin, or Satan incarnate proclaiming to be God!

The next forty-five days are considered as the "days when the seventh angel is about to sound his trumpet." This time period was revealed in Daniel 12:11–12. It begins 1,290 days after the king of the North stops the daily sacrifice from taking place on the Temple Mount. It ends 1,335 days after this event, giving the elect a forty-five-day period of time to be exposed to this strong delusion, just as Jesus foretold in Matthew 24.

In reality, the first sacrifice never takes place. The king of the North will stop it from taking place on the first day it is scheduled to occur. Daniel's prophecy carries through to the rapture, which occurs at the blowing of the seventh trumpet on Daniel's 1,335th day.

The time period between the 1,335th day through the end of Daniel's 2,300th day is the period of time Satan rules and appears to the world as being the Messiah. That's why Daniel 12:12 states, "Blessed is the one who waits for and reaches the end of the 1,335 days." Not only are those who are taken at the rapture blessed, but so are those who die a martyr's death during the time of great tribulation; they will return to earth and rule and reign with Jesus for a thousand years. But our primary focus in this chapter will be the revelation of the Man of Sin posing as the Messiah, which occurs forty-five days prior to the rapture.

THE ABOMINATION THAT CAUSES DESOLATION

Daniel 12:11–12: From the time that the daily sacrifice is abolished and the abomination that causes desolation is set up, there will be 1,290 days. Blessed is the one who waits for and reaches the end of the 1,335 days.

Matthew 24:15–18: So when you see standing in the holy place "the abomination that causes desolation," spoken of through the prophet Daniel—let the reader understand—then let those who are in Judea flee to the mountains. Let no one on the roof of his house go down to take anything out of the house. Let no one in the field go back to get his cloak.

In Matthew 24:15, Jesus said it is very important we understand Daniel 12:11–12. When properly interpreted, Daniel's prophecy provides the important clue we need to establish the fact that the Man of Sin comes after the king of the North.

First, Daniel relates in verse 11 there are two single events that occur 1,290 days apart from each other. The first event involves the king of the North abolishing, or stopping, the daily sacrifice from taking place on the Temple Mount. Daniel then uses the word *and* to build the 1,290-day bridge between the abolishment of the daily sacrifice and the second event, which is the abomination that causes desolation, committed by the king of the South, who becomes the little horn of Daniel 7:8. As Jesus points out, it's not only the daily sacrifice being abolished by the king of the North, but it's also the abomination that causes desolation committed by the king of the South 1,290 days later that we must discern.

Daniel then establishes the time period that the Laodicea church era believers must be exposed to this strong delusion. Forty-five days after the king of the South, posing as the Messiah, commits the abomination that causes desolation, the remaining believers of Jesus Christ on earth will be raptured. Essentially, Daniel tells us not to be deluded by the events that occur during this forty-five-day time frame.

Figure 4-1 shows the outline of Daniel's 2,300-day prophecy, his 1,290-day prophecy, and the events that occur between the 1,290th day and the 1,335th day. We will study all these events in this chapter. But first we need to look at Daniel's prophecies that directly reveal the king of the South is the true Man of Sin. We will also see how John supports all that Daniel writes.

THE TRUE MEANING OF THE FOURTH BEAST

Revelation 13:1–3: And I saw a beast coming out of the sea [this is the king of the North, appearing to the world as being the Man of Sin]. He had ten horns [ten nations that make up his kingdom] and

Satan's Revelation: "I Am The Christ!"

YEARS FOR END-TIME PERIOD

```
3       4       5       6       7       8       9      10
|-------|-------|-------|-------|-------|-------|-------|
```

DANIEL'S 70th WEEK—TRIBULATION PERIOD (DAN. 9:24–27)

| 220 DAYS | TEMPLE DESOLATIONS (DAN. 9:26) 2,300 DAYS (DAN. 8:13–14) |

6th TRUMPET WAR
KING OF THE NORTH DESTROYED BY KING OF THE SOUTH (DAN. 11:40–45) APPEARS AS IF THIS IS THE BATTLE OF ARMAGEDDON (REV. 9:13–21)

DAYS BEFORE THE 7th TRUMPET
MYSTERY OF GOD REVEALED (REV. 10:7)

TWO WITNESSES PROPHESY DURING THE REIGN OF THE MAN OF SIN (REV. 11:3)

THE MAN OF SIN (OR KING OF THE SOUTH), WHO RECEIVED A FATAL HEAD WOUND (DAN. 11:25–26), COMMITS THE ABOMINATION THAT CAUSES DESOLATION (MATT. 24:15) 1,290 DAYS AFTER THE KING OF THE NORTH ABOLISHES THE SACRIFICE— THE WHOLE WORLD IS ASTONISHED (REV. 13:3)

THE MAN OF SIN (OR KING OF THE SOUTH) IS GIVEN POWER TO MAKE WAR AGAINST THE SAINTS (CHURCH) (REV. 13:7)

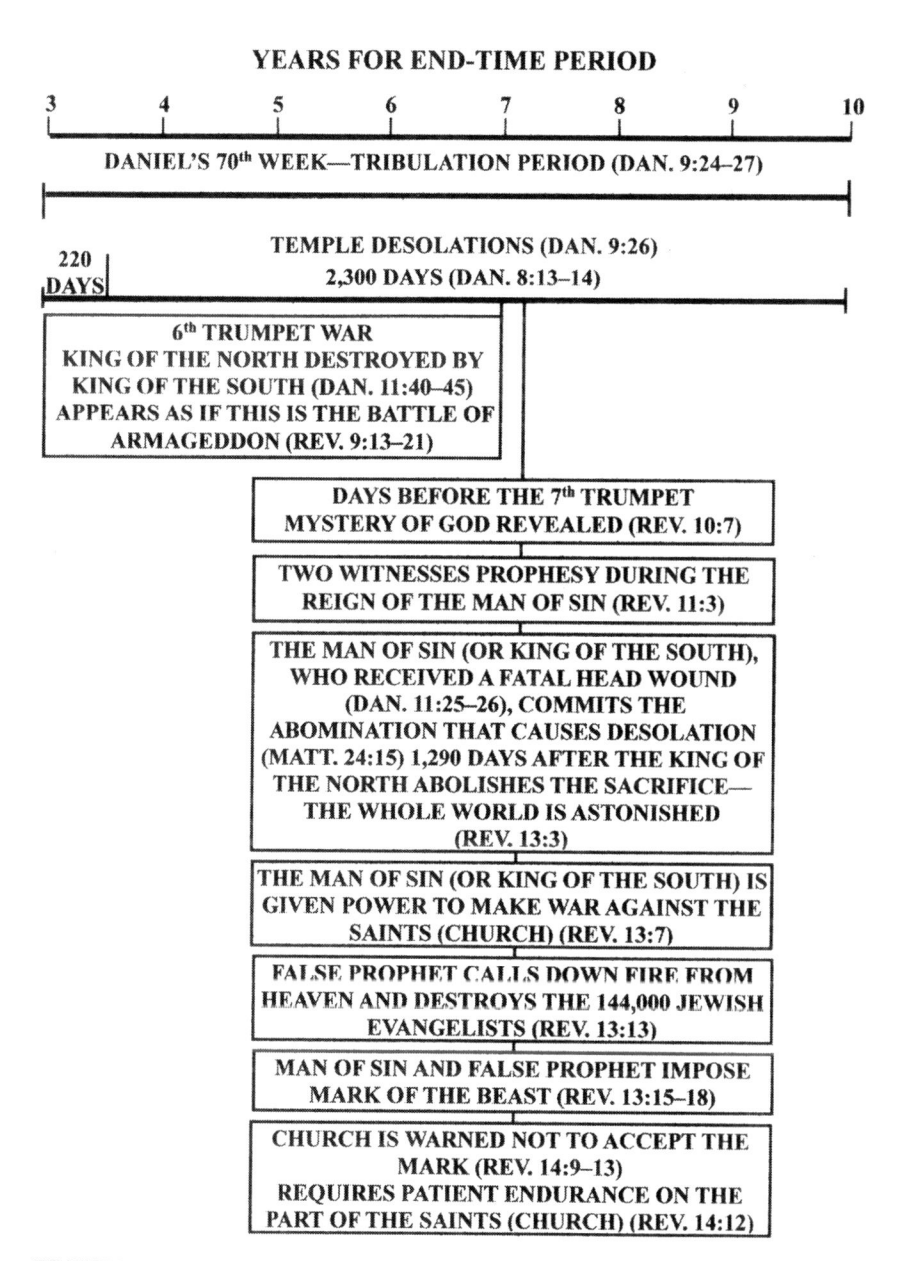

FALSE PROPHET CALLS DOWN FIRE FROM HEAVEN AND DESTROYS THE 144,000 JEWISH EVANGELISTS (REV. 13:13)

MAN OF SIN AND FALSE PROPHET IMPOSE MARK OF THE BEAST (REV. 13:15–18)

CHURCH IS WARNED NOT TO ACCEPT THE MARK (REV. 14:9–13)
REQUIRES PATIENT ENDURANCE ON THE PART OF THE SAINTS (CHURCH) (REV. 14:12)

FIGURE 4-1. DAYS BEFORE THE SEVENTH TRUMPET IS BLOWN

seven heads [which make up the kingdom of the king of the South], with ten crowns on his horns, and on each head a blasphemous name. The beast I saw resembled a leopard [the king of the South's kingdom], but had feet like those of a bear [Russia] and a mouth like that of a lion [America]. The dragon gave the beast [the king of the North] his power and his throne and great authority. One of the heads of the beast [according to Daniel 11:25–26 the king of the South will be betrayed by his own people] seemed to have had a fatal wound, but the fatal wound had been healed. (Explanations in brackets are mine.)

Daniel 7:19–21: Then I wanted to know the true meaning of the fourth beast [the king of the North's purpose is to appear as being the Man of Sin], which was different from all the others and most terrifying, with its iron teeth [the 10 horns that make up his kingdom] and bronze claws [the upcoming king of the South who makes up the seven heads under the king of the North's rule, who is the real Man of Sin]—the beast that crushed and devoured its victims and trampled underfoot whatever was left. I also wanted to know about the ten horns on its head and about the other horn [the king of the South or Man of Sin] that came up, before which three of them fell—the horn that looked more imposing than the others and that had eyes and a mouth that spoke boastfully. As I watched, this horn [the king of the South or Man of Sin posing as the Messiah] was waging war against the saints [implementing the mark of the beast or false salvation] and defeating them, until the Ancient of Days [Jesus] came and pronounced judgment in favor of the saints of the Most High, and the time came when they possessed the kingdom. (Explanations in brackets are mine.)

Daniel infers there is more to the fourth beast, the king of the North, than meets the eye. He discerns that Satan uses this fourth beast to appear as supposedly being the Man of Sin, although he is not. In short order, Daniel exposes this truth by asking for discernment concerning the true meaning behind the king of the North. Although the king of the North appears as the devil, or Man of Sin, Daniel reveals there is another horn (who is the king of the South possessed by Satan) who rebels against the king of the North and attempts to dupe the world into believing he is the Messiah. In reality, he is the real Man of Sin.

We've already studied how the king of the North manipulated Russia into attacking the nation of Israel, trampling underfoot the bear kingdom of Daniel 7:5. We also studied how he eventually overran the leopard kingdom of the king of the South, thereby making the king of the South part of the body of his kingdom, making up the seven heads under the king of the North's rule. We also saw how America became his military might, becoming the god of fortresses that he worshiped. Therefore, using the description of the fourth beast from Daniel 7:19 as a basis for his writings, John describes the first beast in Revelation 13:1–2 as taking on the form of a leopard, bear, and lion. This is the king of the North's empire before he is destroyed at the 6th Trumpet War, which many will believe is Armageddon.

John again supports Daniel by revealing the Man of Sin as being one of those seven heads under the king of the North's rule—the one person who has a healed head wound. Notice it was the heads of the king of the North who had blasphemous names; these are the nations of the king of the South. Daniel 7:21 reveals how it is this imposing horn who goes on to wage war against the saints and defeats them. These saints will become the great tribulation martyrs.

Therefore, the true meaning behind the king of the North is that Satan wants people to believe he is the Man of Sin, the only Antichrist. He essentially uses two different beasts to create this strong delusion. One appears as being the Man of Sin so the other can appear as being the Messiah. In short, this tactic allows Satan himself to appear as the Messiah after the king of the North is destroyed at what appears to be Armageddon.

EYES LIKE THE EYES OF A MAN

Daniel 7:8: While I was thinking about the horns [the king of the North's empire], there before me was another horn, a little one, which came up among them [the king of the South or Man of Sin]; and three of the first horns were uprooted before it. This horn [the king of the South] had eyes like the eyes of a man [Man of Sin] and a mouth that spoke boastfully [he claims to be God]. (Explanations in brackets are mine.)

While Daniel was thinking about the horns, or the European Union and the king of the North, he saw another horn. This little horn is the king of the South, who once ruled the leopard kingdom. This is Daniel's general overview of the king of the South's rebellion. During his rebellion, three of the original horns, or kings, under the rule of the king of the North are destroyed. When the king of the South comes to power, the other seven horns (kings) are stripped of their authority. After he comes to power, Revelation 17:12 tells us he will set up ten new kings.

The king of the South is the person who actually has a head wound from the seven heads of the king of the North's empire. The king of the North overran the king of the South shortly after the failed Russian invasion of Israel. This is how his kingdom included seven heads, of which one of these heads, the king of the South, actually received a head wound that was later healed. Later we'll see how Daniel prophesied the exact time when the king of the South would receive a head wound yet live to conquer the king of the North.

THE BRONZE CLAWS

Daniel 7:19: Then I wanted to know the true meaning of the fourth beast, which was different from all the others and most terrifying, with its iron teeth and bronze claws.

The bronze claws represent the nations of clay that realign themselves under the direction of the king of the North when he moves to stop the daily sacrifice. Originally Daniel depicted them as nations of clay when the king of the South attempted to separate from the king of the North's iron kingdom. *Bronze* refers us to the fact that the Man of Sin has his origins rooted in the ancient Greek empire of Alexander the Great. The king of the South's leopard kingdom will emerge from the geographic region once controlled by Alexander the Great. The king of the South is represented here as the bronze claws of the king of the North's empire, eventually wrapping itself around America after the king of the North is destroyed.

We learn of America's betrayal to the king of the North in Daniel 4:23: "You, O king, saw a messenger, a holy one, coming down from heaven and saying, 'Cut down the tree and destroy it, but leave the stump, bound with iron and bronze, in the grass of the field, while its roots remain in the ground.' " The ancient kingdom of Babylon was destroyed. However, Daniel made it clear that a time was coming when there would be another dominant empire that would become bound by iron and bronze. This new empire would have some similarities to ancient Babylon. This kingdom, Babylon the Great as written by John in Revelation 17 and 18, should be recognized by the last generation. It is America.

It is America that first binds itself to the iron kingdom, serving as his god of fortresses because of SDI and our military strength. Daniel's use of the term *bronze* represents the time of great tribulation when America becomes bound to the king of the South when he appears as being the Messiah. America voluntarily casts off its eagle's wings, which represent religious freedom and liberty for all, and takes on the heart of a man, or the heart of the Man of Sin, or king of the South, believing he is the Messiah. By doing so, this practice of idolatry leads to the persecution of God's holy people by America.

THE IMPOSING HORN

Daniel 7:20–22: I also wanted to know about the ten horns [kings] on its [king of the North's] head and about the other horn [Man of Sin] that came up, before which three of them [kings] fell—the horn that looked more imposing than the others and that had eyes and a mouth that spoke boastfully. As I watched, this horn [king of the South, or Man of Sin] was waging war against the saints [great tribulation martyrs who refuse the Man of Sin's, or Satan's, offer of salvation] and defeating them, until the Ancient of Days [Jesus] came and pronounced judgment in favor of the saints of the Most High, and the time came when they possessed the kingdom. (Explanations in brackets are mine.)

Once again, Daniel writes an overview of the king of the South's reign on earth. It begins with the European Union breaking apart. The king of the North will rule for a little while, and then the king of the South will launch his last attack, according to Daniel 11:40, and defeat him, appearing as the Messiah.

The king of the South, unlike the king of the North, wages war against the saints during the last three years of this ten-year period. He wages war by offering tremendous wealth in exchange for accepting his offer of salvation, or forgiveness for sin.

He implements the mark of the beast as an offer of salvation, or forgiveness for sin. As an incentive to take his offer of salvation, he will entice them with the receipt of tremendous wealth. In fulfillment of 1 Timothy 6:10, it will be for the love of money that many will take his mark, piercing themselves with all kinds of sorrows, even though for a while it will appear as if they have gained the world! But since it will be viewed as an offer of forgiveness for sin, people will fail to recognize their acceptance as an act of taking on the mark of the beast. Those who take his offer will honestly believe—to their own destruction—that he is God in the flesh. This deceptive ploy by Satan is how he truly destroys many through peaceful means.

The saints of the Most High are the great tribulation martyrs John sees in Revelation 7:9, who die for their faith in Jesus and refuse the king of the South's offer of salvation in exchange for wealth.

Those who take the mark will experience a time of unequaled prosperity. They will eventually be gathered to Armageddon and destroyed by Jesus when He returns with all the great tribulation martyrs. That's why Daniel writes here that he saw the Ancient of Days pronounce judgment in favor of the saints. Their martyrdom is just one more method of this generation passing away as Jesus commanded in Matthew 24:34.

ANOTHER KING WILL ARISE

Daniel 7:24–25: The ten horns are ten kings who will come from this kingdom [the king of the North's empire]. After them another king will arise, different from the earlier ones [the king of the South]; he will subdue three kings. He will speak against the Most High and oppress his saints and try to change the set times and the laws. The saints will be handed over to him for a time, times and half a time [the last three and one half years of Daniel's ten-year end-time period]. (Explanations in brackets are mine.)

Here Daniel is first shown the ten-member European Union made up by the king of the North. Then he's shown another king, who is the king of the South. During the sixth trumpet war, the king of the South will subdue three of the kings set up by the king of the North. He will also defeat the king of the North, then pose as the Messiah, thereby changing the set times and laws of God. This passage shows he will rebel and reign for a 3½-year period, or during the time of great distress Jesus spoke of in Matthew 24:21.

DANIEL SAW THE MAN OF SIN DESTROYED BY JESUS

Daniel 7:26: But the court will sit, and his power will be taken away and completely destroyed forever.

The king of the North met his end when the king of the South rose up against him in the land of Israel in what appeared to be the battle of Armageddon. The king of the South meets his end when Jesus returns to earth and destroys the armed forces gathered at Armageddon.

ANOTHER HORN COMES UP

Daniel 8:9: Out of one of them [meaning one of the four geographic regions once controlled by Alexander the Great's generals after Alexander the Great died] came another horn [the king of the South, or Man of Sin], which started small but grew in power to the south and to the east and toward the Beautiful Land [Israel]. (Explanations in brackets are mine.)

Daniel 8:10: It [Satan, through the little horn of Daniel 7:8, or king of the South, who is the Man of Sin) grew until it reached the host of the heavens [Satan, as the prince of the air, possesses the Man of

Sin and poses as the Messiah, portraying Jesus, who is the host of the heavens] . . . (Explanations in brackets are mine.)

Daniel 8:10 (continued): . . . and it threw some of the starry host down to the earth and trampled on them [John shows us in Revelation 13:13 how the 144,000 Jewish-Christian evangelists are destroyed when the False Prophet calls down fire from heaven]. (Explanations in brackets are mine.)

Daniel 8:11: It [Satan, through the Man of Sin] set itself up to be as great as the Prince of the host [Jesus]; it took away the daily sacrifice from him, and the place of his sanctuary was brought low [the Man of Sin sits in the temple and deludes the world into believing he is God]. (Explanations in brackets are mine.)

Daniel 8:12: Because of *rebellion* [the king of the South rebels against the king of the North, appearing as the Messiah, which coincides with 2 Thessalonians 2:3 which speaks of the fact that the *rebellion* must first take place before the Man of Sin is *revealed*], the host of the saints [144,000 Jewish-Christian evangelists] and the daily sacrifice [originally stopped by the king of the North] were given over to it [king of the South, or Man of Sin]. . . . (Emphasis and explanations in brackets are mine.)

Daniel 8:12 (continued): . . . It [the king of the South, or Man of Sin possessed by Satan] *prospered in everything* it did [it is a tremendous time of prosperity for those who accept his offer of salvation, which is really the true mark of the beast], and truth [the fact that salvation comes only by accepting Jesus as Lord and Savior] was thrown to the ground. (Explanations in brackets and emphasis are mine.)

After Alexander the Great died, his empire was divided between four generals. Daniel tells us the king of the South comes from one of the geographic regions once controlled by one of these generals. Therefore, the bronze kingdom, the nations of clay, and the leopard kingdom all represent the king of the South, whose ancestry once ruled one of the geographic regions of the ancient empire of Alexander the Great.

Daniel begins by relating how the king of the South starts out small but grows in power to the south and east and eventually toward the Beautiful Land, which is Israel. Therefore, the king of the South will eventually rule the world from Jerusalem.

After defeating the king of the North and making the sixth trumpet war appear as Armageddon, the king of the South will then sit in the rebuilt temple in Jerusalem and claim to be God. Thus Daniel writes that once again the sanctuary is brought low. We've already seen how the king of the North was the first to desolate the temple, stopping the daily sacrifice from taking place, shortly after the Russian invasion of Israel.

Here Daniel informs us about the second desolation of the temple. In Daniel 9:26 it is recorded there will be more than one temple desolation. The king of the South will pass his desolation of the temple off as supposedly being the wedding supper of the Lamb. However, Daniel later informs us this act is actually the ultimate abomination that causes desolation, as referred to by Jesus in Matthew 24.

Daniel also shows us the king of the South rebels against the king of the North. Second Thessalonians 2:3–4 states the Man of Sin cannot be revealed (meaning as a messiah posing as God) or come to power until this rebellion occurs and the king of the North, who now holds him (the king of the South) back, is taken out of the way. That's because the king of the North must convince the world that he is the Man of Sin, so the king of the South can convince the world that he is the messiah.

Daniel then shows us where the host of the saints, 144,000 Jewish-Christian evangelists, are handed over to him and put to death. We'll see how he accomplishes this when we study John's account of the Man of Sin. Daniel verifies the fact that it will be a wealthy time under this man's reign as he appears as God to the people of earth. He will dole out tremendous wealth to those who will worship him as God.

A MASTER OF INTRIGUE

Daniel 8:19: He [the archangel Gabriel] said: "I am going to tell you what will happen later in the time of wrath [the great tribulation period is considered as the time of God's wrath, when Satan poses as God through the Man of Sin, or king of the South], because the vision concerns the appointed time of the end [last three years of Daniel's ten-year end-time period]. (Explanations in brackets are mine.)

Daniel 8:20–22: The two-horned ram that you saw represents the kings of Media and Persia. The shaggy goat is the king of Greece, and the large horn between his eyes is the first king [Alexander the Great]. The four horns that replaced the one that was broken off represent four kingdoms that will emerge from his [Alexander the Great's] nation but will not have the same power. (Explanations in brackets are mine.)

Daniel 8:23: In the latter part of their reign [end-times], when *rebels* [the king of the South will rebel against the king of the North] have become completely wicked, a stern-faced king, a master of intrigue, will arise [the king of the South rises out of the geographic region of the ancient Greek empire and rebels against the king of the North]. (Explanations in brackets and emphasis are mine.)

Daniel 8:24: He [the king of the South or Man of Sin] will become very strong, but not by his own power [he's empowered by Satan]. (Explanations in brackets are mine.)

Daniel 8:24: He [the king of the South or Man of Sin] will cause astounding devastation [the sixth trumpet war, where one-third of mankind is killed along with the king of the North, appears as Armageddon] and will succeed in whatever he does [deluding the world into believing he is God]. (Explanations in brackets are mine.)

Daniel 8:24: He [the king of the South or Man of Sin] will destroy the mighty men (three kings of the European Union, as well as the king of the North] and the holy people [144,000 Jewish-Christian evangelists, the Jews and any other person who refuses his offer of salvation, which turns out to be the mark of the beast]. (Explanations in brackets are mine.)

Daniel 8:25: He [the king of the South or Man of Sin] will cause deceit to prosper [People will receive tremendous wealth in exchange for taking his offer of salvation, which is actually the mark of the beast. In this passage, Daniel indicates this is a wealthy time for those who take his mark, and he will kill those who refuse.], and he will consider himself superior [God]. (Explanations in brackets are mine.)

Daniel 8:25: When they feel secure [for those who worship him as God, it will be a time of world peace, prosperity, and security], he will destroy many [those who refuse the mark as well as those who take his mark and are destroyed when Jesus returns] and take his stand against the Prince of princes [Jesus]. Yet he [the king of the South or Man of Sin] will be destroyed, but not by human power [he will be destroyed by Jesus]. (Explanations in brackets are mine.)

Gabriel told Daniel the entire strong delusion. Daniel and John fully support all that Gabriel told. The time of wrath is considered the time when the Man of Sin rules, appearing to mankind as the victorious Messiah over the king of the North, the man who appeared to be the Man of Sin.

But when the king of the South comes to power and is revealed to Christians as the true Antichrist, or Man of Sin, we must remember that 1 Thessalonians 5:9 states God has not appointed us to suffer wrath. The last three years of the tribulation period is the time of wrath. The Man of Sin is the beginning of God pouring out His wrath on a wicked and perverse generation. Therefore, all the seal and trumpet judgments of Revelation are only judgments by God in hopes that people will repent and accept the gospel that states Jesus Christ is their only Savior from sin.

Since the Man of Sin is the beginning of God's wrath, the spirits and souls of all true believers in Jesus Christ are taken out of this world (raptured) before God sends unbelievers the entire strong delusion. However, for a short period of time, about forty to forty-five days, God exposes true believers, or the elect as Jesus called them in Matthew 24, to this strong delusion that God sends the rest of the world. We will have a short time to witness the truth to unbelievers.

DESOLATIONS ARE DECREED

Daniel 9:26: The end will come like a flood: War will continue until the end [first seven years of the last ten-year period), and *desolations* have been decreed [by the king of the North, then by the king of the South]. (Explanations in brackets and emphasis are mine.)

Daniel shows us there is more than one temple desolation. It is first desolated when the king of the North invades Israel and stops the daily sacrifice at the very beginning of the tribulation period. Then, 1,290 days later, the abomination that causes desolation occurs when the king of the South, after destroying the king of the North in what will appear to be Armageddon, sits in the holy temple in Jerusalem and claims to be God.

THE MAN OF SIN HAS NO ROYALTY

Daniel 11:21: He [the king of the North] will be succeeded by a *contemptible* [meaning rebellious] person [the king of the South] who has not been given the honor of royalty. (Explanations in brackets and emphasis are mine.)

Daniel 11:21: He [the king of the South] will invade the kingdom when its people feel secure, and he will seize it through intrigue [or idolatry, convincing people to worship him as God when he miraculously heals people around the world from the torture of the great demonic plague of the fifth trumpet judgment]. (Explanations in brackets are mine.)

Daniel 11:22: Then an overwhelming army [the 200-million-man army of the sixth trumpet war fought in the location of Armageddon as recorded by John in Revelation 9:16) will be swept away before him [the king of the South or Man of Sin]; both it [the army] and a prince of the covenant [the king of the North, who confirmed a covenant with many for one "seven" at the very beginning of this ten-year period] will be destroyed [by the king of the South, as recorded by Daniel 11:45, during the sixth trumpet war]. (Explanations in brackets are mine.)

Daniel 11:23: After coming to an agreement with him [the king of the South, or Man of Sin; he will set up ten new kings according to Revelation 17:12], he will act deceitfully [disguise the mark of the beast as an offer of salvation, or forgiveness for sin], and with only a few people [the ten new kings he sets up and the False Prophet] he will rise to power [or portray himself as being God]. (Explanations in brackets are mine.)

Daniel 11:24: When the richest provinces [America, who is Babylon the Great in accordance with Revelation 17 and 18] feel secure, he will invade them [through religious tyranny he will control them by manipulating them into believing he is God, which will be idolatry] and will achieve what neither his fathers [ancient Assyrians] nor his forefathers [ancient Amorites and Hittites] did [rule the world]. He will distribute plunder, loot and *wealth* among his followers [those who take his mark—or offer of salvation—and worship him as God]. (Explanations in brackets and emphasis are mine.)

Daniel 11:24: He will plot the overthrow [through idol worship] of *fortresses* [Revelation 17:16 tells us the Man of Sin and his ten new kings will hate the prostitute America, or Babylon the Great, who served as the king of the North's god of fortresses, as recorded in Daniel 11:38]—but only for a time. (Explanations in brackets and emphasis are mine.)

Daniel 11:21-24 is written by Daniel with the very end in mind. He begins by giving an overview of the end result of the wars that occur between the king of the North and the king of the South. This is how Daniel's book has been kept sealed for all this time. By using juxtaposition, he starts his dissertation on the time of the end with the end result—the coming to power of the real Man of Sin, who ends up being the king of the South. Had Daniel placed these verses in chronological sequence, they would have been placed behind Daniel 11:45, making it clear all along that the king of the South rises to power after the king of the North is destroyed.

In these passages, Daniel begins by giving us a synopsis of the king of the South coming to power after the king of the North. The first line of this passage shows how the king of the North is succeeded by a contemptible person who has not been given the honor of royalty. This is the king of the South. The king of the North, as head of the European Union, will be considered as having royalty when he comes to dominate the world. The next line shows the rebellion initiated by the king of the South to overthrow the king of the North—who must be taken out of the way in accordance with 2 Thessalonians 2:7—so he can be revealed as supposedly being a messiah, seizing the world through intrigue, because he is empowered by Satan.

In Revelation, John tells us about the overwhelming army of 200 million soldiers destroyed during the sixth trumpet war. The king of the South's rebellion against the king of the North results in the sixth trumpet war, where one-third of mankind is killed in the Middle East on the plains of Megiddo, otherwise known as Armageddon. We see ample proof in this passage where a prince of the covenant, or the king of the North, is destroyed as a result of this war, and Daniel 11:45 makes it very clear that the king of the North is destroyed.

In Revelation 17:12, John reveals that when the king of the South comes to power, he will set up ten new kings who will give all their authority to the king of the South. Together they will hate the prostitute—America, or Babylon the Great—and want to bring her to destruction because she still harbors God's chosen people. Daniel backs this up in this passage when he states the king of the South will plot the overthrow of fortresses. This fortress, as we learned earlier, is America.

Figure 4-2 shows all prophecies concerning the prince of the covenant, or the king of the North, and how he must precede the Man of Sin posing as God.

THE DEADLY HEAD WOUND

Daniel 11:25–27: With a large army he [king of the North] will stir up his strength and courage against the king of the South. The king of the South will wage war with a large and very powerful army, but he will not be able to stand because of the plots devised against him. Those who eat from the king's provisions will try to destroy him; his army will be swept away, and many will fall in battle. The two kings, with their hearts bent on evil, will sit at the same table and lie to each other, but to no avail, because an end will still come at the appointed time [for the king of the North first at the sixth trumpet war, then the king of the South at the second coming of Jesus]. (Explanations in brackets are mine.)

This is the very first battle between the king of the North and the king of the South. This battle correlates with the breaking of the first two seals in the book of Revelation. The king of the South is the man on the white horse of the first seal, who has a bow and is bent on conquest.

Here's the crucial passage revealing that the king of the South, who is the true Man of Sin, receives a head wound. Those who eat from the king of the South's own provisions will try to destroy him. In this assassination attempt, he will receive a deadly head wound, but he will live. It will look very gloomy for the king of the South, who is wounded and betrayed by his own people, with his army nearly swept away. Now we know why in Revelation 6:2 John says this man has only a bow but no arrows. He has a large army, but he doesn't have an adequate air force. Because of the might of the king of the North, everyone will overlook the injured king of the South. The king of the North will wreak so much havoc that the real Man of Sin will be missed!

The king of the South is considered the second shepherd Zechariah speaks of in 11:15–16: "Take again the equipment of a foolish shepherd [king of the North]. For I am going to raise up a shepherd [king of the South] over the land who will not care for the lost, or seek the young, or heal the injured, or feed the healthy, but will eat meat of the choice sheep [the people of God or great tribulation martyrs], tearing off their hoofs [killing those who refuse his offer of salvation]." (Explanations in brackets are mine.]

We then see a stiff warning from almighty God to the king of the South and Satan in Zechariah 11:17: "Woe to the worthless shepherd, who deserts the flock! May the sword strike his arm and his right eye! May his arm be completely withered, his right eye totally blinded."

This scripture fully supports Daniel 11:26, which says, "Those who eat from the king's provisions will try to destroy him."

This assassination attempt upon the king of the South takes place at the very beginning of Daniel's ten-year end-time period. Seven years later, as recorded by Daniel 11:40-45, the king of the South defeats the king of the North at what appears to be Armageddon.

Remember earlier how I said the Man of Sin must complete enough prophecies concerning the first coming of Jesus so that he can discredit Jesus as being nothing more than a strong delusion that he, proclaiming to be God, sent two thousand years ago? Just as Judas betrayed Jesus at the Last Supper, those who dine with the king of the South will betray him. This betrayal appears scriptural and appears to fulfill prophecy concerning the coming of the Messiah. This betrayal is designed to lend credibility to the idea that he is the victorious Messiah and Jesus was no more than a strong delusion—just one in many who have claimed to be the Messiah.

Zechariah 13:7–9 also shows the king of the South defeating the king of the North, whom the Lord also calls a shepherd. Remember, during the hour of trial, the king of the South has been under the king of the North's rule, as a wounded head. Zechariah shows the betrayal and rebellion of the king of the South against the king of the North: "Awake, O sword, against my shepherd [king of the North], against the man who is close to me! Strike the shepherd, and the sheep will be scattered, and I will turn my hand against the little ones. . . . Two-thirds will be struck down and perish; yet one-third will be left in it. This third I will bring into the fire [great tribulation]; I will refine them like silver and test them like gold." (Explanations in brackets are mine.)

Zechariah 14:2 tells us about the captives in Jerusalem: "Half of the city will go into exile, but the rest of the people will not be taken from the city." There will be captive Jews in the city of Jerusalem at the time Jesus actually returns, as we'll see later when we study in detail His actual return to earth with His saints.

Now we see why the whole world "will be astonished when they see the beast, because he once was, now is not, and yet will come" (Rev. 17:8). Even John records his own astonishment in Revelation 17:6.

The events that bring this man to power are so real, powerful, and close to the prophetic fulfillment of Jesus' second coming that Jesus admitted in Matthew 24:24 that even the elect—or those who are about to be raptured—could be deceived, if it were possible. Thankfully, by understanding how and when the rapture takes place, it will not be possible for the elect to be deceived.

Let's remember that Daniel 11:27 states the king of the South, like the king of the North, is also "bent on evil." In Revelation 6:2, John states the king of the South is "bent on conquest," meaning world domination. He will conquer, but unlike the king of the North, the king of the South will destroy most of mankind through peace and prosperity as he poses as the Messiah, or God.

Don't ever forget that Daniel states the king of the South is a master of intrigue. His time to rule the world is appointed after the king of the North is destroyed and taken out of his way. In Revelation 6:1–2, John has the king of the South riding a white horse because many will believe he truly is the long-awaited Messiah. But understand that it is God who sets the stage so Satan can be worshiped as God. The world will have just experienced seven years of terror from the king of the North. The king of the South will be able to ride into Jerusalem and appear as God coming to redeem mankind for the first and only time.

THESE ASTONISHING THINGS

Daniel 12:6–7: "How long will it be before these astonishing things [the king of the South rebels against the king of the North and poses as the Messiah] are fulfilled?" The man clothed in linen, who was above the waters of the river, lifted his right hand and his left hand toward heaven, and I heard him swear by him who lives forever, saying, "It will be for a time, times and half a time [3½ years]. When the power of the holy people [144,000 Jewish-Christian evangelists, the Laodicea church era Christians, converted Jews, and those who refuse the Man of Sin's mark of salvation] has been finally broken, all these things will be completed [Jesus will return and reconsecrate the temple]." (Explanations in brackets are mine.)

In Revelation 17:6, John states he was *astonished*. In Revelation 17:8, John records the whole world was *astonished*. In Revelation 17:7, the angel escorting John asks him why he was *astonished*. In this passage from Daniel, an angel asks the Lord how long before these *astonishing* things are fulfilled. The Lord went on to say that this *astonishing* period of time, when the Man of Sin reigns, would cover a 3½-year period. Connecting the word *astonishing* from various sources of Scripture helps bring the strong delusion and John's revelation of the Man of Sin into clearer focus.

DANIEL USES THE CONCEPT OF JUXTAPOSITION TO SEAL HIS BOOK

In Daniel 11:21–45, we find where Daniel uses the concept of juxtaposition to seal the revelation of the true Man of Sin. In Daniel 11:21, he begins his narration of the end-times by first giving an overview of the end result of the wars that occur between the king of the North and the king of the South. He begins with the end in mind.

In verses 21 through 24, Daniel describes the reign of the king of the South, or Man of Sin—a contemptible person who seizes the kingdom of the king of the North through intrigue. Then, beginning in verse 25, Daniel backs up and describes the conflicts that occur between the king of the North and the king of the South. He shows how the king of the North is successful for a little while (Rev. 17:10) over the king of the South. But in the end, Daniel shows how the king of the North is destroyed (Dan. 11:45).

If verses 21 through 24 had been written after verse 45, Daniel's book would have been unsealed, and the mystery of God would have been no mystery at all to previous generations. But it has remained sealed until now because no one has discerned Daniel's writing style and his use of juxtaposition. He purposely wrote verses 21 through 24 out of place so that previous generations would believe there was only one antichrist instead of two.

Even I would not have discerned what Daniel had done had it not been for God imparting His wisdom to me. By understanding how Daniel and John both used the concept of juxtaposition in their writings, only now can we truly know that Daniel is unsealed and fully understand the construction of Revelation. Now that Daniel has been properly unsealed, we can know we are the last generation because we can properly discern the *powerful delusion* (2 Thess. 2:11) God is sending to the world. Figure 4-2 outlines Daniel's use of juxtaposition.

JOHN'S REVELATION OF THE MAN OF SIN

Now, as promised, it's time to see how John reveals the Man of Sin and how the king of the South deludes people into believing he is the Messiah. John first reveals this king when the first seal is opened. Essentially, through seven seal judgments and six trumpet judgments, John describes the seven-year struggle of the king of the South in his bid to appear as the Messiah. For seven years, the king of the South will war against the king of the North. After defeating the king of the North and reigning for a short time, the seven bowls of God's wrath will be poured out on the king of the South and his kingdom when the true Messiah, Jesus, returns.

THE MAN OF SIN HAS NO ARROWS

Revelation 6:1–2: I watched as the Lamb opened the first of the seven seals. Then I heard one of the four living creatures say in a voice like thunder, "Come!" I looked, and there before me was a white horse! Its rider held a bow, and he was given a crown, and he rode out as a conqueror bent on conquest.

I Will Make Myself Like The Most High!

YEARS FOR END-TIME PERIOD

```
0    1    2    3    4    5    6    7    8    9    10
```

DANIEL'S 70th WEEK—TRIBULATION PERIOD (DAN. 9:24–27)

TEMPLE DESOLATIONS (DAN. 9:26) 2,300 DAYS (DAN. 8:13–14)

DANIEL 11:21–24 HE WILL BE SUCCEEDED BY A CONTEMPTIBLE PERSON

DANIEL 11:25 KING OF THE NORTH VS. KING OF THE SOUTH

DANIEL 11:26 THE KING OF THE SOUTH IS BETRAYED

DANIEL 11:27–28 THE KING OF THE NORTH TAKES ACTION AGAINST THE HOLY COVENANT (RUSSIAN INVASION OF ISRAEL)

DANIEL 11:29–30 THE KING OF THE NORTH INVADES THE KING OF THE SOUTH AGAIN

DANIEL 11:31–39 THE KING OF THE NORTH ABOLISHES THE SACRIFICE (DAN. 9:27) EXALTS HIMSELF ABOVE GOD IN AN EFFORT TO DELUDE THE WORLD INTO BELIEVING HE IS THE MAN OF SIN

DANIEL 11:40–45 AT THE TIME OF THE END, THE KING OF THE SOUTH ENGAGES THE KING OF THE NORTH, WHO IS DESTROYED (6th TRUMPET WAR)

DANIEL 11:21–24 HE (THE KING OF THE NORTH) WILL BE SUCCEEDED BY A CONTEMPTIBLE PERSON (THE REBELLION OCCURS, SEE 2 THESS. 2:3–4) THE KING OF THE NORTH, OR *PRINCE OF THE COVENANT*, IS DESTROYED, AND AN *OVERWHELMING ARMY IS SWEPT AWAY BEFORE HIM* (THE 6th TRUMPET WAR, REV. 9:14–19) (APPEARS AS BATTLE OF ARMAGEDDON) THE KING OF THE SOUTH BECOMES THE LITTLE HORN OF DANIEL 7:8 WHO PORTRAYS HIMSELF AS THE MESSIAH, BUT IS THE REAL MAN OF SIN (MATT. 24:23–26)

HAD DANIEL PLACED THESE VERSES AFTER VERSE 45, HIS BOOK WOULD HAVE BEEN UNSEALED.

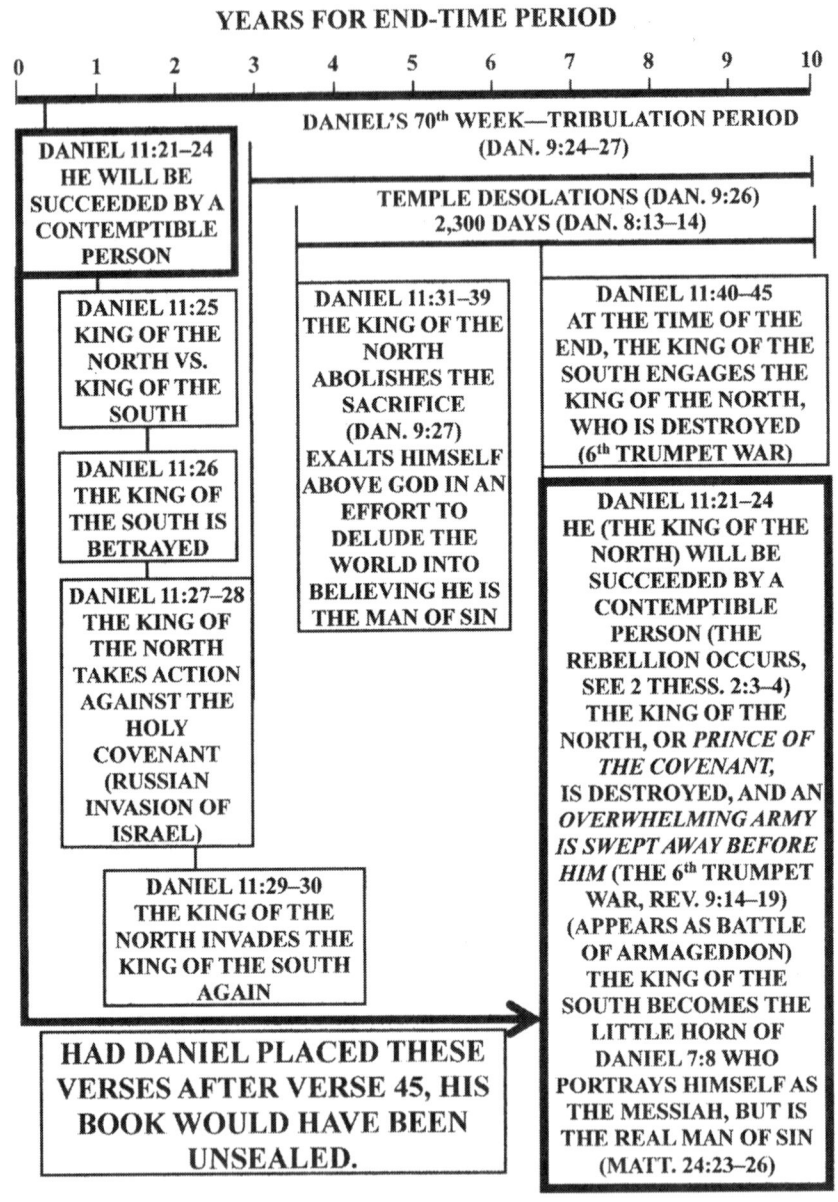

FIGURE 4-2. HOW DANIEL USES THE CONCEPT OF JUXTAPOSITION IN CHAPTER 11 TO SEAL HIS BOOK UNTIL THE TIME OF THE END (DANIEL 12:9)

Daniel 11:25 verifies John's account that the king of the South is not militarily strong. Daniel 8:9 also gives credibility to the fact that the king of the South starts out small but grows in power throughout this ten-year period. Before the king of the South conquers the king of the North, he must serve under the king of the North. Just as Jesus came the first time as a suffering servant, so the Man of Sin must first appear as a suffering servant. During the time the king of the South is serving under the king of the North—serving as one of the seven heads under the king of the North—Satan temporarily gives the king of the North the power to appear as supposedly being the one and only Antichrist.

JOHN OBSERVES THE GREAT CONFLICT

Revelation 10:9–11: So I went to the angel and asked him to give me the little scroll. He said to me, "Take it and eat it. It will turn your stomach sour, but in your mouth it will be as sweet as honey."

Revelation 11:3: And I will give power to my two witnesses, and they will prophesy for 1,260 days, clothed in sackcloth.

Revelation 12:1: A great and wondrous sign appeared in heaven: a woman clothed with the sun, with the moon under her feet and a crown of twelve stars on her head.

John digests the strong delusion that is about to come upon the world as revealed in the little scroll. Immediately, John sees that God sends two witnesses to earth to prophesy during the Man of Sin's reign. Once they are in place, John begins to describe the delusion Satan creates when he makes the king of the North appear as the Man of Sin. We will look at Revelation 12 and see how Satan's plot over the past seven years has brought us to the point of allowing the king of the South to now appear to the world as the Messiah. As John points out in Revelation 12, the great conflict circles around God's most favored nation, Israel, and the Temple Mount, and Satan's desire—through the Man of Sin—to discredit Jesus as the Son of God.

Revelation 12:2: She was pregnant and cried out in pain as she was about to give birth.

Over two thousand years ago, the nation of Israel gave birth to the Lord Jesus Christ.

Revelation 12:3: Then another sign appeared in heaven: an enormous red dragon with seven heads and ten horns and seven crowns on his heads.

In Genesis 3:15, we find a general synopsis of the overall conflict between Satan and God: "And I will put enmity between you and the woman, and between your offspring and hers; he will crush your head, and you will strike his heel."

When Jesus hung from the cross of Calvary, His hands and feet were held in place with spikes. By inciting the Jews to crucify Jesus, Satan thought he would be victorious over God. Although Satan struck the heel of Jesus, it resulted in victory for those of us who have received His offer of salvation through faithful confession. We have seen where Daniel and John show how the other half of this ancient prophecy is fulfilled. During an assassination attempt, the king of the South receives a fatal head wound yet lives.

Notice in this passage that Satan has his crowns on his seven heads, not on his ten horns. Satan's real Man of Sin comes from the seven heads, or is the king of the South, who serves as one of the seven heads under the authority of the king of the North. The king of the North had his crowns on his horns, not on his heads. It was the heads of the king of the North that had blasphemous names.

Revelation 12:4: His tail swept a third of the stars out of the sky and flung them to the earth.

This shows the great rebellion that occurred in heaven when God's most beautiful angel became so filled with pride that he set it in his heart to be worshiped as God. He was able to convince one-third of the angels in heaven to rebel with him. As a result of this rebellion, Satan tempted Adam and Eve to sin against God. As a result, Satan became the prince of the air (earth), with power and authority over sin.

Revelation 12:4: The dragon stood in front of the woman who was about to give birth, so that he might devour her child the moment it was born.

Satan prompted King Herod to send out a search party for the Christ child. Although the search party found the child, they did not return to Herod and report the child's whereabouts. Instead, Mary and Joseph were informed by an angel of the Lord, as recorded in Matthew 2:13, to "take the child and his mother and escape to Egypt. Stay there until I tell you, for Herod is going to search for the child to kill him."

Revelation 12:5: She gave birth to a son, a male child, who will rule all the nations with an iron scepter. And her child was snatched up to God and to his throne.

As a result of Jesus' first coming, He was crucified at Calvary, where He died and rose on the third day. He then ascended to heaven until all his enemies are put underfoot. Therefore, because the Man of Sin has not yet ruled on earth, we still await the day Jesus returns and rules all the nations here on earth for a thousand years.

Revelation 12:6: The woman fled into the desert to a place prepared for her by God, where she might be taken care of for 1,260 days.

Now that John has given us a quick synopsis of the ongoing conflict between Jesus and Satan, he jumps to the time of the end. In chapter 3, we saw where the Russian invasion of Israel starts the final seven-year countdown to the return of Jesus. We also learned that as a result of the Russian invasion, many Israelis are evacuated to America, where religious freedom is considered a basic human right. In this passage, John uses the term *desert* to tie Israel with America.

John supports his claim in Revelation 17:3: "Then the angel carried me away in the Spirit into a desert. There I saw a woman sitting on a scarlet beast that was covered with blasphemous names and had seven heads and ten horns."

This is John's first reference in chapter 12 that America harbors many Jews and Christians during the reign of the king of the North. According to Daniel's parable, this passage supports the plan that Satan is going to use America as a lion's den.

Revelation 12:7–9: And there was war in heaven. Michael and his angels fought against the dragon, and the dragon and his angels fought back. But he was not strong enough, and they lost their place in heaven. The great dragon was hurled down—that ancient serpent called the devil, or Satan, who leads the whole world astray. He was hurled to the earth, and his angels with him.

This war in heaven occurs just prior to the Russian invasion, which starts Daniel's seventieth week, or the actual tribulation period. The first half of the tribulation period is known as the hour of trial. John recounts how Satan is hurled down to the earth at the beginning of the last seven years of this ten-year end-time period. Essentially, John is relating how it is God who controls the events of the entire tribulation period. Satan is given the power to create one delusion after another, first with the king of the North, then with the king of the South.

Revelation 12:10–12: Then I heard a loud voice in heaven say: "Now have come the salvation and the power and the kingdom of our God, and the authority of his Christ. For the accuser of our brothers, who accuses them before our God day and night, has been hurled down. They overcame him by the blood of the Lamb and by the word of their testimony; they did not love their lives so much as to shrink from death. Therefore rejoice, you heavens and you who dwell in them! But woe to the earth [Israel and the Jews] and the sea [or the remaining church that is on the earth], because the devil has gone down to you! He is filled with fury, because he knows that his time is short." (Explanations in brackets are mine.)

Here we see God is ultimately in control. We also see how He uses the tribulation period to bring the last of the church-age saints home to heaven. Although John is given a glimpse of the joy in heaven, he is also informed of the fact that those on the earth will experience Satan's wrath as a result of Satan being thrown out of heaven. John is then informed that Satan's time to create these strong delusions and appear as the Messiah is short. There's much work to be done if Satan is to be successful in portraying himself as God.

Revelation 12:13–14: When the dragon saw that he had been hurled to the earth, he pursued the woman [Israel] who had given birth to the male child [Jesus]. The woman was given the two wings of a great eagle [America], so that she might fly to the place prepared for her in the desert [America], where she would be taken care of for a time, times and half a time [the length of time the king of the North rules, or three and one half years], out of the serpent's reach [meaning Satan's reach through the king of the North, who deludes the world into believing he is the Man of Sin]. (Explanations in brackets are mine.)

As we learned in chapter 2, the very first thing that happens at the beginning of the last seven years on earth is the prompting of Russia to invade the peace-seeking nation of Israel. John once again recounts the fact that many Israelis are evacuated to America. Daniel 7:4 pictured America as a lion nation, having the wings of a great eagle. Naturally, right on schedule, we've seen America reach unprecedented heights in air superiority—and in the course of a single generation! Satan first gives his power and authority to the king of the North so that he might appear as the Man of Sin. John shows how the Israelis remain out of the serpent's reach during the time the king of the North reigns on earth, or the first half of this tribulation period, which is the hour of trial.

Revelation 12:15–16: Then from his mouth the serpent spewed water like a river, to overtake the woman and sweep her away with the torrent. But the earth helped the woman by opening its mouth and swallowing the river that the dragon had spewed out of his mouth.

This is John's brief synopsis of the Russian invasion of Israel. Satan's plan is for the Russian-Arab alliance to basically sweep Israel off the face of the planet. John uses the word *river* to describe this overwhelming army. This coincides with Ezekiel 38:9: "You and all your troops and the many nations with you will go up, advancing like a storm; you will be like a cloud covering the land."

John shows this great invasion metaphorically by describing it as a great river. Then John metaphorically shows how God destroys this invading army by having the earth open its mouth and swallow it, relying on a prophecy from Ezekiel 38:19: "In my zeal and fiery wrath I declare that at that time there shall be a great earthquake in the land of Israel."

In short, these two prophets of God show how Satan's plan to annihilate Israel at the very beginning of the tribulation period is thwarted by almighty God. When God sends an earthquake to the land of Israel, the earth literally opens its mouth and swallows the Russian-Arab alliance.

In chapter 2, we learned the Russian invasion of Israel starts the seventieth week of Daniel, the last seven years preceding the second coming of Jesus. We have seen John's and Ezekiel's accounts of this invasion in terms of a storm, or river. Daniel 9:26 verifies their visions, showing how the Russian invasion of Israel, the beginning of the tribulation period, will come like a *flood*.

Revelation 12:17: Then the dragon was enraged at the woman [Israel and the Jews] and went off to make war against the rest of her offspring—those who obey God's commandments and hold to the testimony of Jesus [the church]. (Explanations in brackets are mine.)

John shows Satan's anger toward Israel as well as the remaining saints of the Laodicea church era who are still on the face of the earth. Satan realizes he won't be able to easily annihilate the Jews, so Satan begins to piece together a strong delusion in an effort to annihilate the church.

His plan begins by bringing to power the king of the North and have him appear as the Man of Sin. Once the world is convinced of this, Satan can then destroy him and bring to power the king of the

South, the real Man of Sin. By doing so, Satan can have him appear to the world as the Messiah. Once Satan convinces the world that he is the Messiah, he can then manipulate the people of America into persecuting the people of God, using America, known by John as Babylon the Great, as a lion's den. Figure 4-3 outlines the plan of Satan.

Revelation 13:1–2: And the dragon stood on the shore of the sea. And I saw a beast coming out of the sea. He had ten horns and seven heads, with ten crowns on his horns, and on each head a blasphemous name. The beast I saw resembled a leopard, but had feet like those of a bear and a mouth like that of a lion. The dragon gave the beast his power and his throne and great authority.

As just explained, John begins the first two verses of chapter 13 by describing the first part of Satan's great scheme. These two verses quickly tell how Satan uses the king of the North to appear to the world, particularly the church, as being the Man of Sin. These two verses are actually the only two verses in all of Revelation 13 that relate anything about the king of the North. The rest of chapter 13 relates to the real Man of Sin, the king of the South, attempting to appear to the world as being the Messiah.

John specifically wrote chapter 13 to make it appear as if he might be talking about the same person, the king of the North. However, close discernment helps us discover that it was written in such a way that Satan can attempt to fulfill the rest of chapter 13 in the person of the king of the North. In reality, we must discern John's purposeful writing style and that he transitions our focus in verse 3 to the real Man of Sin, or the king of the South, who is the little horn of Daniel 7:8.

Revelation 13:3: One of the heads [the king of the South] of the beast [the king of the North] seemed to have had a fatal wound, but the fatal wound had been healed. [Daniel 11:26 tells us how the king of the South was betrayed by his own people who attempted to assassinate him.] (Explanations in brackets are mine.)

I Will Make Myself Like The Most High!

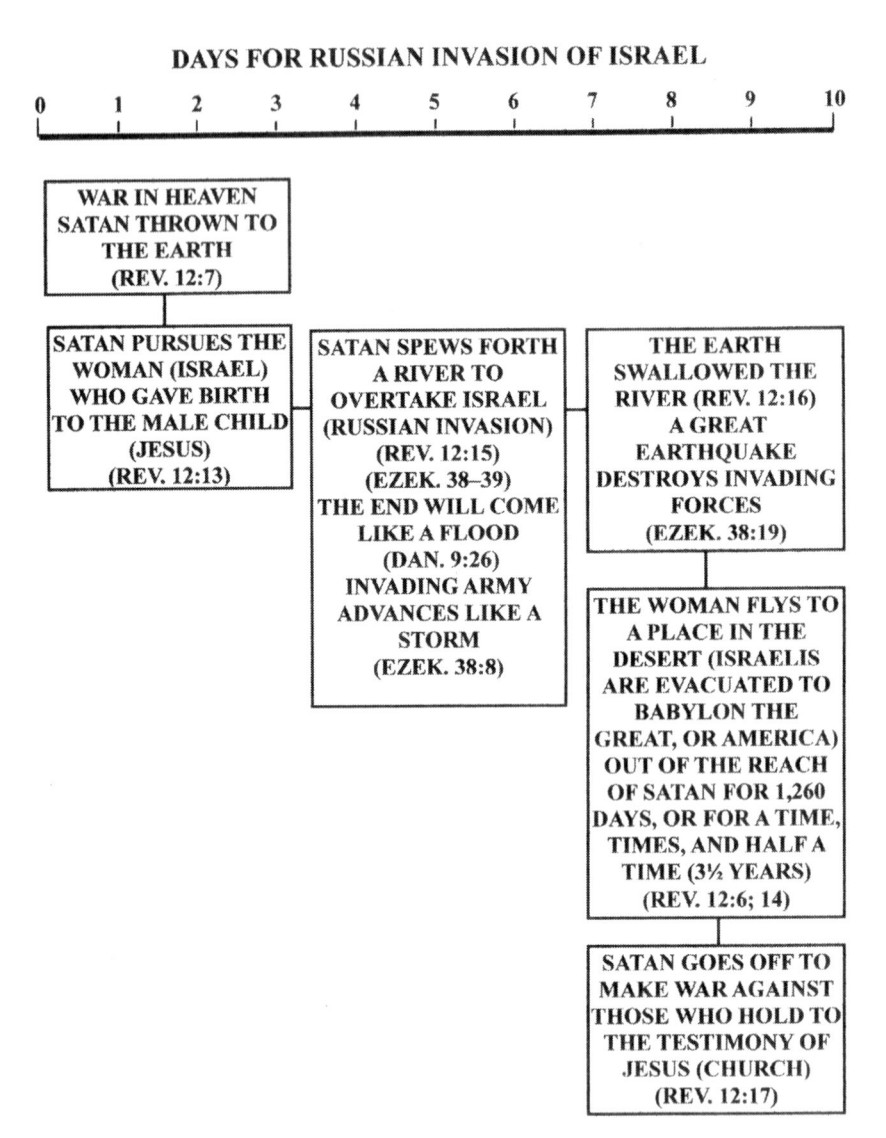

DAYS FOR RUSSIAN INVASION OF ISRAEL

```
0    1    2    3    4    5    6    7    8    9    10
|----|----|----|----|----|----|----|----|----|----|
```

WAR IN HEAVEN SATAN THROWN TO THE EARTH (REV. 12:7)		
SATAN PURSUES THE WOMAN (ISRAEL) WHO GAVE BIRTH TO THE MALE CHILD (JESUS) (REV. 12:13)	SATAN SPEWS FORTH A RIVER TO OVERTAKE ISRAEL (RUSSIAN INVASION) (REV. 12:15) (EZEK. 38–39) THE END WILL COME LIKE A FLOOD (DAN. 9:26) INVADING ARMY ADVANCES LIKE A STORM (EZEK. 38:8)	THE EARTH SWALLOWED THE RIVER (REV. 12:16) A GREAT EARTHQUAKE DESTROYS INVADING FORCES (EZEK. 38:19)
		THE WOMAN FLYS TO A PLACE IN THE DESERT (ISRAELIS ARE EVACUATED TO BABYLON THE GREAT, OR AMERICA) OUT OF THE REACH OF SATAN FOR 1,260 DAYS, OR FOR A TIME, TIMES, AND HALF A TIME (3½ YEARS) (REV. 12:6; 14)
		SATAN GOES OFF TO MAKE WAR AGAINST THOSE WHO HOLD TO THE TESTIMONY OF JESUS (CHURCH) (REV. 12:17)

FIGURE 4-3. HOW REVELATION 12 DETAILS SATAN'S PLAN TO DESTROY ISRAEL AND THE CHURCH AT THE BEGINNING OF DANIEL'S SEVENTIETH WEEK

The beast that comes out of the sea is the king of the North, having ten horns and seven heads. Here in verse 3, John is not telling us that the king of the North has a head wound. This subtle writing style allows John to tell us that a person under the authority of the king of the North is the real Man of Sin. Instead of stating this directly, John chooses to reveal the truth of the little scroll by describing the real Man of Sin as being one of the seven heads under the king of the North. It's actually one of the king of the North's seven heads who has a healed head wound—the king of the South!

By the divine will of God, people have failed for centuries to properly recognize that Revelation 13:3 is a transitional verse, allowing John to write about an entirely different person apart from the king of the North—the little horn of Daniel 7:8, or the king of the South, who is under the authority of the king of the North.

Once he subtly reveals the true Man of Sin in Revelation 13:3, John then goes on to tell how this man deludes people into accepting his mark, which will appear as a form of salvation, or forgiveness for sin. Since he doesn't have the power to forgive anyone for sin, it answers John's perplexing question in Revelation 9:20–21 as to why no one's heart has been changed toward sin when supposedly the Messiah reigns.

If Revelation 13 were written with proper interpretation, this is how it would read:

Revelation 13:1: And I saw a beast [the king of the North] coming out of the sea [he overran the king of the South, crossing the Mediterranean Sea to invade Israel and stop the daily sacrifice from taking place]. He had ten horns [EEC] and seven heads [the king of the South's leopard kingdom), with ten crowns on his horns, and on each head a blasphemous name [meaning that the Man of Sin's empire is actually blasphemous, and it's the king of the South who will perform the ultimate blasphemy against God by claiming to be God, sitting in the temple and passing it off as the wedding supper of the Lamb]. (Explanations in brackets are mine.)

Revelation 13:2: The beast I saw [the iron kingdom of the king of the North, or the terrifying beast of Daniel 7:7] resembled a leopard [king of the South's empire, or the leopard kingdom of Daniel 7:6], but had feet like those of a bear [the king of the North convinced Russia, the bear nation of Daniel 7:5, to invade Israel and was subsequently trampled underfoot by God] and a mouth like that of a lion [as a lion nation, depicted in Daniel 7:4, America is NATO's primary spokesperson]. (Explanations in brackets are mine.)

Revelation 13:2: The dragon [Satan] gave the beast [king of the North] his [Satan's] power and his [Satan's] throne and great authority [in other words, Satan, desiring to be worshiped as God through the king of the South, temporarily gives his evil powers to the king of the North so the king of the North can appear to the world as being the Man of Sin, or devil in the flesh]. (Explanations in brackets are mine.)

Now we'll see that John transitions into telling us what happens when the real Man of Sin, the king of the South, comes to power and attempts to delude people into believing he is the Messiah.

Revelation 13:3: One of the heads [the king of the South] of the beast [the king of the North's empire] seemed to have had a fatal wound [The king of the South received a head wound shortly after the king of the North advanced against him seven years earlier when the first two seal judgments of Revelation were opened. His own people attempted to assassinate him, according to Daniel 11:26.], but the fatal wound had been healed. The whole world was astonished [because he rebelled against and destroyed the king of the North and now appears as and claims to be the Messiah] and followed the beast [the king of the South who is possessed by Satan, believing he is God]. (Explanations in brackets are mine.)

Next, John shows how people who fall for this strong delusion are really worshiping Satan, though they believe they are worshiping God.

Revelation 13:4: Men worshiped the dragon [the king of the South is possessed by Satan, who boasted he would be worshiped as God in Isaiah 14:14] because he had given authority to the beast [the king of the South, who now appears as a victorious Messiah by destroying the king of the North, who many believed was the Man of Sin. Satan withdrew his power from the king of the North and gave it to the king of the South.], and they also worshiped the beast [believing the king of the South is God] and asked, "Who is like the beast? Who can make war against him?" [They don't believe anyone can wage war against the person they believe is God.] (Explanations in brackets are mine.)

After people are convinced the king of the South is now God in the flesh, John provides Satan's objective for betraying the king of the North and establishing the king of the South. After relating the true identity of the Man of Sin, John reverts to using the term *beast* to describe the person who received a head wound yet now lives to appear as the Messiah. Figure 4-4 shows the differences between the king of the North appearing as being the Man of Sin and the king of the South appearing as being the Messiah.

Revelation 13:5: The beast [the king of the South, or Man of Sin] was given a mouth to utter proud words and blasphemies [claiming he is the Messiah, or God. Remember how John said it was the seven heads of the king of the North who had blasphemous names.] and to exercise his authority for forty-two months [fifth trumpet through sixth bowl of wrath]. (Explanations in brackets are mine.)

Revelation 13:6: He opened his mouth to blaspheme God [he discredits Jesus by claiming Jesus was a strong delusion that he, now posing as God, sent to mankind two thousand years ago], and to slander his name [Jesus] and his dwelling place [the Temple Mount in Jerusalem, sitting in the Holy of Holies and passing it off as the wedding supper of the Lamb] and those who live in heaven [the dead in Jesus Christ, or the church, whom John saw as a sea of glass in Revelation 4:6]. (Explanations in brackets are mine.)

THE IRON KINGDOM OF THE KING OF THE NORTH

BEAST OUT OF THE SEA ──────── **KING OF THE NORTH—TEN HORNS**
(NOTE: HE COMES OUT   WITH CROWNS (REV. 13:1)
OF THE SEA OF HUMANITY—   - SEEN AS A TERRIFYING BEAST
HE IS GIVEN THE HONOR   (DAN. 7:7)
OF ROYALTY BY THE   - HE REMAINS FOR A LITTLE WHILE
PEOPLE)   (REV. 17:10)
                            - HE MUST BE *TAKEN OUT OF THE
                              WAY* BEFORE THE MAN OF SIN
                              CAN BE REVEALED (2 THESS. 2:7)
                            - DESTROYED DURING 6TH TRUMPET
                              WAR, WHICH APPEARS AS
                              ARMAGEDDON (REV. 9:13–19)
                              (DAN. 11:40–45)

RESEMBLES A LEOPARD ──────── SEVEN HEADS WITH BLASPHEMOUS
                              NAMES (REV. 13:1)
                            - REPRESENTS THE KING OF THE
                              SOUTH'S LEOPARD KINGDOM
                            - KING OF THE SOUTH BECOMES
                              THE WOUNDED HEAD (REV. 13:3)
                              (DAN. 11:25–26), OR MAN OF SIN

FEET LIKE A BEAR ──────── RUSSIAN INVASION OF ISRAEL
                              (SIXTH SEAL WAR)
                            - RUSSIA DESTROYED (REV. 6:12–17)
                              (EZEKIEL 38–39)

MOUTH LIKE A LION ──────── U.S. SERVES AS GOD OF FORTRESSES
                              (DAN. 11:38)
                            - WINGS OF AN EAGLE—BECOMES A
                              SANCTUARY FOR JEWS AND
                              CHRISTIANS UNDER THE KING OF
                              THE NORTH'S RULE (REV. 12:6; 14)
                            - BECOMES BABYLON THE GREAT
                              (REV. 17–18)
                            - BECOMES CONVINCED THE KING
                              OF THE SOUTH IS GOD (REV. 17:3)
                            - BECOMES DRUNK WITH THE
                              BLOOD OF THE SAINTS (REV. 17:6)

SATAN GIVES THE KING OF THE NORTH HIS (SATAN'S) POWER AND HIS (SATAN'S) THRONE AND GREAT AUTHORITY (REV. 13:2), BUT ONLY FOR A LITTLE WHILE (REV. 17:10) UNTIL HE IS DESTROYED (DAN. 11:40–45).

FIGURE 4-4. DIFFERENCES BETWEEN THE KING OF THE NORTH AND KING OF THE SOUTH, WHO BECOMES THE MAN OF SIN

Satan's Revelation: "I Am The Christ!"

THE BRONZE KINGDOM OF THE KING OF THE SOUTH
(MAN OF SIN)

SATAN HAS SEVEN HEADS WITH CROWNS AND TEN HORNS (REV. 12:3)	KING OF THE SOUTH -HE IS OF THE SEVEN HEADS (REV. 17:11) -HE IS THE ONE WITH A HEAD WOUND (REV. 13:3) BETRAYED BY HIS OWN PEOPLE (DAN. 11:26) -HE IS THE BEAST WHO IS WOUNDED BY THE SWORD AND YET LIVES (REV. 13:14) -HE IS REVEALED AS BEING GOD AFTER THE KING OF THE NORTH IS TAKEN OUT OF THE WAY (2 THESS. 2:3–4) -HE MOUNTS A REBELLION AGAINST THE KING OF THE NORTH (DAN. 11:40–45) (2 THESS. 2:3–4) -HE PROCLAIMS TO BE GOD (REV. 13:6) -HE IS A STERN-FACED KING AND MASTER OF INTRIGUE (DAN. 8:23–25) -OFFERS MARK OF SALVATION (REV. 13:16–18) -OFFERS FOLLOWERS WEALTH (DAN. 11:24) -COMMITS ABOMINATION THAT CAUSES DESOLATION (DAN. 9:26) (REV. 13:6) (MATT. 24:15)	EIGHTH KING (REV. 17:11) -THE KING OF THE SOUTH IS THE ONE WHO WAS, NOW IS NOT, AND YET WILL COME (REV. 17:8, 11) -HE BELONGS TO THE SEVEN (SEVEN HEADS UNDER THE KING OF THE NORTH) -HE SETS UP TEN NEW KINGS (REV. 17:12) -THEY HATE AMERICA, WHO IS BABYLON THE GREAT (REV. 17:16) -HE IS GOING TO HIS DESTRUCTION (REV. 17:11)
FALSE PROPHET HAS HORNS LIKE A LAMB BUT SPEAKS LIKE A DRAGON (REV. 13:11–12) BEAST OUT OF THE EARTH (REV. 13:11) EXALTS KING OF THE SOUTH AS GOD, WHOSE FATAL WOUND HAD BEEN HEALED (REV. 13:12) POSSESSED BY THE ANGEL OF THE ABYSS, KNOWN AS ABADDON, OR APOLLYON (THE DESTROYER) (REV. 9:11)		

NOTE: SATAN HAS HIS CROWNS ON HIS HEADS, NOT HIS HORNS LIKE THE KING OF THE NORTH.

FIGURE 4-4 (CONTINUED). DIFFERENCES BETWEEN THE KING OF THE NORTH AND KING OF THE SOUTH, WHO BECOMES THE MAN OF SIN

SATAN HAS SEVEN HEADS WITH CROWNS AND TEN HORNS

KING OF THE NORTH

HAS TEN HORNS WITH CROWNS AND SEVEN HEADS WITH BLASPHEMOUS NAMES (REV. 13:2–3)

HE RESEMBLES A LEOPARD (KING OF THE SOUTH'S KINGDOM), HAS THE FEET OF A BEAR (RUSSIA), AND THE MOUTH OF A LION (UNITED STATES OF AMERICA) (REV. 13:2)

SATAN TEMPORARILY GIVES HIM HIS POWER, HIS THRONE, AND GREAT AUTHORITY (REV. 13:2) SO HE CAN DELUDE THE WORLD AND THE CHURCH INTO BELIEVING HE IS THE MAN OF SIN

HE MUST REMAIN FOR A LITTLE WHILE (REV. 17:10)

HE IS TAKEN OUT OF THE WAY SO THE REAL MAN OF SIN CAN BE REVEALED (2 THESS. 2:3–4; 8–12) AS SUPPOSEDLY BEING THE MESSIAH

AFTER THEM ANOTHER KING WILL ARISE, DIFFERENT FROM THE TEN HORNS THAT COME FROM THIS KINGDOM (DAN. 7:8, 24)

KING OF THE SOUTH

MAKES UP THE SEVEN HEADS (LEOPARD KINGDOM) WITH BLASPHEMOUS NAMES UNDER THE KING OF THE NORTH (THE IRON KINGDOM)

HE IS THE RIDER ON THE WHITE HORSE WHEN THE FIRST SEAL IS BROKEN (REV. 6:2)

HE IS BETRAYED BY HIS OWN PEOPLE AND RECEIVES A HEAD WOUND (DAN. 11:25–26)

HIS FATAL WOUND IS HEALED (REV. 13:3)

HE IS WOUNDED BY THE SWORD AND YET LIVES (REV. 13:12)

DESTROYS THREE HORNS UNDER THE KING OF THE NORTH WHEN HE REBELS (DAN. 7:8, 24) (DAN. 8:9–12)

AFTER THE REBELLION (SIXTH TRUMPET WAR), HE SETS UP TEN NEW KINGS (REV. 17:12–13)

BABYLON THE GREAT

RIDES THE SCARLET BEAST COVERED WITH BLASPHEMOUS NAMES THAT HAS SEVEN HEADS AND TEN NEW HORNS (REV. 17:3, 7, 12)

FIGURE 4-4 (CONTINUED). DIFFERENCES BETWEEN THE KING OF THE NORTH AND KING OF THE SOUTH, WHO BECOMES THE MAN OF SIN

Revelation 13:7: He [the king of the South] was given power to make war against the saints [during the time of great tribulation, or the last three years of Daniel's ten-year end-time period] and to conquer them. [These will be the great tribulation martyrs John saw in Revelation 7:9–17 and again in Revelation 15:2. John saw them standing beside the church, or sea of glass, which was mixed with fire from those saints who came out of the hour of trial.] And he was given authority over every tribe, people, language, and nation. [This is a reference to America, the melting pot of all people, tribes, and languages into one nation, turning away from the truth that Jesus is God and instead believing the king of the South is God. America helps him convince the whole world that he is God by persecuting those who refuse to worship him as God. The lion nation that once had the wings of a great eagle, representing religious freedom, will now have its wings torn off and be given the heart of a man—the Man of Sin. This is how the lion nation becomes a lion's den during the great tribulation period, killing those who refuse to worship the Man of Sin as God.] (Explanations in brackets are mine.)

Revelation 13:8: All inhabitants of the earth will worship the beast [the king of the South, believing he is God and not recognizing that he is really the Man of Sin]—all whose names have not been written in the book of life belonging to the Lamb [Jesus] that was slain from the creation of the world [all those who refuse to believe and accept Jesus as their personal Savior]. (Explanations in brackets are mine.)

After showing how Satan uses the king of the South to delude the world into believing he is God, John then issues a staunch warning to those who will end up being victorious over this strong delusion. This warning is for those who are temporarily duped by this man's appearance as being the Messiah. Although they may be fooled now and miss the impending rapture, they will discern his true identity sometime after the rapture. Since they fail to accept the truth (that Jesus is Lord, and the king of the South is the Man of Sin) prior to the rapture, John tells them their options once they discern the truth.

I Will Make Myself Like The Most High!

Revelation 13:9–10: He who has an ear, let him hear. If anyone is to go into captivity, into captivity he will go. If anyone is to be killed with the sword, with the sword he will be killed. This calls for patient endurance and faithfulness on the part of the saints [those who miss the rapture but discern the truth, reject the king of the South as God and his offer of salvation and wealth, become great tribulation martyrs]. (Explanations in brackets are mine.)

Next, John describes in detail the delusion Satan creates to convince people that the king of the South is the Messiah, and how he destroys many through peaceful means.

Revelation 13:11–12: Then I saw another beast, coming out of the earth. He had two horns like a lamb, but he spoke like a dragon. [Satan is the voice of the False Prophet, another person he possesses. Satan uses the False Prophet to specifically exalt the king of the South as being God.] He [the False Prophet who appears as the Holy Spirit of God, as portrayed by the king of the South] exercised all the authority of the first beast [the king of the South, who claims to be God] on his [king of the South's/Satan's] behalf and made the earth [the Israelites] and its inhabitants [the Gentiles] worship the first beast [the king of the South] whose fatal wound had been healed. (Explanations in brackets are mine.)

Revelation 13:13: And he [the False Prophet] performed great and miraculous signs [Second Thessalonians 2:9 informs us that "the coming of the lawless one (Man of Sin, or the king of the South) will be in accordance with the work of Satan displayed in all kinds of counterfeit miracles, signs and wonders, and in every sort of evil (offering salvation and wealth) that deceives those who are perishing."], even causing fire to come down from heaven to earth in full view of men [which, as we'll see later, destroys the 144,000 Jewish-Christian evangelists who are preaching that Jesus is God]. (Explanations in brackets and parenthesis are mine.)

Revelation 13:14: Because of the signs he was given power to do on behalf of the first beast [king of the South, who has the head wound], he [the False Prophet] deceived the inhabitants of the earth. He ordered them to set up an image in honor of the beast who was wounded by the sword and yet lived [king of the South]. [Jesus said in Matthew 24:15–16, "So when you see standing in the holy place 'the abomination that causes desolation,' spoken of through the prophet Daniel—let the reader understand—then let those who are in Judea flee to the mountains." What we're supposed to discern is that the king of the South is really the Man of Sin, or Satan incarnate, posing as God!] (Explanations in brackets are mine.)

Revelation 13:15: He [the False Prophet] was given power to give breath to the image of the first beast [king of the South], so that it could speak and cause all who refused to worship the image to be killed. [When the 144,000 Jewish-Christian evangelists refuse to bow their knee and worship the image of the king of the South as being God, the False Prophet will destroy them with fire to gain credibility for the king of the South's proclamation that he is God.] (Explanations in brackets are mine.)

Revelation 13:16–17: He also forced everyone, small and great, rich and poor, free and slave, to receive a mark on his right hand or on his forehead [as we'll see later, this deadly mark will be Satan's subtle offer of wealth in exchange for forgiveness for sin], so that no one could buy or sell unless he had the mark [which appears as an offer of salvation], which is the name of the beast [king of the South] or the number of his name [DNA is unique to each individual]. (Explanations in brackets are mine.)

Revelation 13:18: This calls for wisdom. If anyone has insight, let him calculate the number of the beast [king of the South], for it is man's number. His number is 666 [meaning the king of the South is the ultimate Man of Sin and not God]. Explanations in brackets are mine.)

As we have just seen, Revelation 13:3 transitions from talking about the king of the North to describing the king of the South, who was wounded by the sword and yet lived. Everything thereafter begins to make perfect sense as to the true identity of the Man of Sin and the action Satan takes in order to delude mankind into believing the king of the South is God. This is how Satan achieves being worshiped as God, just as he threatened in Isaiah 14:12–15.

It is now easy to see how Satan has been able to already delude the last generation with a false end-time scenario. Bible scholars have failed to properly divide Revelation 13:1–2 from the rest of Revelation 13. They have attempted to delude us into believing that there is only one Antichrist. Yet even Jesus informs us, in Matthew 24:4–5, that there will be more than one: "Watch out that no one deceives you. For many [meaning both the king of the North and the king of the South] will come in my name [Christ or Godhead], claiming, 'I am the Christ [the Messiah, or God],' and will deceive many." (Explanations in brackets are mine.)

EXALTING THE MAN OF SIN AS GOD

Revelation 13:11–12: Then I saw another beast, coming out of the earth. He had two horns like a lamb, but he spoke like a dragon [False Prophet]. He exercised all the authority of the first beast [king of the South] on his behalf, and made the earth and its inhabitants worship the first beast [king of the South], whose fatal wound had been healed. (Explanations in brackets are mine.)

The beast that has horns like a lamb but speaks like a dragon is the False Prophet. He appears here because he imitates the Holy Spirit. He exalts the king of the South, who rebels against the king of the North, appearing as a victorious Messiah, or God. The False Prophet exercises all the power of the king of the South, just as the Holy Spirit exercises all the power of God, or Jesus, during this age of grace. Just as the Holy Spirit leads believers to worship God, the False Prophet's purpose is to imitate this by having people worship the king of the South, who claims to be God. Having himself exalted by the False Prophet, the king of the South comes to power, through intrigue, on a religious platform.

WORSHIPING DEMONS AND IDOLS

Revelation 9:20–21: The rest of mankind that were not killed by these plagues still did not repent of the work of their hands; they did not stop worshiping demons, and idols of gold, silver, bronze, stone and wood—idols that cannot see or hear or walk. Nor did they repent of their murders, their magic arts, their sexual immorality or their thefts.

After reading Daniel 5:4, the subtle mystery of John's true message can be discerned: "As they [King Belshazzar and all his nobles] drank the wine [from the temple goblets], they praised the gods of gold and silver, of bronze, iron, wood and stone." (Explanations in brackets are mine.)

Remarkably, once again John relies on Daniel's prophetic end-time parable to tell us about the abomination that causes desolation committed by the king of the South, just as Jesus said in Matthew 24:15. Just as Belshazzar desecrated the temple ornaments by holding a grand gala ball, the king of the South desecrates the temple in Jerusalem by holding his own dedication and coronation ceremony. This abomination that causes desolation thereby appears as the marriage supper of the Lamb, as people celebrate the king of the South's victory over the king of the North, and believe he is God.

Notice also how John, unlike Daniel, subtly left the word *iron* out of his list of materials from which idols were made. This is a subtle reference by John that the king of the North and his iron kingdom are history!

THE FORTY DAYS OF TESTING

Luke 21:34–36: Be careful, or your hearts will be weighed down with dissipation, drunkenness and the anxieties of life, and that day will close on you unexpectedly like a trap. For it will come upon all those who live on the face of the whole earth. Be always on the watch, and pray that you may be able to escape all that is about to happen, and that you may be able to stand before the Son of Man.

When Jesus returns, He will hold the marriage supper of the Lamb (Rev. 19:9). The king of the South will imitate this marriage supper as everyone celebrates the arrival and coronation of the person they assume is God.

Additionally, people will be worried about the cares of life: what they will eat, drink, and wear. For them, the king of the South and the False Prophet will have the answers to their dilemma. They will make provision for their needs and more in a world that has been devastated by war. However, their provision for basic food, clothing, and shelter, as well as the riches and luxuries people desire to have, will come with a high price—the eternal damnation of their souls!

Here in Luke, Jesus forewarns us, the true believers of the church, not to participate in this ceremony of deception. Our judgment should not be clouded by the king of the South appearing as the Messiah. We should not be swayed by his offer of wealth in exchange for taking his false form of salvation, or forgiveness for sin. Instead, Jesus tells us, the church, to pray that we might be able to escape from this strong delusion. That method of escape will entail the rapture of our spirits and souls at the blowing of the seventh trumpet.

DELUDING THE SAINTS

Revelation 13:14: Because of the signs he was given power to do on behalf of the first beast, he deceived the inhabitants of the earth. He ordered them to set up an image in honor of the beast who was wounded by the sword and yet lived.

John now describes the delusion Satan creates surrounding the events of the temple-dedication ceremony when the whole world gathers to pay honor to the king of the South, who now claims to be God. Obviously, many will watch this event on television or their smartphones, a prophetic vision that has only been able to be fulfilled in my generation with the advent of television and satellites.

The 144,000 Jewish-Christian evangelists who have been preaching that Jesus is Lord will be present at this ceremony, even given special seating. They preached the gospel of Jesus throughout the hour of trial, along with true believers of the Laodicea church.

This dedication ceremony is a complete fulfillment of the prophetic parable Daniel wrote in chapter 3 of his book when he told the story long ago about Shadrach, Meshach, and Abednego. When King Nebuchadnezzar had his dedication ceremony, three young Jewish men refused to bow their knee to the pagan king's statue, and as a result, they were thrown alive into a furnace of fire. But they were saved by the protecting presence of Jesus.

TRAMPLING ON THE HOST OF THE SAINTS

Revelation 13:15: He was given power to give breath to the image of the first beast, so that it could speak and cause all who refused to worship the image to be killed.

Revelation 13:13: And he performed great and miraculous signs, even causing fire to come down from heaven to earth in full view of men.

Calling fire down from heaven is staged to specifically annihilate the 144,000 Jewish-Christian evangelists. Just as those three young Jews were thrown into a fiery furnace, the 144,000 Jewish-Christian evangelists are about to be killed in their own fiery furnace. After gathering them together to a spot he selects, the False Prophet will have them surgically removed from the face of the earth with the fire that comes down from heaven. They are all destroyed at the same time!

John immediately makes this clear beginning in chapter 14 when he sees the 144,000 evangelists in heaven with Jesus. When people literally see 144,000 evangelists who preached Jesus as God consumed by fire from heaven, it allows Satan to subtly instill the so-called *fear of God* into them. The king of the South, portraying God, will use this opportunity to convince people to worship his image and accept his deadly mark of salvation for economic gain.

THE LAMB AND THE 144,000

Revelation 14:1: Then I looked, and there before me was the Lamb, standing on Mount Zion, and with him 144,000 who had his name and his Father's name written on their foreheads.

Revelation 14:2–3: And I heard a sound from heaven like the roar of rushing waters and like a loud peal of thunder. The sound I heard was like that of harpists playing their harps. And they sang a new song before the throne and before the four living creatures and the elders. No one could learn the song except the 144,000 who had been redeemed from the earth.

Revelation 14:4: They were purchased from among men and offered as first-fruits to God and the Lamb.

How can we discern the 144,000 are killed instantly and at the same time? In Revelation 13:13, we read where the False Prophet calls down fire from heaven. But John doesn't tell the rest of their story until chapter 14. Immediately in chapter 14, John shows us how Jesus stands with the 144,000 in Jerusalem. Suddenly, in a flash, the 144,000 are seen by John standing before the throne of God, learning a new song in heaven, and they are all learning it at the same time.

Revelation 14:4 states they are offered as first-fruits to God and the Lamb. Since they are the first to enter the presence of heaven and stand before the throne of God, the rapture cannot take place until they have been offered up as first-fruits, meaning they are killed and their bodies destroyed, and only their souls and spirits are raised to heaven.

Satan uses this false miracle to simply discredit the validity of Jesus. He makes Jesus out to be the strong delusion that was sent to mankind two thousand years ago. The question Satan wants everyone to ask themselves, including Christians of the Laodicea church who are still alive, is, if Jesus was God, then why didn't He save the 144,000 evangelists preaching His name?

John provides the answer in Revelation 14. Their deaths are divinely willed by God. Their deaths keep with the doctrine Jesus preached in Matthew 24:34, when He stated that everyone must die or pass away. Their deaths do not come as a surprise to God in heaven. The 144,000 have served God's purpose, and now John makes it clear they are brought home first, before the remaining believers of the church are raptured.

The 144,000 evangelists are the first to refuse to worship the king of the South's image. They are the first to be killed during this time of great distress, as both Daniel and Jesus called it, meaning a time of great trouble for true believers.

They are the first to refuse the king of the South's bribe, or receipt of tremendous wealth, in exchange for taking the mark of the beast, which is disguised as an offer of salvation—or the injection of his blood or DNA into a person's body as an atonement for sin!

They are the first members of the church age to be raised in spirit and soul directly before the throne of God, preceding the church, which is the sea of glass John saw in Revelation 4:6. This is in fulfillment of Jesus' prophecies in Matthew 19:30 and 20:16, Mark 10:31, and Luke 13:30, where Jesus said that "the last will be first [they are the last members of the church age] and the first [the church-age believers] will be last."

In an attempt to fulfill Scripture, the king of the South will justify the killing of the 144,000 evangelists who preached Jesus as the Savior. The first commandment given to Moses by God was that we should have no other god before Him. Therefore, the king of the South, working through the False Prophet, or Satan, will have to destroy these evangelists in an effort to show the world that he, now posing as God, is serious. And this helps delude the world into believing that he is God and has the power over life and death.

THE FIRST WARNING—DO NOT BE DECEIVED

Revelation 14:6–7: Then I saw another angel flying in midair, and he had the eternal gospel to proclaim to those who live on the earth—to every nation, tribe, language and people. He said in a loud voice, "Fear God and give him glory, because the hour of his judgment has come. Worship him who made the heavens, the earth, the sea and the springs of water."

2 Thessalonians 3:3: But the Lord is faithful, and he will strengthen and protect you from the evil one.

This angel delivers his message from God to the two witnesses preaching the eternal gospel to the world from the Temple Mount in Jerusalem. People around the world will hear their preaching. This means that television and satellites will still be in place. Thus we now know why John says this angel flies in midair, and his message is heard around the world.

These two witnesses, Elijah and Moses, stand as a witness for Jesus during the great tribulation period, serving as a source of contention against the king of the South. Just as the king of the North was continuously frustrated by the preaching of the gospel by the 144,000 Jewish-Christian evangelists, so the king of the South is given two thorns in his side: Elijah and Moses. Satan will not have the power to kill them at this time. Near the end of his reign, God will allow him to kill these two witnesses in order to serve as yet another strong delusion.

This action shows us how God is never left without a witness here on earth. Empowered by the Holy Spirit of God, these two witnesses preach the everlasting gospel of Jesus, once again fulfilling the words of Jesus in Matthew 24:14.

People who believe their message and refuse the mark of salvation will face martyrdom. They will be killed at the hands of those people who, for the love of money, accept the king of the South's offer of salvation and worship him as God. They will be convinced that by doing so, they are doing God a great service. This is how Satan destroys many through peace!

DO NOT ACCEPT (DNA) HIS SALVATION

Revelation 13:16–18: He also forced everyone, small and great, rich and poor, free and slave, to receive a mark on his right hand or on his forehead, so that no one could buy or sell unless he had the mark, which is the name of the beast or the number of his name. This calls for wisdom. If anyone has insight, let him calculate the number of the beast, for it is man's number. His number is 666.

Only in the last few years has mankind been given the scientific discovery of DNA. From that discovery, medical science and research has grown in leaps and bounds, leading to the ability to clone cells and even create new life. There is significance behind this new God-given knowledge. When we compare this new knowledge against the core truth of Christianity—that we are saved by the shed blood of Jesus Christ—I believe you'll see why mankind has only recently been given the knowledge of DNA. That knowledge is susceptible to the evil ploys of Satan to delude mankind into taking the mark of a blood sacrifice—the blood of the king of the South!

The shed blood of Jesus Christ saves all Christians. Jesus was God coming to mankind in the form and likeness of man. He is the personification of God. To atone for our sins, God poured out His wrath upon Himself in the form of His Son, Jesus Christ. He did this by His own free will in order to restore the broken relationship between God and man.

As John 3:16 states so clearly, "God so loved the world that He gave His only begotten Son, that whoever believes in Him should not perish but have everlasting life" (NKJV). We believe Jesus was the Son of God, based upon faith. When we confess Jesus as our Lord and Savior, it is His shed blood that God imputes to us. While we live in these still-sinful bodies, God spiritually sends us a physical, but spiritual, guarantee of our salvation—the Holy Spirit—living inside each believer and serving as our guide and comforter in this world.

The Holy Spirit is the third person of the Holy Trinity, made up of God the Father, God the Son, and God the Holy Spirit. As a result, even though we are still sinners, God has placed on us—because of our faith and confession—His untold grace and mercy. In other words, when God looks at us, He sees only Himself in the form of His Spirit, who is the likeness of Jesus Christ. Therefore, God dwells inside us because we have believed that He came to us in the form of His only Son, Jesus.

I Will Make Myself Like The Most High!

As far as God is concerned, everyone who has repented of their sins and accepted Jesus as Lord and Savior has the blood of Jesus Christ running through their veins. This belief is critical to the entire doctrine of Christianity. Although I may have type O-positive blood running through my veins, as far as God sees me in the spiritual realm, I have type G blood (for "God") running through my veins. God automatically imputes it to me at the moment of salvation. I didn't earn it, buy it, or deserve it. I just accepted what Jesus did for me, by faith and confession. Therefore, because God decided to freely offer us His salvation, and because we have decided to freely accept it by faith and confession, to the glory of God the Father, we are considered children of God. Have you confessed Jesus as Lord and Savior of your soul?

That's why we are kept from the upcoming wrath of God, which will be poured out in the form of Satan posing as God to the world. God's wrath begins with Satan's reign of religious tyranny immediately after the church is raptured. God's wrath concludes with the seven bowls of wrath being poured out when Jesus returns.

We believers are spared the time of wrath because Jesus has already taken our wrath upon Himself when He was crucified at Calvary. Those of us who are saved by the blood of Jesus will be removed from the earth through a rapture. However, this rapture will include only the taking of our souls and spirits to heaven. It occurs through death, in fulfillment of Jesus' prophecy in Matthew 24:34 that this generation will not pass away, or die off, until all end-time Scripture is fulfilled. Our bodies will appear as dead to unbelievers who are left behind. God will raise only our spirits and souls to heaven.

Those of us who survive the seal and trumpet judgments will be exposed to the true Man of Sin. We will see him try to force everyone, including us, to take his mark, which will physically mirror the spiritual form of true Christianity. He will delude people into accepting physical salvation—his physical blood—instead of spiritual salvation based on faith, which is what Jesus offered. Satan commits this abomination to serve as the ultimate blasphemy against God and what He has already done in the person of Jesus Christ.

Daniel 12:12 tells true believers in Jesus Christ who are exposed to this strong delusion, "Blessed are those who wait for and reach the 1,335 days." Daniel tells us the day the rapture occurs. It can literally be calculated without even using a calendar. That's why 1 Thessalonians 5:4 tells us we have no need to talk about days or seasons. If we understand the truth, that day should not surprise us. That means we will be able to know the day of the rapture, even though we are facing the strong delusion presented by the king of the South.

Since the Man of Sin is portraying himself as God coming to earth for the first and only time, then Satan is going to have to offer the world some form of salvation, or forgiveness for sin. Jesus came and served as an atoning sacrifice, shedding His blood for the forgiveness of sin. If the Man of Sin discredits Jesus, then, as God coming to earth for the first and only time, there will have to be atonement for sin through the shedding of blood. The Old Testament still applies. All have sinned. The wages of sin is death. Therefore, a blood sacrifice must be made to atone for sin.

With the Bible in hand, and quoting Scripture, Satan will commit the ultimate blasphemy against God. Through the king of the South, he will offer the people grace for their sins. Under his twisted terms of grace, he will offer his blood—in the form of DNA—as an atoning sacrifice for sin. The whole world may not have cash registers and computers, but we have demonstrated in these last days that the whole world can easily be vaccinated.

He takes the grace of God and twists it into a physical form of salvation. Physical salvation does not provide the soul eternal life. But under Satan's plan, to be considered as a child of the king, people must accept his offer and take his DNA. Today we know his DNA will be universally unique. He will require his DNA to be injected into each follower's body, much like a vaccination.

The taking of his DNA vaccine will result in an outward mark being tattooed on the body—on the forehead or the hand—for the world to see. This will be proof of a person's public confession they believe the king of the South is God. The tattoo says they are convinced he's God and saved by his blood. By their taking of his DNA, he will claim that a cloning process takes place, claiming people will be reborn of his spirit. He will falsely state that all things, by his blood, are being made new. He will claim that as God he can be pleased only when he sees his own blood sacrifice upon each individual. He will demand that only his blood can cover people for their sins.

By persuading them to take his DNA and convincing them that they are forgiven for their sins, he allows them to freely keep on sinning without guilt, without remorse, and without true repentance. They are falsely convinced, that as God, he is pleased only when he sees his mark. They are oblivious to the fact that their false salvation experience does not result in a change of heart toward sin in their lives. They feel absolutely no guilt or remorse for the sins they continue to commit. Now we can understand why John wrote in Revelation 9:20–21 that people's hearts have not been truly changed toward the sins they commit when the Messiah supposedly reigns in righteousness.

As if this tactic isn't deceptive enough, Satan will then play on the true deceit that lies in the heart of every human being. To sweeten the deal, he will offer tremendous wealth as a reward for their loyalty. By taking his supposedly free gift of salvation, people will be made instantly wealthy beyond their wildest imagination. It will be as if each person just won fifty state lotteries at the same time!

Quoting scripture from the Bible, he'll claim that their teary eyes have not seen and their itching ears have not heard all the glorious things that he as God has longed to bestow upon them. He'll claim that if they truly want to please him, then they will take his blood, or DNA, so he can fulfill the yet-undreamed desires of their hearts.

To their own destruction, many people will not recognize this bizarre method of forgiveness for sin as being the eternal death of their souls. To try to twist salvation into physical reality leaves out the one crucial factor that separates Christianity from all other religions—faith! Faith believes that God can save us from His wrath all by Himself through the person of Jesus Christ. We need not try to save ourselves from God's wrath. We need only to repent of our sins and accept Jesus Christ as our Lord and Savior.

This method of salvation will be Satan's most deceptive and destructive *theory* to date. No wonder Gabriel stated in Daniel 7:25

that "he will speak against the Most High and oppress his saints and try to change the set times and the laws." The *set times* he attempts to change is this age of grace by faith. The *set laws* he attempts to change are the laws of spiritual salvation. In Daniel 8:12, we see where this man prospers in everything he does and throws truth to the ground.

God has recently given mankind a serious demonstration of what happens when people fall for Satan's schemes. We've seen what happens when we are infected with DNA or blood that has a timed-release virus. This is exactly the case with the AIDS virus today. It is brought into the body's system, yet the symptoms have a seven- to ten-year incubation period. Many people carry the HIV virus but don't develop any AIDS-related symptoms for several years.

Once again, Satan will take God's method of true salvation and attempt to delude mankind with what appears to be a suitable, logical, physical replacement. He comes so close to the spiritual truth but remains in the physical realm. People who are not spiritually discerning will be easily deceived. Just as the serpent exclaimed to Eve in the garden, so will Satan exclaim to people in that day, "You will not surely die!" But taking on his DNA will lead them to eternal damnation. So they will die—physically and spiritually for all eternity!

People who take his blood, or DNA mark, will actually be injected with tainted blood that contains an infectious, timed-released virus that won't produce any symptoms for about three years. According to Revelation 16:2, the symptoms of the virus come when the first bowl of God's wrath is poured out just prior to the return of Jesus. Revelation 16:2 helps us understand this: "The first angel went and poured out his bowl on the land, and ugly and painful sores broke out on the people who had the mark of the beast and worshiped his image."

This event occurs three years after people take this deadly mark, or have themselves pierced or vaccinated with his blood. Revelation 16:10–11 further supports the symptoms of the virus: "Men gnawed their tongues in agony and cursed the God of heaven because of their pains and their sores, but they refused to repent of what they had done."

Ironically, John relates how they are still afforded an opportunity to repent and truly be saved. Scripture supports John's statement here. Romans 10:13 states, "In that day, anyone who calls upon the name of the Lord shall be saved." Sadly enough, John tells how their hearts are so hardened that instead of calling upon the name of the Lord Jesus to save them, they curse God. Although someone may be deceived and take his mark, I believe that at any point in time before Jesus returns, by faith (believing in what you cannot see) they can repent of their sin. They can truly change their mind. By doing so, they subject themselves to martyrdom at the hands of the Man of Sin, thereby gaining eternal life for their soul.

DILUTING THE DELUSION

Matthew 24:24: For false Christs and false prophets will appear and perform great signs and miracles to deceive even the elect—if that were possible.

2 Thessalonians 2:11–12: For this reason God sends them a powerful delusion so that they will believe the lie and so that all will be condemned who have not believed the truth but have delighted in wickedness.

Revelation 19:20: With these signs he had deluded those who had received the mark of the beast and worshiped his image.

Ecclesiastes 7:7: Extortion turns a wise man into a fool, and a bribe corrupts the heart.

After displaying the false miracle of calling down fire from heaven and destroying the 144,000 evangelists, the False Prophet now unveils the great plan of the king of the South to offer everyone salvation. It is a great economic plan that helps the king of the South appear as God fulfilling the desires of His followers' hearts.

The millennial reign of Jesus will be a time of great prosperity. There will be no wars. It will be a time of unprecedented peace. Therefore, Satan must duplicate this time of great peace and prosperity in an effort to make people believe the millennial reign of God has begun on earth. However, Satan is forced to use monetary resources natural to mankind. He does not have the miracle wealth-producing power of God, so he's left to fend with that which is physical or natural to mankind—the world's money resources.

He knows if people don't understand the concept of how salvation works, there's one concept they can easily understand—money! Both Daniel and John tell us there is truly much more to this mark, or offer of salvation, than just being able to buy a loaf of bread. Satan knows that at the deepest part of every human heart is the yearning to *have it all*.

It's this deceitfulness of the heart that made Jesus put the Laodicea church through the hour of trial in the first place, in order to test people over the loss of their wealth. The whole reason Jesus issued a strong rebuke to the believers of this end-time church is this warped sense of believing that we can have our heavenly reward here on earth, confusing the receipt of wealth as a sign of our godliness. Satan has been ever mindful that mankind has always been searching for paradise here on earth. Over the past eighty years, he has built up the world through the tremendous wealth generated in America.

However, under the rule of the king of the North, we saw where America continued to be uncooperative with Satan by not persecuting the Jews and Christians. The king of the North was not able to adequately accomplish this goal by brute force. So now, under the rule of the king of the South, Satan uses his most subtle scheme to get America to abandon its Constitution and right of religious freedom. Within the realm of evil, Satan knows there are two basic ways to get people to follow, and brute force is one of them. However, there is a more subtle way to destroy people, and that is to feed them, to give them all they desire. This is the path Satan chooses against America.

The False Prophet devises this diabolical scheme. Knowing America harbors many Jews and Christians, the False Prophet, empowered by Satan, will unveil the new economic plan to make it appear to the world as if the kingdom of heaven is now on earth. His economic recovery plan will have devastating consequences to the lives of Christians and Jews or anyone who refuses to participate.

Additionally, it destroys the eternal destiny of the souls for those who do participate. For Satan, it's the ultimate win-win situation. He doesn't have to outright proclaim that he hates Christians or Jews. He only has to state that he loves all people who worship him, knowing full well that many will reject his offer of wealth and salvation.

BY THE STRENGTH OF MY HAND

Isaiah 10:13–14: For he says: "By the strength of my hand I have done this, and by my wisdom, because I have understanding. I removed the boundaries of nations, I plundered their treasures; like a mighty one I subdued their kings. As one reaches into a nest, so my hand reached for the wealth of the nations; as men gather abandoned eggs, so I gathered all the countries; not one flapped a wing, or opened its mouth to chirp."

How does one gather the wealth of all nations, including America, as one gathers *abandoned* eggs? Consider the fact that almost two-thirds of the world's population has been killed in one form or another over the previous seven-year period. The World Bank came into existence during my grandparents' lifetime. Whoever owns the World Bank controls all the wealth. The king of the South will now control the World Bank by virtue of the fact that the world believes he is God—through the world-wide healing of the 5th trumpet plague and the destruction of the 144,000 evangelists, the whole world will be convinced he has the power over life and death. Of course, the *abandoned eggs* are simply the bank accounts of all the people who have died. There will literally be trillions and trillions of dollars available for the king of the South to offer all individuals the desires of their hearts.

This wisdom and understanding propels the False Prophet to offer millions to everyone who accepts the king of the South's offer of salvation, which is the true mark of the beast. Along with this most generous offer comes the real reason for handing out so much wealth: to get Americans to abandon their Constitution and abolish religious freedom. Therefore, he will offer wealth to all those who accept the mark—men, women, and children alike. Additionally, he will offer them even more wealth if they turn in those who refuse to take the mark and those people who refuse to worship the king of the South as God.

No wonder Paul prophesied to Timothy that the love of money is the root of all kinds of evil, leading many to pierce themselves with all kinds of sorrow. These people pierce themselves by taking on the Man of Sin's blood. They believe they are receiving salvation, or forgiveness for their sins. But there is no salvation, only a smoldering fire that gets fanned into flames—flames of passion for money! No wonder Jesus tells us in Matthew 6:24 that the final conflict for the soul boils down to a person serving one of two masters: God or money. But under the False Prophet's plan, people can worship both!

It's Satan's ultimate slant on prosperity preaching. And since this wealth is available to all, even children can become instantly wealthy. Anyone who takes the mark of salvation will never have to work again. Americans are always seeking ways to be wealthy. But ultimately, more and more people will seek something for nothing. Satan will play on the laziness of mankind and on their ignorance of Scripture. Our recent time of prosperity and mass-marketing ploys has produced massive numbers of people who have become wealthy. Now, by taking the mark of salvation, even children can become rich—without ever having to work a day in their life.

With this much wealth offered in a world where sin is uncontrolled, it's no surprise Jesus prophesied the end of the age would be just like the days of Noah and Lot combined. Just prior to His actual return, He prophesied people would be eating and drinking, buying and selling, and building and planting, fulfilling every desire of their evil hearts.

And people will become even wealthier for turning in family members who refuse to take the mark. Children can turn their parents in for economic gain. Now we know why Jesus said in Matthew 10:35–36 that he came to turn "a man against his father, a daughter against her mother, a daughter-in-law against her mother-in-law—a man's enemies will be the members of his own household." Also, this is the time Jesus spoke of in Matthew 10:21: "Brother will betray brother to death, and a father his child; children will rebel against their parents and have them put to death."

Matthew 10:39 records Jesus' rebuke for those taking the mark in exchange for wealth:

> Whoever finds his life will lose it [his soul will be eternally condemned], and whoever loses his life [by refusing the mark in exchange for wealth] for my sake will find it [will live eternally with Jesus]. (Explanations in brackets are mine.)

In short, accepting the wealth offered through the taking of the mark and believing you're gaining life will result in the loss of eternal life with Jesus. However, refusing the mark, the wealth, the temporary riches of this world, and even your physical life, will gain your soul eternal salvation and eternal life with Jesus.

The False Prophet uses wealth as the final enticement to get people to persecute the Jews who were evacuated to America, as well as the remaining believers of the Laodicea church era. Now, under the strong delusion of the king of the South, many will accept the mark and turn in their loved ones who refuse. This is how he destroys many through peaceful means. He is able to subtly destroy the Jews and Christians without outright claiming to be against them. In Luke 21:16, Jesus warns true believers and those who refuse the Man of Sin's offer, "You will be betrayed even by parents, brothers, relatives and friends, and they will put some of you to death." In verse 19, He gives us hope: "By standing firm you will gain life."

Finally, Jesus tells all of us in John 16:1–2:

> All this I have told you so that you will not go astray. They will put you out of the synagogue; in fact, a time is coming when anyone who kills you will think he is offering a service to God.

This is how Satan wages war on God's saints and destroys those who refuse the mark. John sees the martyred saints of God in Revelation 7:9–17 standing in front of the throne of God, holding palm branches. And in Revelation 15:2, they are standing beside the sea of glass mixed with fire (the church). Thankfully, John sees a great multitude of people who refuse the mark and the offer of wealth; they stand firm in their belief that Jesus is their only means for eternal salvation.

BABYLON THE GREAT TAKES ON THE HEART OF A MAN

Revelation 14:8: A second angel followed and said, "Fallen! Fallen is Babylon the Great, which made all the nations drink the maddening wine of her adulteries."

Daniel 7:4: The first was like a lion, and it had the wings of an eagle. I watched until its wings were torn off and it was lifted from the ground so that it stood on two feet like a man, and the heart of a man was given to it.

It is because of America's great technology, developed over the past century that makes possible both the false mark of the king of the North and the deadly mark of salvation from the king of the South.

The development of computers, bar codes, scanners, social security numbers, and DNA technology were all born in America, seen by John as *Babylon the Great*, the most prosperous kingdom on earth. But here, after the mark of the beast is implemented and a stiff warning of the gospel is preached to the world by the two witnesses, we sadly see where America now gives up its Constitution and the right of religious freedom. This deceptive scheme of the False Prophet now opens the door for everyone to turn against each other, as some choose the mark for economic gain, while others, including the Jews and true believers of the church, refuse to participate.

This is the beginning of the end for America, who up until this time has been used as a golden cup in the Lord's hand, providing a means of protection for the Jews and Christians. But now, collectively as a nation, they fall from God's grace as people elect Satan's monetary offer over God. People now have a legitimate reason to persecute Jews and those who refuse the mark, because they actually think they are doing God—as portrayed by Satan through the king of the South—a great service.

THE MYSTERY OF BABYLON THE GREAT

For the sake of clarity, I will put the correct interpretation of Revelation 17:6–16, in brackets:

Revelation 17:6–7: I saw that the woman [America] was drunk with the blood of the saints, the blood of those who bore testimony to Jesus [America persecutes anyone who does not worship the king of the South as God]. When I saw her, I was greatly astonished. Then the angel said to me: "Why are you astonished? I will explain to you the mystery of the woman and of the beast she rides [king of the South], which has the seven heads [king of the South's leopard kingdom] and ten horns." [Later, in Revelation 17:12, John will reveal that the king of the South will set up ten new kings when he comes to power, different from the ten kings under the reign of the king of the North.]

Revelation 17:8: "The beast [king of the South], which you saw [as the wounded head under the king of the North], once was [he was the king of the leopard kingdom], now is not [he became a wounded head under the king of the North's rule], and will come up out of the Abyss and go to his destruction." [Satan will possess and empower the king of the South at the blowing of the fifth trumpet, and the king of the South will destroy the king of the North during the sixth trumpet war, which many will believe is the great battle of Armageddon. The king of the South will then attempt to pose as the Messiah and will eventually be destroyed when Jesus returns.]

Revelation 17:8: "The inhabitants of the earth whose names have not been written in the book of life from the creation of the world will be astonished when they see the beast [king of the South posing as the Messiah], because he once was [king of the South over the leopard kingdom], now is not [he's been serving under the king of the North as a wounded head], and yet will come [he will defeat the king of the North and appear as the Messiah]."

Revelation 17:9: "This calls for a mind with wisdom. The seven heads are seven hills [America manipulates the governments of all seven continents] on which the woman sits [or represents in its population: Babylonians (Nebuchadnezzar), Persians (Cyrus), Medes (Darius), Greeks (Alexander the Great), Romans (Caesar), Christians and Jews (Jesus), and king of the North—the end-time revived Roman Empire, or fourth end-time beast of Daniel 7:7]."

Revelation 17:10: "They are also seven kings [Nebuchadnezzar, Cyrus, Darius, Alexander the Great, Caesar, Jesus (king of the Jews and church), and the king of the North]."

Revelation 17:10: "Five have fallen [there were five kingdoms preceding the first coming of Jesus: Babylon, Media, Persia, Greece, and Rome], one is [although the world rejected Jesus, He established the kingdom of God here on earth by establishing the church, and His kingdom has been growing on earth for two thousand years], the other has not yet come [here the angel jumps to the end-times and eludes to the fact the king of the North must rise to power]; but when he does come, he must remain for a little while." [In his bid to appear as being the Man of Sin, the king of the North overpowers the king of the South during the seal judgments, becoming the seventh world empire; however, he only remains for a little while until he is taken out of the way. During the trumpet judgments, we saw where the king of the South mounted a rebellion against the king of the North and destroyed him, according to Daniel 11:45.]

Revelation 17:11: "The beast who once was [the king of the South], and now is not [the king of the South and his leopard kingdom served as the seven heads under the reign of the king of the North], is an eighth king." [The king of the South, through rebellion, becomes the little horn of Daniel 7:8, first serving under the rule of the king of the North; when the king of the North is destroyed, the king of the South, posing as the Messiah, becomes an eighth empire.]

Revelation 17:11: "He belongs to the seven [the king of the South served as one of the seven heads under the king of the North, who made up the seventh world empire] and is going to his destruction."

[The king of the South, who is the Man of Sin posing as God, will be destroyed when Jesus returns.]

Revelation 17:12: "The ten horns you saw are ten kings who have not yet received a kingdom, but who for one hour will receive authority as kings along with the beast." [When the king of the South poses as the Messiah, he will set up ten new kings.]

Revelation 17:13: "They [the ten new kings] have one purpose and will give their power and authority to the beast." [They give their authority to the king of the South, believing he is the Messiah.]

Revelation 17:14: "They [king of the South, or Man of Sin, and his ten new kings] will make war against the Lamb [Jesus], but the Lamb will overcome them because he is Lord of lords and King of kings—and with him will be his called, chosen and faithful followers." [In chapter 6, we'll see the return of Jesus and how He destroys the king of the South and his ten new kings.]

Revelation 17:15: Then the angel said to me, "The waters you saw, where the prostitute sits, are peoples, multitudes, nations and languages." [America has become the melting pot of the world, harboring people from all nations and languages, which is why John sees us as Babylon the Great, a reference from ancient Babylon and the Tower of Babel where God implemented the many languages of the nations. And as I stated previously, America, through her wealth, has manipulated the governments of all the nations on all seven continents—a reference to the seven hills upon which she sits.]

Revelation 17:16: "The beast [king of the South, or Man of Sin, posing as God] and the ten horns you saw [the ten new kings he establishes] will hate the prostitute [America—because we are harboring many of God's chosen people, Jews and Christians]. They will bring her to ruin and leave her naked [through religious tyranny they will pluck off the wings of religious freedom and give her the heart of a man—the Man of Sin who is posing as God]; they will eat her flesh [convince the people to persecute those who won't worship the king of the South as God] and burn her with fire [offering the people wealth in exchange for false salvation, which sends their souls to hell]."

When we discern the strong delusion, as well as Daniel's parables about America, we begin to understand the riddles and mysteries that John writes here in Revelation 17. We saw how America became bound to the iron kingdom of the king of the North. Satan deluded the world into believing the king of the North was the Man of Sin. When the king of the North is destroyed, America becomes bound to the bronze kingdom of the king of the South, the real Man of Sin, believing he is the long-awaited Messiah. Later we'll see how Satan uses America as a lion's den, rousing the anger of almighty God against a nation God once used as a golden cup in His hand.

THE FINAL WARNING

Revelation 14:9–12: A third angel followed them and said in a loud voice: "If anyone worships the beast and his image and receives his mark on the forehead or on the hand, he, too, will drink of the wine of God's fury, which has been poured full strength into the cup of his wrath. He will be tormented with burning sulfur in the presence of the holy angels and of the Lamb. And the smoke of their torment rises for ever and ever. There is no rest day or night for those who worship the beast and his image, or for anyone who receives the mark of his name." This calls for patient endurance on the part of the saints who obey God's commandments and remain faithful to Jesus. Then I heard a voice from heaven say, "Write: Blessed are the dead who die in the Lord from now on." "Yes," says the Spirit, "they will rest from their labor, for their deeds will follow them."

Here comes the final warning to the people of the earth that the choosing of money and physical salvation (the mark) over the God of heaven and His Christ (Jesus) will result in their eternal punishment and separation from God. Many will become believers and refuse taking the mark. They will put their trust in the gospel of Jesus preached by the two witnesses and other Christians who are still on earth when this man poses as God. Thus John relates that those who refuse the mark will gain eternal salvation, claiming, "Happy are the dead who die from now on in the Lord."

JESUS TELLS ABOUT THE STRONG DELUSIONS

We have seen how John and Daniel both reveal the Man of Sin, and we have seen Satan's strong delusion by having the king of the North appear as the Man of Sin and the king of the South appear as the Messiah. It is now time to show how Jesus also revealed the plot of Satan's schemes. We turn now to Matthew 24, where Jesus foretold all the end-time events.

Just like John and Daniel, Jesus talked about the end-time period in such a way that it would not be fully understood until God was ready for all prophecies concerning the end-times to be understood— during the last generation. What makes Matthew 24 so remarkable is the fact that it is a fourfold prophecy that describes end-time events in such a way that they are repeated over and over (at least four times) in the span of a single generation's lifetime.

The prophecies are first fulfilled during the last days—that period of time during the last generation's lifetime that includes the fulfillment of many end-time signs up to the Russian invasion of Israel—namely, this past century. The prophecies are repeated again when the king of the North rises to power (the seal judgments of Revelation). They are again repeated as the king of the South rebels against the king of the North and appears as the Messiah (the trumpet judgments). And finally, they are repeated again just prior to the return of Jesus to earth. Jesus accurately supports Daniel's prophecies as well as John's account of end-times in Revelation. Figure 4-5 depicts how Matthew 24 is completed four times in the last generation's lifetime, up to and including the time when Jesus returns to earth.

Matthew 24:4–5: Jesus answered: "Watch out that no one deceives you. For many will come in my name, claiming, 'I am the Christ,' and will deceive many."

Jesus begins His discourse by stating up front that more than one person will attempt to appear as being the Messiah. He warns us of the great deception Satan brings against mankind. So strong will be the delusion that Jesus forewarns us many will be deceived and believe the lie.

Matthew 24:6–8: You will hear of wars and rumors of wars, but see to it that you are not alarmed. Such things must happen, but the end is still to come. Nation will rise against nation, and kingdom against kingdom. There will be famines and earthquakes in various places. All these are the beginning of birth pains.

Here Jesus gives us an account of the first three years of the last ten-year period. The king of the South will rise up and become public enemy number one for the king of the North. War will rage across Europe as the king of the North rises to power. This gives us one kingdom pitted against another. We also saw in chapter 3 where the king of the North prompts Russia and many other nations to invade the nation of Israel. God thwarts the invasion with an earthquake. The Russian-Arab alliance is destroyed by chemical and biological agents intended to be used against Israel. In humiliation, Russia launches a full-scale nuclear strike against the United States. However, because of our superior space technology, Russia is again humiliated and defeated.

We then saw how the king of the North overruns the king of the South, invades Israel, and attempts to claim himself as the Messiah, stopping the daily sacrifice and desolating the temple in Jerusalem—all as an attempt to delude the world into believing he is the Man of Sin. We saw that because of war, inflation in America results in people working all day just to afford the necessities of life. We also saw how the war in Europe brings excessive famine to other countries. And of course we saw how a great earthquake in the land of Israel annihilates the Russian-Arab alliance. Daniel and John (writing about the seal judgments) describe these events. Jesus said all these things were just the beginning of birth pains, meaning they would all be repeated again in preparation for the next person who would come and claim to be the Messiah.

After the king of the North rises to power, we saw through the trumpet judgments of Revelation how the Man of Sin mounts a rebellion against the king of the North, once again giving us kingdom against kingdom. We also saw Iran's/Iraq's defiance against the United States, resulting in nation rising against nation and the ultimate annihilation of Iraq/Iran, ancient Babylon, and the city of Rome—whom many falsely believe is Babylon the Great. Finally, we saw the opening of the Abyss and the great war (sixth trumpet war; see also Daniel 10:1 concerning this great war). We saw the destruction of the king of the North and the rise to power of the king of the South, who will claim to be the Messiah.

Later, in chapter 6, we will see how these prophecies are once again repeated when the true Messiah, Jesus, returns to earth with His saints, destroying the Man of Sin, who is the king of the South.

Matthew 24:9–14: Then you will be handed over to be persecuted and put to death, and you will be hated by all nations because of me. At that time many will turn away from the faith and will betray and hate each other, and many false prophets will appear and deceive many people. Because of the increase of wickedness, the love of most will grow cold, but he who stands firm to the end will be saved. And this gospel of the kingdom will be preached in the whole world as a testimony to all nations, and then the end will come.

In this passage, Jesus describes the time of the seventh seal, when the king of the North implements his new economic program. The false prophets within the church will deceive many into believing this new economic program is the mark of the beast. As a result of their being deluded, the hypocrites within the church will turn away from the truth and persecute the members of their church who accept and comply with this new economic program. They will believe that they are doing God a favor by ridding their ranks of these so-called evil people. We saw how this activity takes place during the hour of trial, for which the Laodicea church generation is spit out to endure. Those who survive this hour of trial and the strong delusion that is created when the king of the South destroys the king of the North will be saved during the rapture. We also saw how the 144,000 Jewish-Christian evangelists preach the gospel of Jesus Christ throughout the world prior to their destruction.

In chapter 6, we will learn that many people will fall away from the truth and believe the lie that the king of the South is the Messiah. We will see how those who accept the mark of this beast will instead believe they are accepting salvation from God. We will also see how, believing they are doing God a favor (as portrayed by the king of the South), these people who accept his false salvation will turn against those who refuse, putting them to death. We will also see how many will stand firm in their faith of Jesus, thereby being martyred for their faith. Also, we will see how the two witnesses preach the gospel of Jesus Christ throughout the reign of the king of the South.

"And then the end will come." is a threefold prophecy that works for the king of the North appearing as the Man of Sin, the king of the South appearing as the Messiah, and again when Jesus actually returns.

Matthew 24:15–25: So when you see standing in the holy place "the abomination that causes desolation," spoken of through the prophet Daniel—let the reader understand—then let those who are in Judea flee to the mountains. Let no one on the roof of his house go down to take anything out of the house. Let no one in the field go back to get his cloak. How dreadful it will be in those days for pregnant women and nursing mothers! Pray that your flight will not take place in winter or on the Sabbath. For then there will be great distress, unequaled from the beginning of the world until now—and never to be equaled again. If those days had not been cut short, no one would survive, but for the sake of the elect those days will be shortened. At that time if anyone says to you, "Look, here is the Christ!" or, "There he is!" do not believe it. For false Christs and false prophets will appear and perform great signs and miracles to deceive even the elect—if that were possible. See, I have told you ahead of time.

This prophecy describes the 1,290-day interval when the king of the North abolishes the daily sacrifice (which many will falsely interpret as the abomination that causes desolation) and the time when the king of the South commits the actual abomination that causes desolation, appearing as the Messiah.

When the king of the North invades Israel and stops the daily sacrifice, the false prophets within the church will delude people into believing he is committing the *abomination that causes desolation*. They will determine the king of the North is the Man of Sin, and many will fall for their lies. The king of the North's reign will appear to be cut short as a result of the king of the South's rebellion and appearance as the Messiah.

Next we see how this same passage fits the rise of the king of the South as he attempts to delude the world into believing he is the Messiah. When he commits the actual *abomination that causes desolation*, the false prophets will delude the world into believing he is the Messiah, rightfully assuming his throne here on earth. He will enter the Holy of Holies in the temple in Jerusalem in preparation for the wedding supper of the Lamb.

Of course, Daniel 12:12 informs us that the believers in Jesus Christ are exposed to this strong delusion for only forty-five days, until the rapture occurs. Jesus also proclaims that for the sake of the elect, their exposure to this powerful delusion will be cut short—inferring that the rapture will shortly take place. In Matthew 24:23, Jesus zeroes in on the fact that many will fall for this grand scheme, claiming, "Look, here is the Christ!" Jesus makes it very clear that we should not fall for Satan's evil plot, exclaiming, "See, I have told you ahead of time."

Matthew 24:26: So if anyone tells you, "There he is, out in the desert," do not go out; or, "Here he is, in the inner rooms," do not believe it.

So strong will be this delusion and the false miracles they perform that Jesus warns us not to believe them. First, He tells us not to go out chasing this man—the king of the South—who appears as the Messiah, because he is the Man of Sin.

Matthew 24:27–28: For as lightning that comes from the east is visible even in the west, so will be the coming of the Son of Man. Wherever there is a carcass, there the vultures will gather.

Obviously, the true meaning of this passage is Jesus' description of His own return when His coming will light up the entire sky. We'll look more at the fulfillment of this prophecy in chapter 6. Also, Jesus includes the fact that at His coming, many will be destroyed at Armageddon, allowing the vultures to feast on the dead remains.

However, Jesus included this passage so that the Man of Sin could also use it to support his rise to power. Remember, Satan wants everyone to believe that the sixth trumpet war is the battle of Armageddon. This is when the king of the North is destroyed, making many believe he is the Man of Sin.

Also, if people are not convinced that Jesus is Lord, they will not discern that the rapture occurs through the death of millions of people after the king of the South appears as the Messiah. When the rapture occurs through the death of millions, many will be convinced that the king of the South is God when vultures are once again allowed to feast on the dead remains of those, who in fact, went to be with Jesus during the rapture. We'll look more closely at this delusion in chapter 5.

Matthew 24:30–31: At that time the sign of the Son of Man will appear in the sky, and all the nations of the earth will mourn. They will see the Son of Man coming on the clouds of the sky, with power and great glory. And he will send his angels with a loud trumpet call, and they will gather his elect from the four winds, from one end of the heavens to the other.

In chapter 6, we'll see how Jesus returns and gathers those saints who are still alive at His second coming. For now, I want to point out how, once again, the king of the South will copy Jesus' return. He will serve as a suffering servant under the king of the North, and many will weep and mourn when the king of the South appears as the Messiah—bewildered at how they could have missed the signs.

After the king of the South appears as the Messiah and is revealed to believers as really being the Man of Sin, their time to this exposure will be cut short through a rapture by death. Those saints who are still alive when the rapture takes place will meet Jesus in heaven as He stands amongst that great cloud of witnesses, the elders John wrote about in Revelation. At the sounding of the seventh trumpet, the remaining saints of the Laodicea church will have their spirits and souls raised to heaven in front of the throne of God, alongside the 144,000 who were offered up as first fruits. It is this great rapture through death that we will study in the next chapter. We also will learn how to accurately calculate Daniel's 1,335 days prophecy (see Daniel 12:12), which is the day the Lord calls up the spirits and souls of believers at the blowing of the seventh trumpet.

HOW MATTHEW 24 IS FULFILLED PRIOR TO THE TEN-YEAR END-TIME PERIOD

LAST GENERATION'S LIFETIME		
LAST GENERATION	**HOW JESUS' PROPHECIES ARE FULFILLED**	**MATT.**
THE TIME PRECEDING THE TEN-YEAR END-TIME PERIOD (1900–PRESENT) MATT. 24:34: "I TELL YOU THE TRUTH, THIS GENERATION [THE LAST GENERATION] WILL CERTAINLY NOT PASS AWAY UNTIL ALL THESE THINGS HAVE HAPPENED [MEANING ALL THE FOURFOLD PROPHECIES OF MATTHEW 24 ARE COMPLETED]. (EXPLANATIONS IN BRACKETS ARE MINE.)	- DAYS OF NOAH/LOT COMBINED PEOPLE EATING, DRINKING, MARRYING, GIVING IN MARRIAGE; BUYING, SELLING, BUILDING, PLANTING (INDICATING A TIME OF GREAT PROSPERITY/TECHNOLOGY)	24:37–39 LUKE 17:26-29
	- HITLER— "I AM THE CHRIST" (DESTROYED JEWS)	24:5
	- WARS AND RUMORS OF WARS (WWI AND II)	24:6
	- KINGDOM VS. KINGDOM (HITLER VS. EUROPE/JEWS)	24:7
	- NATION VS. NATION (GERMANY/RUSSIA; RUSSIA/AFGHANISTAN; IRAN/IRAQ; AFGHANISTAN/IRAN; IRAQ/KUWAIT; U.S./IRAQ; VIETNAM WAR; KOREAN WAR; U.S./JAPAN; NATO/KOSOVO, ETC.)	24:7
	- EARTHQUAKES IN VARIOUS PLACES	24:7
	- BEGINNING OF BIRTH PAINS (LEADING UP TO THE 10-YEAR END-TIME PERIOD)	24:8
	- PERSECUTION (OF THE CHURCH FOR PREACHING TRADITIONAL CHRISTIAN BELIEFS)	24:9
	- MANY TURNING AWAY FROM THE FAITH (SEPARATION OF CHURCH AND STATE)	24:10
	- MANY FALSE PROPHETS RISING (THE TRUTH OF END-TIMES HAS BEEN PURPOSELY FALSIFIED BY PROSPERITY PREACHERS DURING THESE LAST DAYS)	24:11
	- INCREASE IN WICKEDNESS/LOVE GROWS COLD (MASS MURDERS/ABORTIONS/ DRUG USAGE/CORRUPT GOVERNMENTS)	24:12
	- THOSE WHO STAND FIRM TO THE END WILL BE SAVED	24:13
	- GOSPEL PREACHED TO THE WORLD BY THE CHURCH AND WORLDWIDE MINISTRIES (BILLY GRAHAM/RADIO AND TELEVISION MINISTRIES)	24:14

FIGURE 4-5. THE FOURFOLD PROPHECIES OF MATTHEW 24

HOW MATTHEW 24 IS FULFILLED THREE MORE TIMES IN A TEN-YEAR PERIOD DURING THE LAST GENERATION'S LIFETIME

EVENT	HOW JESUS' PROPHECIES ARE BEING FULFILLED IN THE LAST GENERATION'S LIFETIME	MATT.
	TRANSITION PERIOD	
1st SEAL	- KING OF THE SOUTH—"I AM THE CHRIST!"	24:5
2nd SEAL	- WARS/RUMORS OF WARS (DAN. 11)	24:6
3rd SEAL	- KINGDOM VS. KINGDOM (KING OF THE NORTH VS. KING OF THE SOUTH) (DAN. 11:25–30)	24:7
4th SEAL	- NATION VS. NATION (RUSSIAN-ARAB INVASION OF ISRAEL)	24:7
5th SEAL	- GREAT EARTHQUAKE (IN ISRAEL DESTROYS RUSSIAN-ARAB ALLIANCE) (SEE EZEKIEL 38–39)	24:7
	HOUR OF TRIAL	
6th SEAL	- KINGDOM VS. KINGDOM (KON VS. KOS)	24:7
	- NATION VS NATION (RUSSIA VS. U.S.) (THE 6th SEAL WAR IS RUSSIA'S ARMAGEDDON; IT STARTS THE 70th WEEK OF DANIEL, THE TRIBULATION PERIOD)	24:7
	- VULTURES GATHER (EZEK. 38–39)	24:28
7th SEAL	- KON DEFEATS KOS—"I AM THE CHRIST!"	24:5
	- SACRIFICE STOPPED BY KON (DAN. 9:26–27)	24:15
	- UNHEARD OF DISTRESS (HOUR OF TRIAL)	24:16–22
	- "HERE IS THE CHRIST!" – DON'T BELIEVE IT	24:23
	- FALSE CHRISTS AND FALSE PROPHETS	24:24
	- PERSECUTION (BY KING OF THE NORTH)	24:9
	- MANY WILL TURN FROM THE FAITH	24:10
	- MANY FALSE PROPHETS ARISE (TO CONVINCE THE WORLD THAT THE KING OF THE NORTH IS THE MAN OF SIN)	24:11
	- INCREASE IN WICKEDNESS/LOVE GROWS COLD/GOVERNMENT CORRUPTION	24:12

FIGURE 4-5 (CONTINUED). THE FOURFOLD PROPHECIES OF MATTHEW 24

HOW MATTHEW 24 IS FULFILLED THREE MORE TIMES IN A TEN-YEAR PERIOD DURING THE LAST GENERATION'S LIFETIME

EVENT	HOW JESUS' PROPHECIES ARE BEING FULFILLED IN THE LAST GENERATION'S LIFETIME	MATT.
	HOUR OF TRIAL (CONTINUED)	
7th SEAL	- HE WHO STANDS FIRM WILL BE SAVED (BY THE UPCOMING RAPTURE)	24:13
	- GOSPEL OF JESUS PREACHED TO THE WORLD (BY THE CHURCH AND 144,000 EVANGELISTS)	24:14
	- DAYS OF NOAH/LOT COMBINED (SEE LUKE 17:26–29)	24:37–39
1st TRUMPET	- WARS AND RUMORS OF WARS (KING OF THE NORTH INVADES ISRAEL)	24:6
2nd TRUMPET	- NATION VS. NATION (U.S. VS IRAQ/IRAN) (IRAQ/IRAN REBELS AGAINST THE KING OF THE NORTH)	24:7
3rd TRUMPET	- KINGDOM VS. KINGDOM (THE KING OF THE SOUTH REBELS AGAINST THE KING OF THE NORTH) (SEE DAN. 11:40–45) (SEE ALSO 2 THESS. 2:3–4)	24:7
4th TRUMPET	- EARTHQUAKE (ROME IS DESTROYED TO TO MAKE IT APPEAR AS IF BABYLON THE GREAT IS DESTROYED)	24:7
5th TRUMPET	- BIRTH PAINS (KING OF THE SOUTH MOVES TO DEFEAT KING OF THE NORTH) (ALL NATIONS MEET IN THE VALLEY OF MEGGIDO TO DEFEAT THE KING OF THE NORTH, WHO MANY NOW BELIEVE IS THE MAN OF SIN AND THE KING OF THE SOUTH IS THE MESSIAH)	24:8
	GREAT TRIBULATION PERIOD	
6th TRUMPET	- VULTURES GATHER (THE 6th TRUMPET WAR APPEARS AS ARMAGEDDON FOR THE KING OF THE NORTH, WHO MANY WILL BELIEVE IS THE MAN OF SIN)	24:28

FIGURE 4-5 (CONTINUED). THE FOURFOLD PROPHECIES OF MATTHEW 24

HOW MATTHEW 24 IS FULFILLED THREE MORE TIMES IN A TEN-YEAR PERIOD DURING THE LAST GENERATION'S LIFETIME

EVENT	HOW JESUS' PROPHECIES ARE BEING FULFILLED IN THE LAST GENERATION'S LIFETIME	MATT.
7th TRUMPET	**GREAT TRIBULATION PERIOD (CONTINUED)** - KING OF THE SOUTH PROCLAIMS, "I AM THE CHRIST!" (JESUS SAID, "DON'T BELIEVE IT.")	24:5
	- TEMPLE IS DESECRATED (KING OF THE SOUTH COMMITS ABOMINATION THAT CAUSES DESOLATION (DAN. 9:27))	24:15
	- MANY ARE TAKEN; MANY LEFT BEHIND VULTURES GATHER (THE RAPTURE TAKES PLACE THROUGH THE DEATH OF MILLIONS OF CHRISTIANS WORLDWIDE)	24:31
	- UNEQUALED DISTRESS (FOR THOSE WHO REFUSE TO TAKE THE KING OF THE SOUTH'S MARK OF SALVATION)	24:16-22
	- MANY WILL PROCLAIM, "HERE IS THE CHRIST!" (JESUS WARNS, "DON'T BELIEVE IT!")	24:23
	- FALSE CHRISTS (PLURAL—MEANING BOTH THE KING OF THE NORTH AND THE KING OF THE SOUTH ARE POSSESSED BY SATAN) WILL APPEAR, AS WELL AS FALSE PROPHETS	24:24
	- "THERE HE IS!"—DO NOT BELIEVE IT	24:26
	- PERSECUTION (FOR THOSE WHO REFUSE HIS MARK OF SALVATION)	24:9
	- MANY WILL TURN AWAY FROM THE FAITH (ACCEPTING HIS MARK OF SALVATION BECAUSE THEY BELIEVE HE IS THE MESSIAH)	24:10
	- MANY FALSE PROPHETS APPEAR TO DECEIVE MANY (SATAN AND THE FALSE PROPHET WILL CONVINCE PEOPLE THAT THE TWO WITNESSES SENT BY GOD ARE FALSE PROPHETS)	24:11

FIGURE 4-5 (CONTINUED). THE FOURFOLD PROPHECIES OF MATTHEW 24

HOW MATTHEW 24 IS FULFILLED THREE MORE TIMES IN A TEN-YEAR PERIOD DURING THE LAST GENERATION'S LIFETIME

EVENT	HOW JESUS' PROPHECIES ARE BEING FULFILLED IN THE LAST GENERATION'S LIFETIME	MATT.
7th TRUMPET	**GREAT TRIBULATION PERIOD (CONTINUED)** - INCREASE IN WICKEDNESS/LOVE GROWS COLD (ALTHOUGH MANY TAKE THE KING OF THE SOUTH'S MARK OF SALVATION, THEY KEEP ON SINNING [SEE REV. 9:20–21], AND THEIR LOVE FOR MONEY [OFFERED BY THE KING OF THE SOUTH] MAKES THEM KILL THOSE WHO REFUSE HIS MARK. A BOUNTY IS PLACED ON THEIR LIVES [SEE DAN. 8:12 AND 25, WHERE IT STATES THE KING OF THE SOUTH WILL MAKE DECEIPT PROSPER.])	24:12
	- HE WHO STANDS FIRM (REFUSES THE MARK) WILL BE SAVED (EITHER THROUGH MARTYRDOM OR WHEN JESUS RETURNS WITH HIS SAINTS)	24:13
	- GOSPEL OF JESUS PREACHED TO THE WORLD (BY THE TWO WITNESSES AND BY THOSE WHO ARE MARTYRED)	24:14
	- DAYS OF NOAH/LOT COMBINED (FOR THOSE WHO FOLLOW THE KING OF THE SOUTH, IT WILL BE A TIME OF TREMENDOUS PROSPERITY. IN EXCHANGE FOR TAKING HIS SO-CALLED OFFER, OR MARK OF SALVATION [MARK OF THE BEAST], PEOPLE WILL RECEIVE UNTOLD WEALTH. FOR THEM IT WILL BE A TIME OF EATING, DRINKING, MARRYING, GIVING IN MARRIAGE [MEANING ALTERNATIVE FORMS OF MARRIAGE], BUYING, SELLING, BUILDING AND PLANTING. [SEE ALSO LUKE 17:26–29.])	24:37–39

FIGURE 4-5 (CONTINUED). THE FOURFOLD PROPHECIES OF MATTHEW 24

HOW MATTHEW 24 IS FULFILLED THREE MORE TIMES IN A TEN-YEAR PERIOD DURING THE LAST GENERATION'S LIFETIME

EVENT	HOW JESUS' PROPHECIES ARE BEING FULFILLED IN THE LAST GENERATION'S LIFETIME	MATT.
	APPOINTED TIME OF THE END (SEE DAN. 8:19–25)	
1st BOWL	- WARS AND RUMORS OF WARS/FAMINES/ DISEASE (ALL THOSE WHO TOOK THE MARK BREAK OUT WITH SORES AS RUMORS ABOUND OF THE IMPENDING SPACE INVASION, WHICH IS JESUS RETURNING WITH THE SAINTS OF HEAVEN. HOWEVER, THE KING OF THE SOUTH WILL CONVINCE THE WORLD THAT IT IS SATAN AND HIS EVIL DEMONS COMING TO EARTH.)	24:6
2nd BOWL	- NATION VS. NATION (REV. 17:16 STATES THE KING OF THE SOUTH (BEAST) AND THE TEN NEW KINGS HE SETS UP WILL HATE AMERICA, WHO IS BABYLON THE GREAT. SATAN WILL BRING HER UNDER GOD'S JUDGMENT WHEN AMERICA PERSECUTES CHRISTIANS AND JEWS, OR THOSE WHO REFUSE THE MARK.)	24:7
3rd BOWL	- KINGDOM VS. KINGDOM (SATAN VS. JESUS)	24:7
4th BOWL	- EARTHQUAKE (AMERICA, OR BABYLON THE GREAT, IS DESTROYED)	24:7
5th BOWL	- BIRTH PAINS (JESUS RETURNS)	24:8
6th BOWL	- VULTURES GATHER (THE 6th BOWL WAR IS THE GATHERING OF THE NATIONS TO ARMAGEDDON TO MAKE WAR AGAINST JESUS AND HIS SAINTS)	
7th BOWL	- JESUS ACTUALLY RETURNS (SATAN IS BOUND. THE KING OF THE SOUTH AND THE FALSE PROPHET ARE DESTROYED. JESUS' RETURN APPEARS AS LIGHTNING.)	24:27
	- THE ELECT (THOSE NOT MARTYRED FOR REFUSING THE MARK OF SALVATION AND ARE STILL ALIVE) ARE GATHERED FROM THE FOUR WINDS	24:31

FIGURE 4-5 (CONTINUED). THE FOURFOLD PROPHECIES OF MATTHEW, CHAPTER 24

CHAPTER 5

THE DAY OF THE ANTICHRIST

2 Thessalonians 2:3-4: Don't let anyone deceive you in any way, for that day [the day of the rapture] will not come, until the rebellion occurs [the king of the South rebels against and destroys the king of the North] and the man of lawlessness [the king of the South, or Man of Sin] is revealed [portrays himself as God], the man doomed to destruction. (Explanations in brackets are mine.)

John purposely wrote Scripture so that all generations prior to the last generation would believe the sixth trumpet war brings in the kingdom of the Messiah. However, at the end of the sixth trumpet war, we saw where John subtly reveals that nobody's heart had been changed as a result of the Messiah supposedly reigning. The answer to John's perplexity comes when John eats the little scroll and hears the seven thunders speak. Had the Messiah, or Jesus, truly returned, John would have had no need to prophesy again.

Although John places the blowing of the seventh trumpet in chapter 11 of Revelation, it actually occurs shortly after the Man of Sin attempts to reveal himself as the Messiah. The blowing of the seventh trumpet will conclude the hour of trial, ending with the spirits and souls of all true believers being caught up to heaven to be with Jesus Christ.

Using the concept of juxtaposition, John places the seventh trumpet in chapter 11 and then goes back and shows us the details that lead up to that event. That's what John is doing as he writes chapters 12, 13, and 14. John begins the details of this powerful delusion in chapter 12 by giving a brief historical review of the ancient and continuous war between God and Satan.

In chapter 13, John briefly reveals the true identity of the king of the North. This chapter answers Daniel's original question concerning the true meaning behind the fourth beast, or the king of the North's iron kingdom, which was very terrifying. John shows us how it is actually the king of the South who has a head wound and is the Man of Sin. He also tells about the strong delusion that is created when the False Prophet exalts the Man of Sin as being God and destroys the 144,000 who are preaching Jesus is Lord. The False Prophet relegates Jesus to appear as if He were the strong delusion sent to mankind two thousand years ago.

In chapter 14, after showing how the 144,000 are offered up as first-fruits to God, John merges the details of the blowing of the seventh trumpet back together, telling how it results in a great harvest of souls.

BLESSED ARE THEY WHO WAIT

Daniel 8:14: He said to me, "It will take 2,300 evenings and mornings; then the sanctuary will be reconsecrated."

Daniel 12:11–12: From the time that the daily sacrifice is abolished [by the king of the North, portraying himself as the Man of Sin] and the abomination that causes desolation [image of the king of the South, who is the real Man of Sin, but portrays himself as the Messiah] is set up, there will be 1,290 days. Blessed is the one who waits for and reaches the end of the 1,335 days [because the seventh trumpet blows and the rapture occurs]." (Explanations in brackets are mine.)

Two thousand three hundred days will pass from the time the king of the North stops the daily sacrifice on the Temple Mount until Jesus reconsecrates the temple. One thousand two hundred ninety days after the king of the North stops the daily sacrifice, the king of the South will commit the abomination that causes desolation, proclaiming to be God. He will hold what appears to be the marriage supper of the Lamb. The king of the South's rebellion and reign will take place during the last 1,260 days of this 2,300-day period, or the last 3½ years of Daniel's ten-year period. That's why at the end of the sixth trumpet war, which concludes the first seven years of this ten-year end-time period, John was told to prophesy again about another 3½-year period.

But Daniel also tells believers they will be blessed if they wait until the 1,335th day after the king of the North abolishes the sacrifice. In other words, believers will face about forty days of testing after the king of the South attempts to pass himself off as the redeemer of mankind.

Figure 5-1 clearly depicts how both kings come to desolate the temple, but at different times; it also shows the exact time the rapture occurs for believers shortly after the Man of Sin is revealed.

JUDGING THE DEAD

Revelation 11:15: The seventh angel sounded his trumpet, and there were loud voices in heaven, which said: "The kingdom of the world has become the kingdom of our Lord and of his Christ, and he will reign for ever and ever."

Revelation 14:14–16: I looked, and there before me was a white cloud, and seated on the cloud was one "like a son of man" with a crown of gold on his head and a sharp sickle in his hand. Then another angel came out of the temple and called in a loud voice to him who was sitting on the cloud, "Take your sickle and reap, because the time to reap has come, for the harvest of the earth is ripe." So he who was seated on the cloud swung his sickle over the earth, and the earth was harvested.

1 Thessalonians 4:16–17: For the Lord himself will come down from heaven, with a loud command, with the voice of the archangel and with the trumpet call of God, and the dead in Christ will rise first. After that, we who are still alive and are left will be caught up together with them in the clouds to meet the Lord in the air.

YEARS FOR END-TIME PERIOD

```
0     1     2     3     4     5     6     7     8     9     10
```

| TRANSITION PERIOD (DAN. 11:25-31) 3 YEARS | HOUR OF TRIAL (REV. 3:10) 3½ YEARS | GREAT TRIBULATION (DAN. 12:1) (MATT. 24:21) 3½ YEARS |

THE KING OF THE NORTH CONFIRMS COVENANT WITH MANY (DAN. 9:26)

TEMPLE DESOLATIONS (DAN. 9:26)
2,300 DAYS (DAN. 8:13–14)

KING OF THE NORTH ABOLISHES SACRIFICE IN THE MIDDLE OF THE FIRST SEVEN YEARS (DAN. 9:27; 11:31–32) WORLD BELIEVES HE IS THE ANTICHRIST, OR MAN OF SIN

1,290 DAYS AFTER THE KING OF THE NORTH ABOLISHES THE SACRIFICE, THE MAN OF SIN, OR KING OF THE SOUTH, WILL COMMIT THE ABOMINATION THAT CAUSES DESOLATION (DAN. 12:11) (MATT. 24:15) SATAN PORTRAYS HIMSELF AS GOD THROUGH THE LITTLE HORN OF DANIEL 7:8

JESUS RETURNS (DAN. 8:14, 25)

1,335 DAYS AFTER THE KING OF THE NORTH ABOLISHES THE SACRIFICE, THE RAPTURE OCCURS AT THE SEVENTH TRUMPET (REV. 11:15–19) (DAN. 12:12) (1 COR. 15:51) (1 THESS. 4:15–17) HAPPY ARE THEY WHO WAIT (DAN. 12:12) HARVEST OF THE CHURCH (REV. 14:14–16) VULTURES GATHER TO FEAST ON DEAD BODIES OF THOSE RAPTURED (MATT. 24:28) JOHN HEARS LOUD VOICES IN HEAVEN (REV. 11:15)

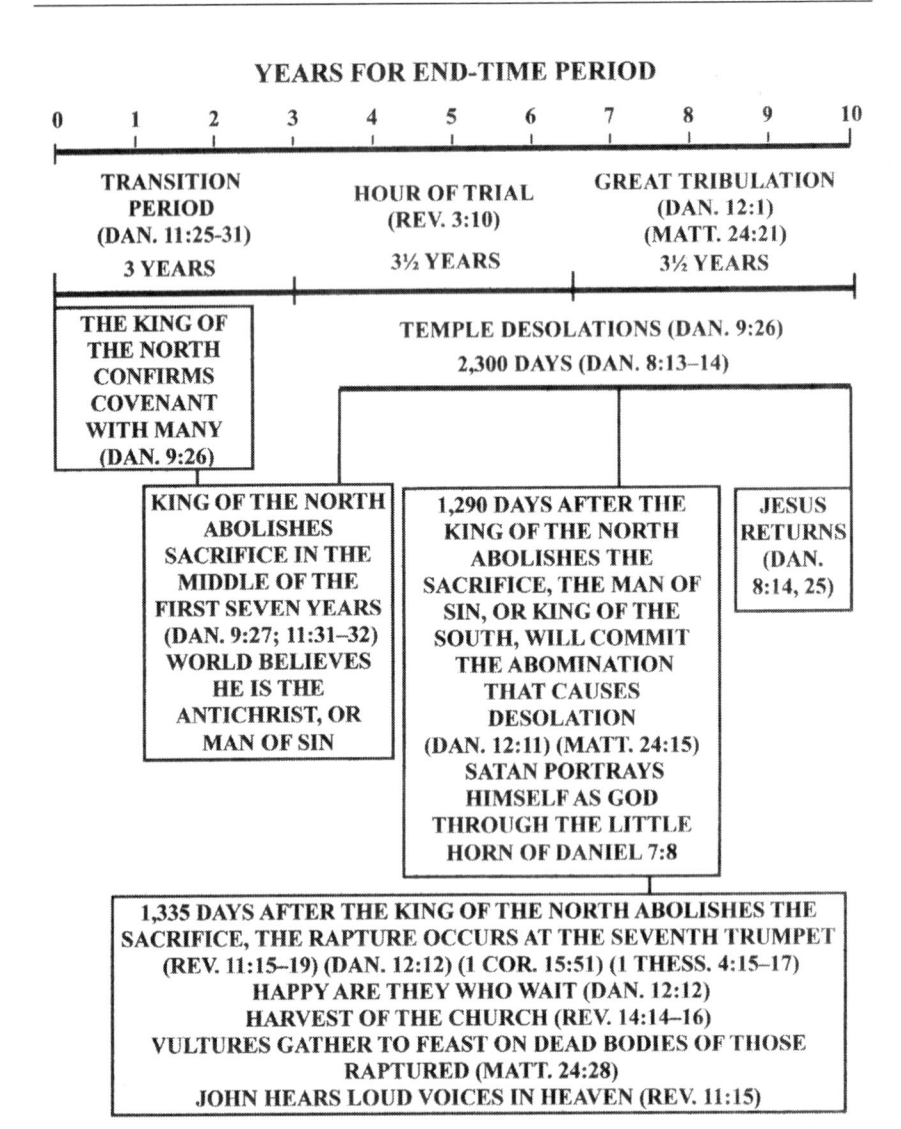

FIGURE 5-1. DANIEL'S 2,300/1,290/1,335-DAY PROPHECIES AND METHOD FOR CALCULATING THE DAY OF THE RAPTURE

NOTE: *RAPTURE BY DEATH* MEANS ONLY THE SPIRITS AND SOULS OF THOSE WHO HAVE ACCEPTED JESUS CHRIST AS THEIR PERSONAL SAVIOR ARE CAUGHT UP TO HEAVEN. THE BODY OF EACH BELIEVER IS LEFT BEHIND TO APPEAR AS BEING DEAD. THE RAPTURE WILL APPEAR AS THE SUDDEN DEATH OF MILLIONS OF PEOPLE AROUND THE WORLD.

Here we see where the elders in heaven, as well as the 144,000, serve as a great cloud of witnesses to the rapture of all the souls and spirits of believers who are still alive. This happens shortly after the Man of Sin attempts to portray himself as God. This message is the hope of our salvation—the saving power of Jesus Christ.

MILLIONS SUDDENLY DIE

Revelation 11:18: The time has come for judging the *dead*, and for rewarding your servants the prophets and your saints and those who reverence your name, both small and great. (Emphasis is mine.)

Zechariah 14:12: This is the plague with which the Lord will strike all the nations that fought against Jerusalem: Their flesh will rot while they are still standing on their feet, their eyes will rot in their sockets, and their tongues will rot in their mouths.

Zechariah 14:13: On that day men will be stricken by the Lord with great panic.

2 Peter 2:9: If this is so, then the Lord knows how to rescue godly men [meaning true believers in Jesus Christ] from trials [meaning the great tribulation period—which is the time of God's wrath] and to hold the unrighteous for the day of judgment [the return of Jesus Christ], while continuing their punishment [the time of great tribulation, when the Man of Sin appears as God]. (Explanations in brackets are mine.)

The king of the South, imitating Jesus Christ's actual return, will attempt to make people believe that he is fulfilling the prophecies described in Zechariah 14, when the rapture occurs. Zechariah 14:2 states all the nations will come together at the city of Jerusalem. We saw this occur as all the armies of the world converged on Jerusalem in the process of destroying the king of the North. The king of the South will come from the Mount of Olives into Jerusalem, taking victory for defeating the king of the North, who many will be convinced was the Man of Sin.

After establishing himself as the Messiah and destroying the 144,000, he will offer everyone salvation, or forgiveness for their sins. During the forty days of testing, believers will still resist him. Daniel 12:3 helps us understand how the remaining church-age saints serve as a witness to those who stand to be deluded: "Those who are wise will shine like the brightness of the heavens, and those who lead many to righteousness, like the stars for ever and ever." Daniel paints a beautiful picture of these witnesses just prior to the rapture.

By the divine will of God, there will be a very short time to witness to others about the saving power of Jesus Christ. Then, on Daniel's 1,335th day, believers are stricken with death and their souls and spirits are snatched up to be with the Lord Jesus, who is in heaven, encircled by a great cloud of witnesses, the elders and the 144,000 who were offered up as first-fruits.

Although the world will be stricken with panic, the king of the South will have the answer to this dilemma. He will simply turn to Zechariah 14:12 and delude the people left behind into believing the mysterious and instant death of millions of people was only another one of his divine acts of judgment.

Zechariah 14:12 states the nations, or enemies of God, will be stricken with a terrible disease. This lines up perfectly with the rapture occurring through death for believers. The king of the South and Satan steal God's glory by using the rapture of God's people as a means to delude unbelievers into believing the king of the South is truly God. The king of the South will claim to have power over life and death, taking credit for the divine power of God.

The instant infliction of this disease occurs worldwide. It occurs so fast that Zechariah 14:12 states that people's eyes and tongues will rot in their sockets before they can fall to the ground dead.

Zechariah 14:13 tells us, "On that day men will be stricken by the Lord with great panic." This divine act of God will nonetheless capture the attention of every unbeliever left behind after the rapture. Only through discernment will people understand that what just took place was the rapture of Christians—by death! Their spirits and souls were instantly snatched from their bodies, leaving their bodies behind to appear as if they instantly died from a wasting disease.

The king of the South, empowered by Satan, will use this opportunity as an advantage to strengthen his base of power and appear as God to those who are still alive. Speaking from Jerusalem and claiming to be God, the king of the South will claim to have wiped out many evil people—those who believe Jesus is the Christ. He will delude the people left behind into believing that as God he sent Jesus to mankind as his strong delusion two thousand years ago. He will take credit for killing all of his enemies, claiming they perished because they believed a lie. He simply twists 2 Thessalonians 2:3–4 to his advantage, using the Word of God as a weapon against unbelievers.

Through panic and fear of reprisal, he hopes that those who are still alive and left behind will now be convinced he is the true Messiah, or God revealing Himself to mankind for the first and only time. He deludes them into believing that he served as a suffering servant under the king of the North, but now rules with a rod of iron.

After what appears to be another miracle by this man who proclaims to be God, he will then attempt to portray himself as a caring and loving God, offering salvation to all people. He'll claim that he stands ready to fulfill the desires of every person's heart that believes in him.

THE DOCTRINE OF PASSING AWAY

Matthew 24:34: I tell you the truth, this generation [meaning the generation that sees all the signs of the last days and the events described in Matthew 24, Daniel, and Revelation] will certainly not pass away until all these things have happened [this provides about a 120-year time frame for all events to take place in the span of a single generation]. (Explanations in brackets are mine.)

Revelation 3:10: Since you have kept my command to endure patiently, I will also keep you from the hour of trial that is going to come upon the whole world to test those who live on the earth. [Jesus is speaking to the Philadelphia church. The last true believers of this church generation passed away during the Russian invasion of Israel, which began the hour of trial, or began the tribulation period, the last seven years preceding the second coming of Jesus Christ, or Daniel's seventieth week.] (Explanations in brackets are mine.)

Revelation 3:16: So, because you are lukewarm—neither hot nor cold—I am about to spit you out of my mouth. [Jesus is speaking to the Laodicea church. They have a form of godliness—wealth—but essentially have no personal relationship with Jesus Christ. Even true believers are *spit out* to endure the hour of trial, as previously forewarned to the Philadelphia church.] (Explanations in brackets are mine.)

1 Thessalonians 5:4: But you, brothers, are not in darkness so that this day [the day Jesus calls up our spirits and souls, known as the rapture] should surprise you like a thief. [Daniel tells us when the rapture takes place: 1,335 days after the king of the North first abolishes the sacrifice.] (Explanations in brackets are mine.)

The Bible is very specific that believers should not only understand why the rapture must happen through death, but also know the day of the rapture. This event is not supposed to come upon true believers like a thief, meaning suddenly and without discernment for when it occurs.

Over the past century, we've had our knowledge deluded by theories inside and outside the church that go completely against all the predetermined laws of God. That's because Satan likes sensationalism. Everyone suddenly disappearing sounds good, and the last church era having no trial or tribulation sounds even better. Ever so slowly and subtly, Satan's false prophets, masquerading as angels of light, have been setting up the world and the church for this strong delusion for many reasons:

(1) By teaching a disappearing rapture theory, they trap those who refuse to believe the gospel of Jesus Christ and are waiting to see if there really is a great disappearance; they'll base their faith on this event, which will prove in their minds that God really exists. Therefore, since the rapture truly doesn't happen through a worldwide disappearance

of Christians, God says in 2 Thessalonians 2:11 that those who are left behind when millions of people suddenly die will come to believe the lie, which is the king of the South claiming to be God Almighty!
(2) With no pretribulation rapture for this wealthy generation, Satan incites anger and bitterness toward God in those whose hearts are deceived through prosperity preaching. Unlike Job, many in this generation have not yet learned and do not understand that God gives the blessings and can also take away the blessings to test a person's heart. It will incite anger toward God when they find themselves forced to give up and forsake their wealth during the hour of trial.
(3) It will bring on the mockers spoken of in 2 Peter 3:3–4. They have not discerned the sign that starts the tribulation period—the Russian invasion of Israel—because they have been deluded with false teaching. When all of the events they're expecting to occur never materialize, their widespread loss of faith in Christianity (because of false teaching) will delude people into believing life goes on.

In Matthew 24:10, Jesus confirms that many "will turn away from the faith" at the time of the end. This prophecy has at least a double fulfillment:

(1) As America's wealth has grown, its citizens have increasingly turned away from God's laws and the Bible as fundamental truths for mankind. In just the past thirty years, we have completely turned away from the faith of our forefathers and have come to rely on our own ingenuity, wealth, and technological advancements to save us. We have literally fulfilled Jesus' prophecy in Revelation 3:17 by believing and saying to ourselves, "I am rich; I have acquired wealth and do not need a thing."
(2) When this wealthy generation realizes they are facing the hour of trial Jesus said was coming upon the whole world, many will turn away from God through anger and bitterness. They have been told—and have believed to their own lustful

satisfaction— they will be spared any trial or suffering for their faith. They have been deluded into believing their wealth is a sign of their godliness and God has favored this generation above all generations.

For now, I want to bring to light a time when Jesus made a profound proclamation that completely supports the original law of Genesis 3:19, that the body must die for the spirit and soul to be resurrected. In Matthew 24:34, Jesus declared this generation, meaning the generation that sees all the signs fulfilled, will not pass away until all the signs have been fulfilled (remember how Matthew 24 is a fourfold prophecy, completed four times in the span of a single generation). In an eighty-year period, ending with the worldwide preaching of the gospel by Billy Graham and other worldwide church ministries, all the signs of Matthew 24 have virtually been completed the first time around. The same prophecies must be repeated three more times before this last generation passes away, or reaches 120 years old. The last three completions of these prophecies occur during the last ten-years preceding the second coming of Jesus Christ—and must be completed with ever-increasing speed like labor pains.

When does the last generation begin the 120-year countdown? The year Israel was granted statehood, or 1948. Right now, this last generation is over sixty-five years old. The entire life span of a single generation is considered as being 120 years. That means the last of the Philadelphia church age believers will be gone within another fifty-five years. Their deaths will keep them from the hour of trial.

It's serious business, and I'm trying to shed light on the reality of our situation. Jesus is fulfilling His prophecy by allowing an entire generation to pass away while the last sign of His near return—worldwide evangelism—is completed around the world.

Why is it necessary for the Philadelphia church generation to pass away before the hour of trial begins? In Revelation 3:10, Jesus promised the believers of that generation He would keep them from the hour of trial that is about to come upon the entire world. He didn't make this promise to the Laodicea generation—not even true believers! Jesus supports God's claim that He will not violate the original law set forth in Genesis 3:19. Therefore, He removes the Philadelphia church-age believers through death. As a matter of fact, in order for God to keep the original law of Genesis 3:19 intact, He removes all believers, even when the rapture occurs, through death.

We have an example of an entire generation passing away when the Israelites refused to enter the Promised Land. It is the same for the Philadelphia church-era believers before Daniel's seventieth week can begin. You can rest assured, Jesus will carry this promise out to the last person, even though we won't know the name of that person. And since we won't be able to discern this, Jesus, in Matthew 24:6–8, points us to the sign that starts the hour of trial: the Russian invasion of Israel.

The death of the last Philadelphia church-age believer will go unnoticed after the hour of trial begins because unbelievers from that generation will not be kept from experiencing the hour of trial. Therefore, we will find people from that last generation going through the hour of trial. The Philadelphia church believers pass away between the completion of the worldwide preaching of the gospel (happening during these last days) and the beginning of the hour of trial—or the Russian invasion of Israel. Of course, at the same time, people of all ages—saved or unsaved—will continue to naturally die, or pass away.

The unbelievers still alive from the Philadelphia church generation, along with believers and nonbelievers of all ages from the Laodicea church era, will go into the hour of trial. At the end of the hour of trial, everyone who has accepted Jesus Christ as their personal Savior will have their spirits and souls caught up to heaven through a rapture that will appear to be the death of millions of people around the world.

Unbelievers of all ages still alive after the rapture will go into the time of great tribulation. They will face the strong delusion that God sends to an unbelieving world—Satan, through the little horn of Daniel 7:8, or king of the South, posing as the Messiah. They will face great tribulation because they have rejected the worldwide preaching of the gospel through evangelism such as done by Billy Graham and other ministries during these last days. They will have rejected the 144,000 Jewish-Christian evangelists and rejected the

Christians from the Laodicea church era who go through the hour of trial with them.

When the Man of Sin poses as God, the only way to truly be saved (spiritually and eternally) is to refuse the mark of this beast, which appears as an offer of salvation, or forgiveness for sin. Refusal to accept his mark of salvation may result in death by martyrdom. But some people who refuse this offer of salvation may remain alive and live into the millennium with Jesus. At the end of the millennium, Jesus puts down another rebellion. That will result in the death of a great multitude. After this rebellion is put down, the spirits and souls of remaining believers will be snatched out of their bodies and raised to heaven, where all true believers will live with Jesus.

John sees a great multitude in heaven that specifically comes out of great tribulation. They are martyred for their steadfast faith in Jesus, refusing to participate in the Man of Sin's twisted offer of wealth in exchange for physical salvation.

As you can see, this prophecy is always completed and fulfilled in accordance with God's command that the body return to the dust or be destroyed in this world. The body is sinful. The world is tainted with sin. Therefore, at the end of the millennium, Jesus destroys the old heaven and old earth. Both have been tainted with sin; the devil and his angels tainted heaven, and through our sins committed in the body, the earth has been tainted.

WHY EVERYONE MUST PASS AWAY

Genesis 3:19: By the sweat of your brow you will eat your food until you return to the ground, since from it you were taken; for dust you are and to dust you will return.

Matthew 24:34: I tell you the truth, this generation will certainly not pass away until all these things have happened.

Satan has done his best to ensure this generation has not understood God's self-imposed eternal laws concerning life and death, or what truly happens to the body, soul, and spirit at the point of death. Careful study reveals that God has never violated his laws concerning the body (the sinful flesh) dying or being destroyed and only the spirit and soul taken to heaven. We will review the death of those who were supposedly raptured in the body and see how their bodies were actually destroyed.

In Genesis 3:19, we clearly read that the body of every single person must return to the dust. This is an operative law that was established by God Himself over six thousand years ago as a result of Adam's sin. God has never changed the law, nor has He made any exceptions to it. That's because God will never violate His own laws.

I know many want to believe "all things are possible with God." To quote this scripture, we must remember that it is correct only as long as we don't have God violating laws that He Himself sets. To think or believe otherwise is to call God a sinner! That is impossible, and it is blasphemous.

Satan knows that it is impossible for God to sin or break any law that He establishes. God has never changed the laws of gravity, life and death, seedtime and harvest, sowing and reaping, and a host of other universal laws in order to suit our daily whims and wishes. What's truly possible with God is for God to work within the framework of His own set laws to accomplish His purposes.

Genesis 3:19 is the basic law imposed by God concerning the destruction of the body, because it is sinful. Hebrews 9:27 states that it is "appointed once for man to die, then the judgment." Therefore, we can factually conclude that nobody ever escaped death.

Romans 5:12 states "death came to all men, because all sinned." And in verse 14, the apostle goes on to say that "death reigned from the time of Adam to the time of Moses, even over those who did not sin."

Concerning Enoch, for the author to say that God "took him away" (Gen. 5:24), is another expression for stating Enoch died. Even today, if we were to attend a funeral or memorial service and hear someone exclaim, "The Lord took him away," we would not assume the person was raptured to heaven in the body—even if a body was never found.

Concerning Elijah, let me begin by stating the reality of 1 Corinthians 15:20–22: "But Christ has indeed been raised from the dead, the *first-fruits* of those who have fallen asleep. . . . For as in Adam *all die*, so in Christ all will be made alive." (Emphasis is mine.)

To believe the false notion that Enoch and Elijah were physically raptured in their bodies (which are sinful) would be to believe that death was overcome by some method other than Jesus Christ dying on the cross of Calvary. In other words, if death was not allowed to occur in their bodies, then Jesus was crucified in vain. That would mean that almighty God overcame death by some other means. If God had overcome the physical death that came as a result of sin through Adam in some way other than Jesus' death, then all of Christianity would be a hoax.

Because of Adam's sin, the penalty for sin was the experience of physical death for all people. Since this penalty became God's own judgment for sin, to assume He made exceptions to that law for mere men would be to make the assumption that God changed the penalty for sin—that some die and some don't.

If God is allowed to violate His own laws, then why was Jesus so set on keeping the laws, even to the point of death? He asked God in the Garden of Gethsemane if there was any other way to bring salvation short of dying on the cross. Evidently, there was no other way that would be pleasing to God; therefore, Jesus died so that we might spiritually live forever.

Second Corinthians 5:8 states that we "prefer to be away from the body and at home with the Lord." Therefore, because death had not been overcome until Jesus was crucified, no person prior to Him could have entered heaven physically. Nor can anyone enter heaven physically now, because eternal life is only granted for the soul and the new body each person will receive, not the bodies we now inhabit. Therefore, the rapture can occur only through death, where only the spirit and soul are caught up to heaven. The body will be left behind. And to those people left behind, it will appear as if we instantly died.

Consider Moses. Deuteronomy 34:10 tells us that "no prophet has risen in Israel like Moses, whom the Lord knew face to face." Concerning the fact that Moses died and yet his body was never found is ample proof God does not make exceptions to His laws, not even for the greatest prophets who ever lived. In Deuteronomy 34:5, we find God Himself buried the body, and to this day no one knows where the grave is located.

The same is true for Elijah. The spiritual vehicle God used to take Elijah's soul and spirit to heaven is described in 2 Kings 2:10–11 as being a chariot of fire and chariot of horses. The physical reality of this spiritual vehicle and method for death to the body is described as being a whirlwind. Another name for a whirlwind is *tornado*. This fierce, violent storm is the physical vehicle God used to accomplish a spiritual purpose. One vehicle served two separate and distinct purposes of God: to take Elijah's soul and spirit to heaven, while disposing of the prophet's physical and sinful body.

Even those who saw this event understood this concept. The whirlwind was used to cause immediate death to Elijah and was also used to separate the spirit and soul from the body. The men who were present believed God may have discarded the body in a nearby valley or on the mountains, leading them to search for three days. However, this was not the case. God could have disposed of Elijah's body in a multitude of different ways, precluding anyone from ever finding the remains. The lightning from the storm could have disintegrated the body much like cremation, spreading Elijah's ashes. God could have used the whirlwind to dig Elijah's grave, resulting in it never being found. God could have carried the body the entire distance of the storm's route, discarding the body in a location where no one could locate the remains. The possibilities are endless when proper discernment concerning God's laws are applied to Elijah's death.

The whole concept of a physical rapture either through disappearance or ascension in the body makes a mockery of all that God has predetermined for the sinful flesh and accomplished through His Son, Jesus Christ. The fact that we are all changed in the twinkling of an eye simply means that death occurs instantly, and we are changed from physical mortal beings to immortal spiritual beings—instantly, in the twinkling of an eye—so fast that we won't even experience the sting of death. God uses a vehicle whereby death occurs in order to take our soul out of this body so He may shroud it with a glorified body. Since the dawn of man, it has always occurred in this manner—even when a body is never found.

We who are still alive at the time of the rapture will have our spirits and souls caught up to heaven. We will not experience death. That's simply because 2 Thessalonians 2:3–6 says it will happen so suddenly—in a flash, in the twinkling of an eye. Although we will not experience death in our minds, be assured, our sinful bodies will be left behind and will either appear as dead, destroyed, or missing to those who are still alive. Instead of people instantly disappearing, it will appear as if death instantly occurred to millions of people who believed in Jesus or were younger than the age of understanding.

THERE THE VULTURES WILL GATHER

Luke 17:34–37: "I tell you, on that night two people will be in one bed; one will be taken and the other left. Two women will be grinding grain together; one will be taken and the other left." Then, in verse 37: "Where, Lord?" they asked. He replied, "Where there is a *dead* body, there the vultures will gather." (Emphasis is mine.)

Another strong piece of evidence that the rapture actually occurs through the death of millions of people is found in Luke 17:34–37, where Jesus is talking about one person being taken and another being left behind. His disciples asked Him a question concerning the mass death of millions of people. The word *taken* is a reference that once again God takes the spirit and soul of a person through death. The disciples asked the Lord what would happen to those who were taken. Jesus replied in verse 37, "Where there is a dead body, there the vultures will gather."

They asked no further questions because the disciples clearly understood that the rapture, or the taking of believers' spirits and souls to heaven, would appear as the instantaneous death of millions of people on a worldwide basis. Their taking would result only in their spirits and souls being caught up to be with the Lord, leaving their bodies behind for the vultures to feed on before any proper burial could be performed.

We can see where death occurs on a worldwide scale and to so many at the same time that the vultures move in to feast on the dead remains before burial can occur to all those who died. There are three times when the vultures move in to feast on dead remains during the last ten-year period preceding the return of Jesus Christ: (1) The Russian invasion of Israel; (2) the rapture, because it occurs through death; and (3) Armageddon, when Jesus returns.

It's evident in this passage that Jesus was not talking about the war of Gog and Magog (Russian invasion of Israel) where all the birds of the air are invited to a sacrificial feast prepared by God (Ezekiel 38 and 39). Nor was He talking about His return at Armageddon where the birds are invited to the great supper of God (Revelation 19). This passage refers to a rapture of millions by death. The fact that he referenced some would be sleeping and others working indicates that it occurs instantly around the world.

THE LAST TRUMPET

1 Corinthians 15:51: Listen, I tell you a mystery: We will not all sleep, but we will all be changed—in a flash, in the twinkling of an eye, at the last trumpet.

To think that the apostle's words "we will not all sleep" is the same as "we will not all die" is in error. The apostle is saying that not all Christians will enter the place of rest. The place of rest is the sea of glass that John saw in Revelation 4:6. This is the place where the dead in Christ remain until the rapture occurs. John also saw these souls under the altar of God when the fifth seal was opened. When the rapture occurs, the dead in Christ (those souls that make up the sea of glass) are raised from *under the altar* of God to *in front of the throne* of God. We who are alive on earth bypass the sea of glass, or place of rest, and enter directly into the presence of God's throne, along with the dead in Christ who are raised from under the altar. At the rapture's occurrence, all true believers—those who make up the dead in Christ and those caught up from the earth—are then made alive in Christ. Essentially, the apostle is simply telling us that those who are raptured from the earth never become part of the dead in Christ.

Also, in this passage, the apostle tells us when to expect the timing of the rapture's occurrence. All we have to do is look in the book of Revelation to find that the last trumpet mentioned in the entire Bible is the seventh trumpet judgment.

Revelation 10:7 states, "But in the days when the seventh angel *is about to sound his trumpet*, the mystery of God [which is the Man of Sin attempting to pass himself off as God] will be accomplished." (Emphasis is mine.) This mystery, or secret, is the strong delusion that is created when the Man of Sin poses as the Messiah. But when the seventh trumpet is actually blown, millions of Christians will suddenly die when they experience the catching away of their souls and spirits on a one-time worldwide basis. It's the completion of 1 Thessalonians 4:16 and 2 Corinthians 15:51.

We know there are still three years to go because the angel tells John in Revelation 10:11, "You must prophesy again about many peoples, nations, languages, and kings." Immediately following that command, John is told to measure the temple. He's told it will be trampled for forty-two months. This is the great tribulation period Jesus spoke of in Matthew 24.

CAUGHT UP IN THE CLOUDS OF WITNESSES

1 Thessalonians 4:17: After that, we who are still alive and are left will be caught up [meaning our spirits and souls] together with them [the dead in Christ in paradise, or sea of glass] in the clouds [the elders and the 144,000 are the great clouds of witnesses] to meet the Lord in the air [or throne of God in heaven]. (Explanations in brackets are mine.)

Revelation 5:6: Then I saw a Lamb, looking as if it had been slain, standing in the center of the throne, encircled by the four living creatures and the elders.

Hebrews 12:1: Therefore, since we are surrounded by such a great cloud of witnesses [these are the elders whom John saw sitting in front of the throne of God in heaven], let us throw off everything that hinders and the sin that so easily entangles, and let us run with perseverance the race marked out for us. (Explanations in brackets are mine.)

Revelation 14:14: I looked, and there before me was a white cloud [the elders sitting before the throne of God], and seated on the cloud [In Revelation 5:6, John sees Jesus, the Lamb, looking as if He had been slain, encircled by the elders, who will be a great cloud of witnesses to the rapture. Here John sees Jesus as the victorious King of Kings, still encircled by the elders.] was one "like a son of man" with a crown of gold on his head and a sharp sickle in his hand. (Explanations in brackets are mine.)

The twenty-four elders serve as clouds, or witnesses, to the rapture. These elders are mentioned as a great cloud of witnesses in Hebrews 12:1. They sit before the throne of God and encircle the Lamb, Jesus Christ. Therefore, when the seventh trumpet is blown, Jesus steps down from His throne and stands amongst the great cloud of elders, as well as the 144,000 Jewish-Christian evangelists, to welcome all the saints from the church age—the dead in Christ from the sea of glass, first, then those who are raptured from the earth—to heaven, which is considered to be *in the air*. Therefore, when the rapture takes place, we don't meet Jesus in the clouds of the sky. The elders encircle Jesus like a great cloud and witness the rapture take place—in heaven, or in the air.

The sharp sickle held by the one who appeared like a son of man, or Jesus, is a subtle reference by John that the rapture occurs through the death of believers here on earth.

THE SAINTS COME MARCHING IN

1 Thessalonians 4:16: For the Lord Himself will come down from heaven, with a loud command, with the voice of the archangel and with the trumpet call of God, and the dead in Christ will rise first. After that, we who are still alive and are left will be caught up together with them in the clouds to meet the Lord in the air.

Now we can clearly see how 1 Thessalonians 4:16 lines up directly with the blowing of the seventh trumpet. The rapture is the great harvest by one who appears as the Son of Man, as described in Revelation 11:15–19 and 14:14–16. These scriptures line up perfectly with the different groups of souls John describes in Revelation 4:6, 7:9–17, and 15:2. The scriptures also line up perfectly with 1 Corinthians 15:51 and Hebrews 12:1.

- (1) The sea of glass is the dead in Christ up to Daniel's seventieth week, which is the last seven years of this ten-year period, or the tribulation period.
- (2) At the time of the rapture by death, or seventh trumpet, the souls and spirits of the dead in Christ in paradise are immediately called up from under the altar to in front of the throne of God. Immediately after them, the souls and spirits of those believers who are still alive on earth will also be brought up to the throne of God. They will all stand in front of the elders, who serve as a cloud of witnesses that encircles Jesus.
- (3) The souls John sees under the altar at the breaking of the fifth seal are the dead in Christ from paradise, or the sea of glass John saw in Revelation 4:6. At the beginning of the tribulation period (the last seven years of Daniel's ten-year end-time period, started by the Russian invasion of Israel). They were given white robes and told to wait until their fellow brethren were slain or killed or had passed away just as they were. Essentially, the last of these brethren are slain as a result of the rapture occurring. The rapture occurs through death so the spirits and souls of the remaining church-age saints can be called up to heaven.
- (4) After the rapture by death occurs at the seventh trumpet, it is time for us to meet the judgment seat of Christ while the great tribulation saints are added, just as John sees in Revelation 15:2 and seven years before that time in Revelation 7:9–17. These are the saints John saw in white robes, but holding palm branches. They immediately precede the return of Jesus to earth. They come out of great tribulation when the king of the South, or Man of Sin, poses as God.

In Revelation 7:15–17, we find that the great tribulation martyrs who refuse the mark of the Man of Sin bypass paradise and go directly into the presence of God and serve Him day and night. That's because their final judgment is their refusal to take the Man of Sin's mark of salvation and their overcoming the strong delusion sent to them by God according to 2 Thessalonians 2:11–12. Therefore, they stand beside the sea of glass mixed with fire (the church), or those souls that met the judgment seat of Christ.

The great tribulation saints are a great multitude, and they are holding palm branches, unlike the first group John saw under the altar in paradise who were given white robes and told to wait. For all practical purposes, they are told to wait until the end of the hour of trial when the rapture occurs through the death of their fellow brethren, although John doesn't write it in those terms.

The reason the great tribulation martyrs are holding palm branches is because they immediately precede the second coming of Jesus to earth, as King of Kings and Lord of Lords. This parallels Jesus' first coming when He rode into Jerusalem on a donkey while people were hailing Him by waving palm branches.

As you can see, John left us a detailed outline of what happens to the church-age saints during the tribulation period. His writings and these scriptures give us sound doctrine on which to base the rapture occurring through the death of remaining Christians at the blowing of the seventh trumpet. All the scriptures—Genesis 3:19, Matthew 24:34, 1 Thessalonians 4:16, 2 Corinthians 15:51, Revelation 4:2, 7:9–17, and 15:2—line up perfectly. It also helps us distinguish exactly when the rapture will occur: at the seventh trumpet, or the last trump, and, according to Daniel, 1,335 days after the king of the North first abolishes the sacrifice from taking place on the Temple Mount. Figure 5-2 shows how all these scriptures fit neatly together.

WOE TO PREGNANT WOMEN AND NURSING MOTHERS

Matthew 24:19–22: How dreadful it will be in those days for pregnant women and nursing mothers! Pray that your flight will not take place in winter or on the Sabbath. For then there will be great distress, unequaled from the beginning of the world until now—and never to be equaled again. If those days had not been cut short, no one would survive, but for the sake of the elect those days will be shortened.

I Will Make Myself Like The Most High!

YEARS FOR END-TIME PERIOD

```
0    1    2    3    4    5    6    7    8    9   10
|    |    |    |    |    |    |    |    |    |    |
```

TRANSITION PERIOD
(DAN. 11:25-31)

HOUR OF TRIAL
(REV. 3:10)

GREAT TRIBULATION
(DAN. 12:1)
(MATT. 24:21)

3 YEARS   3½ YEARS   3½ YEARS

144,000 SEALED DURING THE RUSSIAN INVASION OF ISRAEL
(REV. 7:1–8)

1,290th DAY AFTER SACRIFICE IS ABOLISHED BY THE KING OF THE NORTH, THE MAN OF SIN (OR KING OF THE SOUTH) COMMITS THE ABOMINATION THAT CAUSES DESOLATION (DAN. 12:11) (MATT. 24:15) SATAN PORTRAYS HIMSELF AS GOD THROUGH THE LITTLE HORN OF DANIEL 7:8, WHO IS THE KING OF THE SOUTH

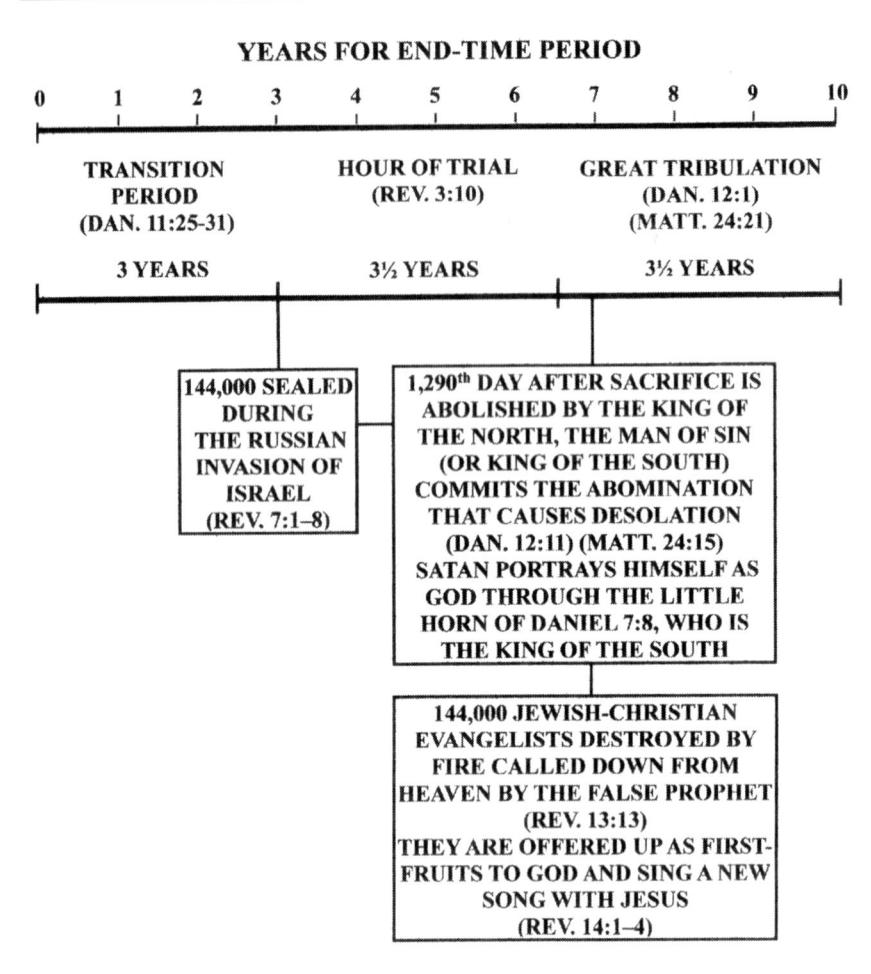

144,000 JEWISH-CHRISTIAN EVANGELISTS DESTROYED BY FIRE CALLED DOWN FROM HEAVEN BY THE FALSE PROPHET (REV. 13:13) THEY ARE OFFERED UP AS FIRST-FRUITS TO GOD AND SING A NEW SONG WITH JESUS (REV. 14:1–4)

FIGURE 5-2. SHOWING THE ORDER IN WHICH JESUS BRINGS HOME THE SAINTS

YEARS FOR END-TIME PERIOD

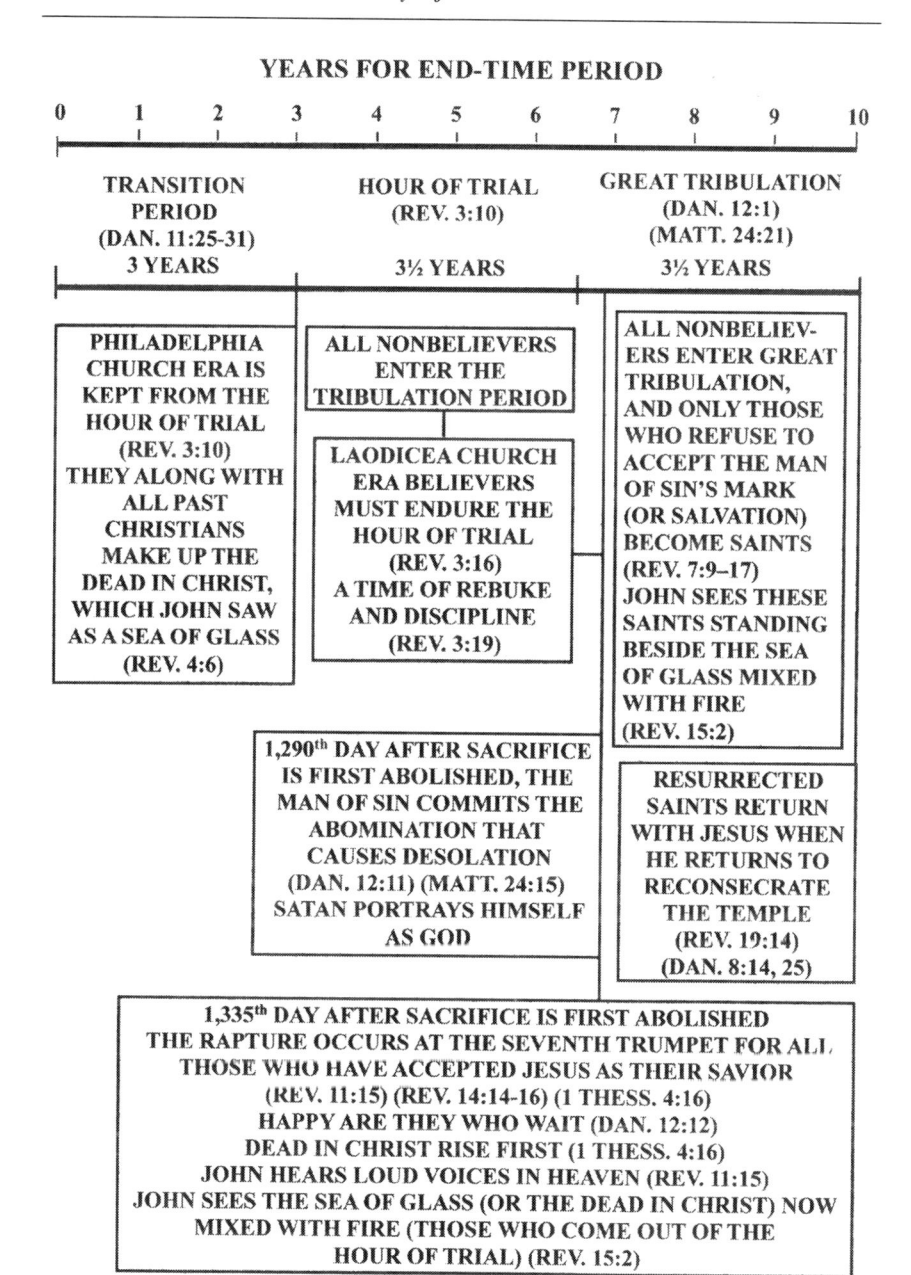

```
0     1     2     3     4     5     6     7     8     9     10
```

| TRANSITION PERIOD (DAN. 11:25-31) 3 YEARS | HOUR OF TRIAL (REV. 3:10) 3½ YEARS | GREAT TRIBULATION (DAN. 12:1) (MATT. 24:21) 3½ YEARS |

PHILADELPHIA CHURCH ERA IS KEPT FROM THE HOUR OF TRIAL (REV. 3:10) THEY ALONG WITH ALL PAST CHRISTIANS MAKE UP THE DEAD IN CHRIST, WHICH JOHN SAW AS A SEA OF GLASS (REV. 4:6)

ALL NONBELIEVERS ENTER THE TRIBULATION PERIOD

LAODICEA CHURCH ERA BELIEVERS MUST ENDURE THE HOUR OF TRIAL (REV. 3:16) A TIME OF REBUKE AND DISCIPLINE (REV. 3:19)

ALL NONBELIEVERS ENTER GREAT TRIBULATION, AND ONLY THOSE WHO REFUSE TO ACCEPT THE MAN OF SIN'S MARK (OR SALVATION) BECOME SAINTS (REV. 7:9–17) JOHN SEES THESE SAINTS STANDING BESIDE THE SEA OF GLASS MIXED WITH FIRE (REV. 15:2)

1,290th DAY AFTER SACRIFICE IS FIRST ABOLISHED, THE MAN OF SIN COMMITS THE ABOMINATION THAT CAUSES DESOLATION (DAN. 12:11) (MATT. 24:15) SATAN PORTRAYS HIMSELF AS GOD

RESURRECTED SAINTS RETURN WITH JESUS WHEN HE RETURNS TO RECONSECRATE THE TEMPLE (REV. 19:14) (DAN. 8:14, 25)

1,335th DAY AFTER SACRIFICE IS FIRST ABOLISHED THE RAPTURE OCCURS AT THE SEVENTH TRUMPET FOR ALL THOSE WHO HAVE ACCEPTED JESUS AS THEIR SAVIOR (REV. 11:15) (REV. 14:14-16) (1 THESS. 4:16) HAPPY ARE THEY WHO WAIT (DAN. 12:12) DEAD IN CHRIST RISE FIRST (1 THESS. 4:16) JOHN HEARS LOUD VOICES IN HEAVEN (REV. 11:15) JOHN SEES THE SEA OF GLASS (OR THE DEAD IN CHRIST) NOW MIXED WITH FIRE (THOSE WHO COME OUT OF THE HOUR OF TRIAL) (REV. 15:2)

FIGURE 5-2 (CONTINUED). SHOWING THE ORDER IN WHICH JESUS BRINGS HOME THE SAINTS

When Jesus harvests the earth of all believers, their bodies will instantly be struck with a plague. Now, since this plague will really be the rapture occurring to all believers through the death of their bodies, it means that all babies not yet born will die in each mother's womb. Unborn babies are clearly under the age of understanding. The worldwide death of all unborn babies should stand as a clear indicator to all unbelievers who miss the rapture that the rapture occurred through the death of millions of people, not by disappearance or bodily ascension.

Also, all children who have not yet reached the age of understanding will also die instantly in the twinkling of an eye. Therefore, mothers who are not saved at the time of the rapture by death will experience the horror of their babies and young children dying, all over the world. No wonder Jesus called it a time of great distress!

I think Jesus specifically pointed this fact out so that those who are discerning will have a great sign that the Man of Sin, although posing as God and claiming to be God, is truly the Man of Sin. One thing is for sure: this event will cause the greatest fear and panic and confusion the world has ever known.

The Man of Sin will use this divine act of calling the souls and spirits of believers to heaven as an opportunity to sway people into believing that he is God. He'll claim that he has the power over life and death. He will convince the people left behind that only his blood saves people from their sins and that only his blood can make them have life everlasting. But the death of all children will spark one of two reactions from parents. They will hate this man entirely and rebel by refusing to take his mark and offer of wealth, or they will believe his lie to the eternal destruction of their souls.

THE PENALTY FOR SIN IS DEATH

1 Thessalonians 5:9: For God did not appoint us to suffer wrath but to receive salvation through our Lord Jesus Christ.

Under God's law of salvation by grace, the only sin that absolutely cannot be forgiven is the sin of hearing the gospel of Jesus

Christ and then failing to accept Him as your Lord and Savior before you die. Every other sin a person commits can be forgiven.

In an effort to copy God, the Man of Sin will claim to have judged all those struck by the plague for the unpardonable sin: accepting salvation from Jesus, rather than from himself, now posing as God. The Man of Sin will state that since they claimed to be saved by Jesus, he as God marked them and reserved them for judgment. Thus he poured out his fierce wrath upon them, killing them instantly with a plague.

The truth is, the Man of Sin is part of God's wrath. Although believers will be exposed to the revelation of this man, they will not endure the full wrath this man unleashes on those who refuse to worship him as God. Therefore, after the elect are exposed to the strong delusion of this man, they are shortly removed through death, because God has not appointed believers to suffer the upcoming wrath of God, through the person of the Man of Sin. So everything that occurs up to the seventh trumpet is only a judgment of God. Judgments are used in hopes that people will repent, accept Jesus Christ as their Savior, be raptured, and thus be spared the time of great tribulation.

However, the Man of Sin will use the rapture as an attempt to copy the time when Jesus returns and separates the sheep from the goats; that is, His followers from those who refuse to believe He is God. After claiming the death of millions of followers of Jesus Christ was his act of wrath, the Man of Sin simply turns around and offers all unbelievers forgiveness for their sins. He does this by offering salvation through the taking of his blood, or DNA, so their uncontrolled sins will supposedly be covered or atoned for.

Their doing so will negate any reason for him to judge them through death. This shows you the great lengths Satan will go in copying God's method of salvation by grace so that no man can boast. But here, under this false method of salvation, those who accept it and take the money will be able to boast and gloat over the belief that they are now a favored child of God. Believing their sins are forgiven through the shedding of his blood, their continual sinning is completely justified, sanctified, endorsed and condoned without judgment, as far as the Man of Sin is concerned.

THE HARVEST OF GREAT TRIBULATION SAINTS

Revelation 14:17–20: Another angel came out of the temple in heaven, and he too had a sharp sickle. Still another angel, who had charge of the fire, came from the altar and called in a loud voice to him who had the sharp sickle, "Take your sharp sickle and gather the clusters of grapes from the earth's vine, because its grapes are ripe." The angel swung his sickle on the earth, gathered its grapes and threw them into the great winepress of God's wrath. They were trampled in the winepress outside the city, and blood flowed out of the press, rising as high as the horses' bridles for a distance of 1,600 stadia.

After the rapture occurs, only unbelievers will be left to endure the time of great tribulation. This part of the harvest lasts for the next three-year period as people who accept the mark put to death those who refuse. That's why we see the angel holding a sickle, an indicator that once again all must die. But this death by martyrdom will gain people instant entrance to heaven and eternal salvation for their souls. This harvest will last during most of the reign of the king of the South, until just before Jesus comes. Because of the wealth offered to those who capture and kill others who refuse the mark, Americans will literally be consumed with hunting down these so-called traitors around the world to receive a rich bounty.

Just as ancient Babylon was used as a judgment against Israel and the Jews were taken captive and killed, so will America, the daughter of Babylon, hunt for Jews, take them captive, and kill them, along with any other person who refuses the false mark of salvation.

Evidently, the price for those who refuse the mark is so great that Americans will search the world for those without the mark and ship these captives to Israel, where they will be tortured and killed. John gives evidence of this in Revelation 18:13 when he sees ships loaded with "bodies and souls of men" coming from the most prosperous nation on earth—Babylon the Great, the harlot, or America.

Jeremiah further backs this up when he quotes the very words of God in Jeremiah 16:16:

But now I will send for many fisherman [144,000 Jewish Christian evangelists] . . . and they will catch them [they will witness to believers who will eventually be caught up to heaven in the rapture]. After that I will send for many headhunters [those who take the false mark of salvation], and they will hunt them down [those who refuse the mark] on every mountain and hill and from the crevices of the rocks. (Explanations in brackets are mine.)

Remember how Jesus informed the Jews in Matthew 24:16 to flee to the mountains of Judea when they see the *abomination of desolation* that the prophet Daniel spoke of standing where it doesn't belong, on the Temple Mount? Jesus knew they would be hunted down for a price.

Thus Satan accomplishes the destruction of mankind in two ways: (1) bringing physical death to those who maintain a witness and faith for Jesus and (2) destroying the eternal destiny of those who accept the false mark of salvation offered by Satan's real Man of Sin. And he does it all in the name of peace, prosperity, and safety—in the name of God!

In the next chapter, we'll piece together John's final prophecies concerning the Man of Sin's reign of terror. We will discern the horrible fate of those who reject the gospel of Jesus Christ and persist in being deluded by the Man of Sin, or Satan, posing as God.

CHAPTER 6

THE DAY OF THE LORD

In chapter 5, we studied the delusion Satan creates when the Man of Sin attempts to copy the day of the Lord. We saw how the Man of Sin turns the stakes on God's holy people. We saw the strong delusion he presents by destroying the 144,000 Jewish-Christian evangelists, how he makes the rapture by death appear as the separation of the sheep from the goats, how he offers salvation in exchange for wealth, and how he convinces his followers to destroy those who refuse his offer of salvation.

In this chapter, we will study the real day of the Lord—that day when Jesus returns as the victorious Messiah. This time, however, instead of it being a blessed day for the inhabitants of the earth, Joel 1:15 reminds us of the reality of Jesus' return to earth: "Alas for that day! For the day of the Lord is near; it will come like destruction from the Almighty."

Just as we saw in the last chapter how Satan twisted events around to appear as the outpouring of his wrath upon mankind (devising ways to kill Jews and Christians), in this chapter we will see the fierceness with which God exacts His punishment upon an evil and perverse and deluded generation that has refused to believe the truth.

As a strong delusion, Satan almost achieves his goal of destroying all of mankind. Acting as God and offering salvation in exchange for wealth, he is able to physically destroy the people of

The Day Of The Lord

God: Jews who refuse his offer of salvation, along with remaining Gentiles who continue to stand steadfast in their faith that Jesus is the true Messiah. Although he has been able to destroy these saints physically, he has not destroyed them spiritually. Their faith in Jesus and refusal of wealth, and their subsequent martyrdom, gains them eternal life with God.

Satan's thirst to destroy mankind appears victorious in that he is able to delude many people into believing he is God and convince them to take his mark of salvation in exchange for having every desire of their hearts fulfilled. He is successful in deluding his followers with the riches of this world. Isaiah 2:7 tells us "their land is full of silver and gold; there is no end to their treasures."

In Revelation 17:18, John describes America, Babylon the Great, as a great city. Isaiah 1:21–23 gives a befitting picture of America in the days just before Jesus returns: "See how the faithful city has become a harlot! She once was full of justice; righteousness used to dwell in her—but now murderers! Your silver has become dross, your choice wine is diluted with water. Your rulers are rebels, companions of thieves; they all love bribes and chase after gifts."

Second Timothy 3:1–5 gives us a snapshot of people's hearts as they fall for Satan's evil scheme, considering themselves as righteous children of the king:

> But mark this: There will be terrible times in the last days [during the great tribulation when Satan rules the world as God through the Man of Sin]. People will be lovers of themselves, lovers of money, boastful, proud, abusive, disobedient to their parents, ungrateful, unholy, without love, unforgiving, slanderous, without self-control, brutal, not lovers of the good, treacherous, rash, conceited, lovers of pleasure rather than lovers of God— having a form of godliness [taking the Man of Sin's, or Satan's, offer of salvation in exchange for wealth] but denying its power [that Jesus is God]. Have nothing to do with them. (Explanations in brackets are mine.)

With all this wealth fueling the deceit of people's hearts, Jesus provides a startling picture of the world, particularly America, at the onset of His near return, in Matthew 24:37–39:

> As it was in the days of Noah, so it will be at the coming of the Son of Man. For in the days before the flood, people were eating and drinking, marrying and giving in marriage, up to the day Noah entered the ark; and they knew nothing about what would happen until the flood came and took them all away. That is how it will be at the coming of the Son of Man.

He compares these times not only with the days of Noah, but also with the days of Lot, in Luke 17:28–30:

> It was the same in the days of Lot. People were eating and drinking, buying and selling, planting and building. But the day Lot left Sodom, fire and sulfur rained down from heaven and destroyed them all. It will be just like this on the day the Son of Man is revealed.

Now we know why Daniel 8:25 could be written with such conviction about the Man of Sin portraying himself as God:

> He [the Man of Sin, who is the king of the South, or the little horn of Daniel 7:8] will cause deceit [the offer, or mark, of false salvation] to prosper [by offering them tremendous wealth], and he will consider himself superior [God]. When they feel secure [because of their wealth], he will destroy many and take his stand against the Prince of princes [Jesus]. Yet he will be destroyed, but not by human power [he's destroyed by Jesus]. (Explanations in brackets are mine.)

It is the destruction of the Man of Sin, the False Prophet, and Satan that we will study in this chapter. This strong delusion and America's thirst for wealth at the expense of God's holy people arouse the fierce destruction of the wrath of almighty God.

POURING OUT THE BOWLS OF GOD'S WRATH

Revelation 15:1: I saw in heaven another great and marvelous sign: seven angels with the seven last plagues—last, because with them God's wrath is completed.

Joel 1:15: Alas for that day! For the day of the Lord is near; it will come like destruction from the Almighty.

The 144,000 have been killed. The church has been raised from paradise (sea of glass) and from the earth through a rapture by death (John saw the sea of glass mixed with fire). The harvest of the great-tribulation saints is now finished (in Revelation 15:2, John saw the great tribulation saints standing *beside* the sea of glass mixed with fire, or the church). Although there are people still alive who have refused to accept the mark of the beast, Jesus will divinely protect them as He begins to destroy the evil forces of the world. These people will be spared from God's wrath that is about to be poured out on an evil world. This is in fulfillment of Romans 5:9, where Paul tells us, "Since we have now been justified by his blood, how much more shall we be saved from God's wrath through Him!"

Up until this time, God has only been meting out judgments upon the world. But now, because all nations, including America, have treated His holy people with contempt, His anger is completely aroused against the world. John now begins to describe the actual preparation and return of Jesus Christ, beginning with a heavenly picture of all the saints throughout the entire church age.

THE LAST SAINT COMES HOME

Revelation 15:2–3: And I saw what looked like a sea of glass mixed with fire and, standing beside the sea, those who had been victorious over the beast and his image and over the number of his name. They held harps given them by God and sang the song of Moses the servant of God and the song of the Lamb: "Great and marvelous are your deeds, Lord God Almighty. Just and true are your ways, King of the ages. Who will not fear you, O Lord, and bring glory to your name? For you alone are holy. All nations will come and worship before you, for your righteous acts have been revealed."

Here we see all the saints of the church age in heaven, standing before the throne of God, holding harps and praising God and Jesus. Before long, they will return to earth with Jesus Christ. But first, there's still work that must be done on earth. We are now at the very end of the great-tribulation period. We are about to see the kingdom of the king of the South come to ruin, as well as America, Babylon the Great.

PEACE AND SAFETY

1 Thessalonians 5:1-3: Now, brothers, about times and dates we do not need to write to you, for you know very well that the day of the Lord will come like a thief in the night. While people are saying, "Peace and safety," destruction will come on them suddenly, as labor pains on a pregnant woman, and they will not escape.

Here at the end of the king of the South's reign, people are secure in their conviction he is God. People will be talking about what great peace and safety they have experienced under his reign, even though it has actually been a reign of terror for God's holy people. Unaware they have been duped by the Man of Sin, they will not escape the destruction that will suddenly come upon them.

Against their positive-thinking opinions and the resounding cries of their prosperity-preaching false prophets, they have no idea they are not at peace and certainly are not safe. Instead, they have allowed themselves to be deluded by Satan into a false sense of security. They don't realize their eating and drinking and sinning have only fattened them for the day of slaughter.

As a matter of fact, they are actually anticipating this time. That's because the Man of Sin will convince them that the *day of the Lord* (with Satan posing as God) is the day that Satan is unbound and destroyed according to Revelation 20:7–10. They believe that after it is over, then it's a new heaven and a new earth. In Amos 5:18, we see where God asks these people a revealing question: "Woe to you who long for the day of the Lord! Why do you long for the day of the Lord? That day will be darkness, not light."

These people have been deluded into believing the *day of the Lord* is the day when Satan is unbound and the king of the South puts down the final rebellion by Satan. But just as the day of the rapture by death was a day of darkness, so the second coming of Jesus will be a day of darkness.

Amos 6:4 states they have such a peace about this upcoming day that they "lie on beds inlaid with ivory and lounge on your couches. You dine on choice lambs and fattened calves. You strum away on your harps like David and improvise on musical instruments. You drink wine by the bowlful and use the finest lotions."

Amos 9:10 goes on to tell us that these people will actually say, "Disaster will not overtake or meet us." Joel 2:3 states that the people have been so wealthy that before this invading army arrives, the "land is like the garden of Eden." Amos 3:15 states people will have a winter house and a summer house, and their mansions will be adorned with ivory.

So secure have they become in their wealth that they are not aware of God's word in Zephaniah 1:18: "Neither their silver nor their gold will be able to save them on the day of the Lord's wrath." Their security and contempt of God are seen in the way John writes about America in Revelation 18:7: "I sit as queen; I am not a widow, and I will never mourn."

In 1 Timothy 6:3–10, we find the root of their arrogance. They have failed to agree to the "sound instruction of our Lord Jesus Christ and to godly teaching . . . robbed of the truth and who think that godliness is a means to financial gain. . . . People who want to get rich fall into temptation and a trap and into many foolish and harmful desires that plunge men into ruin and destruction. For the love of money is a root of all kinds of evil. Some people, eager for money, have wandered from the faith and pierced themselves with many griefs."

In Revelation 18:12–13, we find that American trade and commerce will be unprecedented. John describes the ships of cargo traded by the merchants of the world: ". . . cargoes of gold, silver, precious stones and pearls; fine linen, purple, silk and scarlet cloth;

every sort of citron wood, and articles of every kind made of ivory, costly wood, bronze, iron and marble; cargoes of cinnamon and spice, of incense, myrrh and frankincense, of wine and olive oil, of fine flour and wheat; cattle and sheep; horses and carriages; and bodies and souls of men."

DRUNK WITH THE BLOOD OF THE SAINTS

Revelation 18:13: . . . and bodies and souls of men.

Excluding the "shiploads of bodies and souls of men," John writes a startling resemblance of America today! But in this one short line, John gives the reason for God's wrath being poured out double against this nation. These shiploads of *bodies and souls of men* are what made the woman, America, "drunk with the blood of the saints, the blood of those who bore testimony to Jesus" (Rev. 17:6).

Earlier, seven years prior to this event, at the beginning of Daniel's seventieth week, John saw these souls, the tribulation martyrs, in Revelation 7:9–17. He was told previously by an elder that they would be a "great multitude that no one could count, from every nation, tribe, people and language, standing before the throne and in front of the Lamb." Now here in Revelation 18:13, John sees them as shiploads of "bodies and souls of men." John was told in Revelation 7:14 that "these are they who have come out of the great tribulation."

These shiploads of *bodies and souls of men* are a result of Satan's anger toward those who held to the testimony of Jesus Christ. John revealed Satan's hatred for them in Revelation 12:17: "Then the dragon was enraged at the woman and went off to make war against the rest of her offspring—those who obey God's commandments and hold to the testimony of Jesus."

These are the *bodies and souls of men* whom John warned in Revelation 13:10: "If anyone is to go into captivity, into captivity he will go. If anyone is to be killed with the sword, with the sword he will be killed. This calls for patient endurance and faithfulness on the part of the saints."

These shiploads of *bodies and souls of men* prompted John to write in Revelation 13:15 that the False Prophet "was given power to give breath to the image of the first beast, so that it could speak and cause all who refused to worship the image to be killed."

These shiploads of *bodies and souls of men* contained those people John previously saw in Revelation 13:16 as being "small and great, rich and poor, free and slave." They refused to "receive a mark on his right hand or on his forehead" so they could buy or sell and enjoy the luxury of tremendous wealth.

John forewarned these shiploads of *bodies and souls of men* in Revelation 14:12: "This calls for patient endurance on the part of the saints who obey God's commandments and remain faithful to Jesus."

These are the *bodies and souls of men* John was speaking to in Revelation 14:13: "Write: Blessed are the dead who die in the Lord from now on. 'Yes,' says the Spirit, 'they will rest from their labor, for their deeds will follow them.'"

These shiploads of *bodies and souls of men* make up the great-tribulation martyrs, or saints, that John saw in Revelation 15:2: "And I saw what looked like a sea of glass mixed with fire and, standing beside the sea, those who had been victorious over the beast and his image and over the number of his name."

These shiploads of *bodies and souls of men* made John stand astonished as he wrote in Revelation 17:6, "I saw that the woman was drunk with the blood of the saints, the blood of those who bore testimony to Jesus."

These are the *bodies and souls of men* whom John sees the sea captains cry out to in Revelation 18:20, when they realize their awful sin and see America sinking into the sea: "Rejoice over her, O heaven! Rejoice, saints and apostles and prophets! God has judged her for the way she treated you."

The bounty on these shiploads of *bodies and souls of men* made people want to kill and torture them as the angel revealed in Revelation 18:24: "In her was found the blood of prophets and of the saints, and all who have been killed on the earth."

And finally, these shiploads of *bodies and souls of men* make up the first resurrection, as recorded by John in Revelation 20:4–6:

"And I saw the souls of those who had been beheaded because of their testimony for Jesus and because of the word of God. They had not worshiped the beast or his image and had not received his mark on their foreheads or their hands. They came to life and reigned with Christ a thousand years. (The rest of the dead did not come to life until the thousand years were ended.) This is the first resurrection. Blessed and holy are those who have part in the first resurrection. The second death has no power over them, but they will be priests of God and of Christ and will reign with him for a thousand years."

Because the people of God are being outright murdered for the sake of money, John writes in Revelation 18:21–23: "The great city of Babylon will be thrown down, never to be found again. . . . Your merchants were the world's great men."

GOD TAKES VENGEANCE FOR HIS HOLY TEMPLE

Revelation 15:5–8: After this I looked and in heaven the temple, that is, the tabernacle of the Testimony, was opened. Out of the temple came the seven angels with the seven plagues. They were dressed in clean, shining linen and wore golden sashes around their chests. Then one of the four living creatures gave to the seven angels seven golden bowls filled with the wrath of God, who lives forever and ever. And the temple was filled with smoke from the glory of God and from his power, and no one could enter the temple until the seven plagues of the seven angels were completed.

Finally, John begins to tell how the wrath of God is poured out on a world that has refused to acknowledge the mighty power and glory of God in heaven and His Son, Jesus Christ. The bowls of God's wrath will conclude the reign of the king of the South and bring in the kingdom of the real Messiah, Jesus Christ.

THE MARK PROVES FATAL

Revelation 16:2: The first angel went and poured out his bowl on the land, and ugly and painful sores broke out on the people who had the mark of the beast and who worshiped his image.

To understand the first four bowls of God's wrath, we must look at the power God gives to His two witnesses who have been preaching the gospel of Jesus for the past three and one-half years. In Revelation 11:5–6, John writes: "If anyone tries to harm them, fire comes from their mouths and devours their enemies. This is how anyone who wants to harm them must die. These men have power to shut up the sky so that it will not rain during the time they are prophesying; and they have power to turn the waters into blood and to strike the earth with every kind of plague as often as they want."

It is actually these two witnesses who have the power to inflict this plague upon those who accepted the mark, or blood sacrifice, of the king of the South.

THE SEA TURNS TO BLOOD

Revelation 16:3: The second angel poured out his bowl on the sea, and it turned into blood like that of a dead man, and every living thing in the sea died.

Here John is speaking about the Mediterranean Sea, the same sea from which Daniel saw four end-time beasts emerge. Once again the two witnesses, Elijah and Moses, have the power to turn the sea into blood.

RIVERS AND SPRINGS BECOME BLOOD

Revelation 16:4–7: The third angel poured out his bowl on the rivers and springs of water, and they became blood. Then I heard the angel in charge of the waters say: "You are just in these judgments, you who are and who were, the Holy One, because you have so judged; for they have shed the blood of your saints and prophets, and you have given them blood to drink as they deserve." And I heard the altar respond: "Yes, Lord God Almighty, true and just are your judgments."

Once again the two witnesses have this power, as the saints in heaven praise God.

GLOBAL WARMING

Revelation 16:8-9: The fourth angel poured out his bowl on the sun, and the sun was given power to scorch people with fire. They were seared by the intense heat and they cursed the name of God, who had control over these plagues, but they refused to repent of what they had done.

By now, it is no secret to the world that the two witnesses are producing real miracles and have the Spirit of God resting on them. But people still reject their gospel of Jesus Christ. Instead, they would rather continue to use His name in vain rather than change their evil hearts. Instead of the miracles producing a change of heart and a renewal of their thinking, people only become more embittered as these miracles disrupt their prosperous lifestyles.

CELEBRATING THE DEATH OF THE TWO WITNESSES

Revelation 11:7–12: Now when they have finished their testimony, the beast that comes up from the Abyss will attack them, and overpower and kill them. Their bodies will lie in the street of the great city, which is figuratively called Sodom and Egypt, where also their Lord was crucified. For three-and-a-half days men from every people, tribe, language and nation will gaze on their bodies and refuse them burial. The inhabitants of the earth will gloat over them and will celebrate by sending each other gifts, because these two prophets had tormented those who live on the earth.

This is where Satan begins to create his last delusion. Essentially, Satan's Man of Sin will claim that he bound Satan for a thousand years. Of course he'll open up the Bible and quote Revelation 20:7–10:

> When the thousand years are over, Satan will be released from his prison and will go out to deceive the nations in the four corners of the earth—Gog and Magog—to gather them for battle. In number they are like the sand on the seashore. They marched across the breadth of the earth and surrounded the camp of God's

people, the city he loves. But fire came down from heaven and devoured them. And the devil, who deceived them, was thrown into the lake of burning sulfur, where the beast and the false prophet had been thrown. They will be tormented day and night for ever and ever.

In a last-ditch effort to convince the world he is God, the Man of Sin will claim that the destruction of these two witnesses is the beginning of Satan being unbound for the last time, and then once-and-for-all destroyed. Of course, he'll claim that the thousand years is to be translated into the last thousand days of his reign. In Revelation 20:3, we see where Satan is bound by Jesus for a thousand years and then is set free for a short time so that he can go out and deceive the nations to mount a rebellion against Jesus in Jerusalem. Since Jesus quickly puts this rebellion down, the Man of Sin will attempt to make people believe that this prophecy is about to come true.

When we look at our calendar of this ten-year period, we see where the Man of Sin has about a thousand days to rule and reign after the fifth/sixth trumpet war. Of 1,260 days, the fifth/sixth trumpet war will last about 250 days. That leaves 1,010 days. Since he claims that this is Satan's last rebellion, he begins this last delusion by convincing people that the thousand years must be interpreted as a thousand days.

After the two witnesses are killed and their deaths celebrated, he will then inform the people of the incoming invasion, claiming it's the devil and his angels "numbered like the sand of the seashore." Of course, it's not the devil and his angels who are coming toward earth—it's Jesus and His saints! Those shiploads of bodies and souls of men who were martyred for their faith now return with Jesus to rule and reign with Him.

But just as he supposedly called fire down from heaven and destroyed the 144,000 Jewish-Christian evangelists, he tells his followers they have nothing to be concerned about. The reason John makes a reference to Gog of Magog is due to the fact that American technology defeated the Russian missiles. And since SDI worked then, it will also work against this invading space force—or so he makes them believe. He will convince them that he will put down this last great rebellion by Satan simply by calling down fire from heaven again, from American space-based technology. As we saw earlier, he invested a tremendous amount of money in space technology for this very purpose; he worships this so-called god of fortresses, just like his predecessor, the king of the North.

The people of the earth who have taken this man's mark and believe that he is God will simply believe that what he says is the truth. That's why they talk peace and safety. In other words, his followers buy into the lie that Satan has been unbound and the millennium is supposed to last only a thousand days. They don't realize they have been deluded and that it is really Jesus and His saints coming to earth.

John goes on to tell us that the real rebellion by Satan against Jesus will be put down just outside Jerusalem. In other words, it's Armageddon all over again at the end of Jesus' 1,000 year reign on earth. The Man of Sin, arrogantly claiming that this invading force will be put down, will muster all the world's forces to Armageddon to show how this apparent rebellion by Satan is supposedly put down by God, as portrayed by the king of the South. Through this delusion, people are more than willing to assemble for battle at Armageddon. They believe they are going to put down this rebellion by Satan. They have no idea that Satan is possessing the king of the South.

Joel 3:10 provides us insight into just how deluded these people are as the Man of Sin convinces them to "beat your plowshares into swords and your pruning hooks into spears." This is in contrast to Isaiah 2:4, during the reign of Jesus: "They will beat their swords into plowshares and their spears into pruning hooks." Joel is talking about the time just before Jesus returns, when the king of the South has the world convinced that Jesus is the devil let loose for a season. It is an indication of the prosperity and peace that people have enjoyed under the king of the South. The mere fact that the people labor in preparation for war should be an indicator that the king of the South is not God as he proclaims. During the actual reign of Jesus, the people will never have to prepare for war when Satan is let loose to deceive the nations.

Since Jesus is God, He doesn't need our weapons of war to put down any rebellion. However, we see here that even though the king of the South proclaims to be God, Satan must rely on mankind's developed resources in order to wage war—a strong indication that he is not who he appears to be.

THE KINGDOM IS COVERED IN DARKNESS

Revelation 16:10–11: The fifth angel poured out his bowl on the throne of the beast, and his kingdom was plunged into darkness. Men gnawed their tongues in agony and cursed the God of heaven because of their pains and their sores, but they refused to repent of what they had done.

To understand this darkness that comes upon the throne of the beast and the entire world, we once again must see what John has to say about the two witnesses. In Revelation 11:7–12, we find why the beast's kingdom is thrust into darkness:

> But after the three and a half days a breath of life from God entered them, and they stood on their feet, and terror struck those who saw them. Then they heard a loud voice from heaven saying to them, "Come up here." And they went up to heaven in a cloud, while their enemies looked on.

When the two witnesses are killed, brought back to life, and ascend to heaven on a cloud, the whole world is plunged into spiritual darkness. Between the time of their ascension and the actual return of Jesus Christ, for the first and only time the world is left without a witness. But in reality, there are still people alive who have continued to overcome the taking of the mark. Many of them are still in prison awaiting their execution.

Their ascension to heaven now prepares the way for the return of Jesus and the final conflict between the King of Kings and Lord of Lords, and Satan, the king of the South and the False Prophet, as well as their gathered forces at Armageddon.

DRYING UP THE ANCIENT RIVER

Revelation 16:12–14: The sixth angel poured out his bowl on the great river Euphrates, and its water was dried up to prepare the way for the kings from the East. Then I saw three evil spirits that looked like frogs; they came out of the mouth of the dragon, out of the mouth of the beast and out of the mouth of the false prophet. They are spirits of demons performing miraculous signs, and they go out to the kings of the whole world, to gather them for the battle on the great day of God Almighty.

The forces of America are undergoing destruction as a result of a powerful earthquake that John writes about in Revelation 16:18–19: "Then there came flashes of lightning, rumblings, peals of thunder and a severe earthquake. No earthquake like it has ever occurred since man has been on earth, so tremendous was the quake. The great city [America, termed Babylon the Great] split into three parts, and the cities of the nations collapsed. God remembered Babylon the Great and gave her the cup filled with the wine of the fury of his wrath." (Explanation in brackets is mine.) We'll study the prophetic details of America's destruction in more detail later.

With America undergoing destruction by almighty God, the only forces really available to the king of the South are the ground forces of the kings of the East. The three frogs are John's best attempt to describe our modern telecommunications systems. Imagine a first-century apostle trying to describe the telephone and how it works or our vast system of radio communications. On one end, John sees the world leaders speaking into telephones, or frogs. Somehow, thousands of miles away, the kings of the world are able to understand the message and respond to the call. In this case, because this concept is so foreign to John and because the impending message comes from two diabolical evil leaders empowered by Satan, John naturally calls the transmission of their voices "spirits of demons, which have power to do miracles."

Once again, this lends complete credibility to the fact that Satan has the power only to use what is natural or developed by mankind.

In this case, he uses the recently developed mass-communications systems of the world to assemble all the forces together.

THE FINAL WARNING

Revelation 16:15: Behold! I come like a thief! Blessed is he who stays awake and keeps his clothes with him, so that he may not go naked and be shamefully exposed.

Here Jesus issues one last warning of hope to those who have refused the mark of the beast and have put their trust in Jesus (clothing themselves with the righteousness of Jesus). Happy will be those people who hold firm to their faith and wait patiently for His coming. Even though the world is assembling for war, the words of Jesus' prophecy in Matthew 24:6 ring out:

> You will hear of wars and rumors of wars, but see to it that you are not alarmed. Such things must happen, but the end is still to come. Nation will rise against nation, and kingdom against kingdom [the kingdom of Jesus comes against the kingdom of Satan and his Man of Sin]. There will be famines and earthquakes in various places [America is destroyed by the largest earthquake in mankind's history]. All these are the beginning of birth pains [the return of Jesus]. (Explanations in brackets are mine.)

Just as Jesus accurately predicted, the world is full of rumors of an impending war with the kingdom of the king of the South rising against the kingdom of Jesus Christ. Famines are rampant because of the first four bowls of God's wrath, and an earthquake literally annihilates Babylon the Great, America, sending shock waves around the world. But here, just as He cautioned in Matthew 24:6, Jesus tells the saints who have refused the mark to not be alarmed and to hold on to the faith that they have maintained throughout this time of great tribulation.

BABYLON THE GREAT IS DESTROYED

Revelation 16:17–21: The seventh angel poured out his bowl into the air, and out of the temple came a loud voice from the throne, saying, "It is done!" Then there came flashes of lightning, rumblings, peals of thunder and a severe earthquake. No earthquake like it has ever occurred since man has been on earth, so tremendous was the quake. The great city split into three parts, and the cities of the nations collapsed. God remembered Babylon the Great and gave her the cup filled with the wine of the fury of his wrath. Every island fled away and the mountains could not be found. From the sky huge hailstones of about a hundred pounds each fell upon men. And they cursed God on account of the plague of hail, because the plague was so terrible.

Revelation 17:16: The beast and the ten horns you saw will hate the prostitute. They will bring her to ruin and leave her naked; they will eat her flesh and burn her with fire.

Zechariah 9:3-4: Tyre [Zechariah compares America to the ancient city of Tyre] has built herself a stronghold [SDI]; she has heaped up silver like dust, and gold like the dirt of the streets [the people have become extremely prosperous by accepting false salvation from the Man of Sin]. But the Lord will take away her possessions and destroy her power on the sea, and she will be consumed by fire. (Explanations in brackets are mine.)

Revelation 18:8: She will be consumed by fire.

Obadiah 4: Though you soar like the eagle [America] and make your nest among the stars [a reference to our space program and SDI], from there I will bring you down. (Explanations in brackets are mine.)

Isaiah 24:18–23: The floodgates of the heavens are opened, the foundations of the earth shake. The earth is broken up, the earth is split asunder [this is where America is split into three parts, sinking into the sea, causing worldwide calamities through tsunamis going around the world to other nations], the earth is thoroughly shaken. The earth reels like a drunkard, it sways like a hut in the wind; so heavy upon it is the guilt of its rebellion that it falls—never to rise again. [America is literally sunk into the oceans of the world, causing worldwide destruction to the other cities of the world.] (Explanations in brackets are mine.)

Zephaniah 3:7: I said to the city, "Surely you will fear me and accept correction!" Then her dwelling would not be cut off, nor all my punishments come upon her. But they were still eager to act corruptly in all they did.

Zephaniah 3:8: I have decided to assemble the nations, to gather the kingdoms and to pour out my wrath on them—all my fierce anger. The whole world will be consumed by the fire of my jealous anger.

These are the true birth pains of the promised Son coming to rule the earth with an iron rod for the next thousand years. Just as Jesus declared, "It is finished!" from the cross of Calvary, once again His words echo through time and space to the present.

The last great nation to be born on earth is the last nation to become an enemy of Christ. Here at the seventh bowl of God's wrath, we see the complete destruction of Babylon the Great, or America. It's ironic that America was founded upon godly principles, biblical theologies, and the commands of God. Sadly enough, this most blessed nation turned away from the wisdom and teachings of its forefathers and instead began to rely on the wisdom of mankind.

In Daniel's vision of America, he writes in Daniel 7:4 that the prominent empire of America "was like a lion, and it had the wings of an eagle. I watched until its wings were torn off and it was lifted from the ground so that it stood on two feet like a man, and the heart of a man was given to it."

Just as this passage appears to describe the kingdom of ancient Babylon under the rule of King Nebuchadnezzar, so it now describes the "daughter of Babylon" spoken of by the prophet Jeremiah. Just as ancient Babylon was represented by a head of gold in Daniel

2:38, so John later reveals that America, as Babylon the Great in Revelation 17:4, holds the golden cup of her abominations. Once used as a golden cup in the hands of the Lord, America finally abandons its own Constitution and hands itself over to the king of the South. Thus, just as Daniel envisioned, it is given "the heart of a man."

The impending result is that America gives itself over to killing the holy people of God in exchange for the riches of this world. So great is her sin of greed and murder that John records in Revelation 17:6, "I saw that the woman was drunk with the blood of the saints, the blood of those who bore testimony to Jesus."

So great is God's anger against America that John records in Revelation 18:8 that in one single day her "plagues will overtake her: death, mourning and famine. She will be consumed by fire, for mighty is the Lord God who judges her."

John records in Revelation 18:17 that the merchants on the seas will cry out bitterly, "In one hour such great wealth has been brought to ruin!"

Amongst all this weeping over America, John sees the forces of heaven rejoicing in Revelation 19:3: "Hallelujah! The smoke from her goes up for ever and ever."

John further records in Revelation 18:21: "With such violence the great city of Babylon will be thrown down, never to be found again."

America's doom is recorded in Jeremiah 51:49: "Babylon must fall because of Israel's slain, just as the slain in all the earth have fallen because of Babylon."

The shiploads of bodies and souls of men that had been transported from America and slain during the past three years, recorded in Revelation 18:13, serve as a striking testimony to Jeremiah's vision. Through the prophet Jeremiah, God prophesied the day when America would become dependent upon its space-based defense system. Listen to Him in Jeremiah 51:53: "Even if Babylon reaches the sky and fortifies her lofty stronghold, I will send destroyers against her."

God's primary weapon of choice is an earthquake. No technology in the world can defend a nation against an earthquake. In this case, SDI and space-based defense systems do America absolutely no good. In Jeremiah 51:58, we see the Lord declare, "Babylon's thick wall will be leveled and her high gates set on fire; the peoples exhaust themselves for nothing, the nations' labor is only fuel for the flames."

The destruction of this nation—termed a *great city* by John in Revelation 16:19; 17:18; 18:10; 18:18; 18:19; and 18:21—is so complete that John records how the nation will actually split in three parts. In Jeremiah 51:42, we see where "the sea will rise over Babylon; its roaring waves will cover her."

John supports Jeremiah's prophecy in Revelation 18:21, where he records that "a mighty angel picked up a boulder the size of a large millstone and threw it into the sea" as an example of America's total annihilation. This exact same scenario was envisioned in Jeremiah 51:64 by Seraiah, who said as he dropped Jeremiah's scroll into the great Euphrates River, "So will Babylon sink to rise no more because of the disaster I will bring upon her. And her people will fall."

Isaiah 65:11–12 expresses the anger God has for this evil and perverse generation: "But as for you who forsake the Lord and forget my holy mountain, who spread a table for Fortune and fill bowls of mixed wine for Destiny, I will destine you for the sword, and you will all bend down for the slaughter; for I called but you did not answer; I spoke but you did not listen. You did evil in my sight and chose what displeases me."

For the sake of fortune, the people of America freely and willingly shed the blood of saints and prophets—those who refused the mark—believing they were performing a service to God, portrayed by the Man of Sin, or king of the South. Therefore, America is completely destroyed and sunk into the oceans, causing tremendous destruction to other nations and cities of the world.

Isaiah also predicted the shedding of blood by Americans when he wrote in Isaiah 47:5–7: "Sit in silence, go into darkness, Daughter of the Babylonians; no more will you be called queen of kingdoms. I was angry with my people and desecrated my inheritance; I gave them into your hand, and you showed them no mercy. Even on the aged you laid a very heavy yoke. You said, 'I will continue forever —the eternal queen!' But you did not consider these things or reflect on what might happen."

At the Lord's coming, Joel 2:20 describes the Lord's plan of destruction for American armed forces: "I will drive the northern army far from you, pushing it into a parched and barren land, with its front columns going into the eastern sea and those in the rear going into the western sea. And its stench will go up; its smell will rise. Surely he has done great things."

As America, the great city, splits apart, the eastern coast sinks into the Atlantic Ocean and the western United States will sink into the great Pacific Ocean. The rest of the land will be covered completely from the resulting tsunami shock waves that will literally rock the earth. John records the words of a great and powerful angel in Revelation 18:2: "Fallen! Fallen is Babylon the Great! She has become a home for demons and a haunt for every evil spirit, a haunt for every unclean and detestable bird."

HEAVEN REJOICES

Revelation 19:1–2: After this I heard what sounded like the roar of a great multitude in heaven shouting: "Hallelujah! Salvation and glory and power belong to our God, for true and just are his judgments. He has condemned the great prostitute who corrupted the earth by her adulteries. He has avenged on her the blood of his servants."

Here we see the forces of heaven praising the mighty power of God, who has destroyed America for abandoning religious freedom and killing the people of God.

THE SAINTS PREPARE TO RIDE

Revelation 19:6–9: Then I heard what sounded like a great multitude, like the roar of rushing waters and like loud peals of thunder, shouting: "Hallelujah! For our Lord God Almighty reigns. Let us rejoice and be glad and give him glory! For the wedding of the Lamb has come, and his bride has made herself ready. Fine linen, bright and clean, was given her to wear." (Fine linen stands for the righteous acts of the saints.) Then the angel said to me, "Write: 'Blessed are those who are invited to the wedding supper of the Lamb!' "

We must note here that the only righteous thing done by God's holy people is that they laid down their own pride and self-righteous acts and instead clothed themselves with the righteousness of Jesus Christ. Our good deeds are as filthy rags compared to the righteousness of Jesus Christ and the giving of His life on the cross so that our sins may be remembered no more. It was strictly their acceptance of Jesus Christ and their profession of faith and confession of their sins and their realization of their inability to save themselves that gained them entrance to heaven. Nobody made it into heaven because of their own good deeds alone. The acceptance of Jesus as the Lord and Savior of their souls is the only thing that gained them entry to heaven.

Here, now that they have been fully clothed with the righteousness of Jesus Christ and have met the judgment seat of Christ and have been rewarded with new heavenly bodies for their souls and spirits, they prepare to follow Jesus during His triumphal return to earth.

THE SECOND COMING

Revelation 19:11–14: I saw heaven standing open and there before me was a white horse, whose rider is called Faithful and True. With justice he judges and makes war. His eyes are like blazing fire, and on his head are many crowns. He has a name written on him that no one knows but He himself. He is dressed in a robe dipped in blood, and his name is the Word of God. The armies of heaven were following him, riding on white horses and dressed in fine linen, white and clean. Out of his mouth comes a sharp sword with which to strike down the nations. "He will rule them with an iron scepter." He treads the winepress of the fury of the wrath of God Almighty. On his robe and on his thigh he has this name written: KING OF KINGS AND LORD OF LORDS.

Joel 2:2: Like dawn spreading across the mountains a large and mighty army comes, such as never was of old nor ever will be in ages to come.

Joel 2:4: They have the appearance of horses; they gallop along like cavalry.

Joel 2:6: At the sight of them, nations are in anguish; every face turns pale.

Joel 2:10: Before them the earth shakes, the sky trembles, the sun and moon are darkened, and the stars no longer shine.

Joel 2:11: The Lord thunders at the head of his army; his forces are beyond number, and mighty are those who obey his command. The day of the Lord is great; it is dreadful. Who can endure it?

There will be no mistaking the coming of Jesus—the real Messiah—who is King of Kings and Lord of Lords. In Matthew 24:27, Jesus tells how we will be able to know His actual return: "For as lightning that comes from the east is visible even in the west, so will be the coming of the Son of Man."

Just as lightning lights up the entire sky from horizon to horizon, so will be the brightness of His coming to earth with all his saints. The prophet Joel described Jesus' return as the dawn breaking over the mountains.

Zechariah 14:3 paints a beautiful picture of the return of Jesus.

Then the Lord will go out and fight against those nations, as He fights in the day of battle. On that day His feet will stand on the Mount of Olives, east of Jerusalem, and the Mount of Olives will be split in two from east to west, forming a great valley, with half of the mountain moving north and half moving south.

At this time, Jerusalem experiences an earthquake, spoken by John in Revelation 11:26. Now is when God's holy people still alive in Jerusalem will flee from Jerusalem by this newly formed mountain valley. This is how Jesus protects the remnant of Jews from His coming wrath upon the gathered forces.

THE GREAT SUPPER OF GOD

Revelation 19:17–19: And I saw an angel standing in the sun, who cried in a loud voice to all the birds flying in midair: "Come, gather together for the great supper of God, so that you may eat the flesh of kings, generals, and mighty men, of horses and their riders, and the flesh of all people—free and slave, small and great." Then I saw the beast and the kings of the earth and their armies gathered together to make war against the rider on the horse and his army.

Picture about a billion people assembled on the plain of Megiddo, a twenty-five-square-mile piece of real estate surrounded by mountains, giving it the appearance of a bowl-shaped valley—which God will use as a great winepress—to destroy all His enemies. Zechariah 14:12–13 paints the picture of this event:

> This is the plague with which the Lord will strike all the nations that fought against Jerusalem: Their flesh will rot while they are still standing on their feet; their eyes will rot in their sockets, and their tongues will rot in their mouths. On that day men will be stricken by the Lord with great panic. Each man will seize the hand of another, and they will attack each other.

This is not nuclear annihilation of these forces. Jesus does not need man's developed weapons of mass destruction to annihilate the enemy forces of this world. Zechariah is specific about the use of a plague, not weapons of mass destruction. John writes in Revelation 19:15 that "out of the rider's mouth comes a sharp sword that He will use to defeat the nations."

In an instant, with one single command and without a single shot being fired, people will literally and instantly turn to jelly and simply begin to rot away while standing on their feet! Those who do not immediately begin to rot away will be struck with such confusion that they will literally turn on others and kill them. This is another war of confusion brought on by the victorious Messiah. Ironically, not a single shot is fired at the battle of Armageddon!

THE BEAST AND FALSE PROPHET ARE DESTROYED

Revelation 19:20–21: But the beast was captured, and with him the false prophet who had performed the miraculous signs on his behalf. With these signs he had deluded those who had received the mark of the beast and worshiped his image. The two of them were thrown alive into the fiery lake of burning sulfur. The rest of them were killed with the sword that came out of the mouth of the rider on the horse, and all the birds gorged themselves on their flesh.

Amazingly, John wraps up the end of this ten-year period of trial and great tribulation with a few short sentences. The king of the South or Man of Sin, the False Prophet, and those who had worshiped the king of the South, are quickly and without remorse destroyed. Zechariah 14:9 gives a befitting tribute to the end of Satan's reign of terror on earth: "The Lord will be king over the whole earth. On that day there will be one Lord, and his name the only name."

That name, of course, is the name of Jesus.

The Day Of The Lord

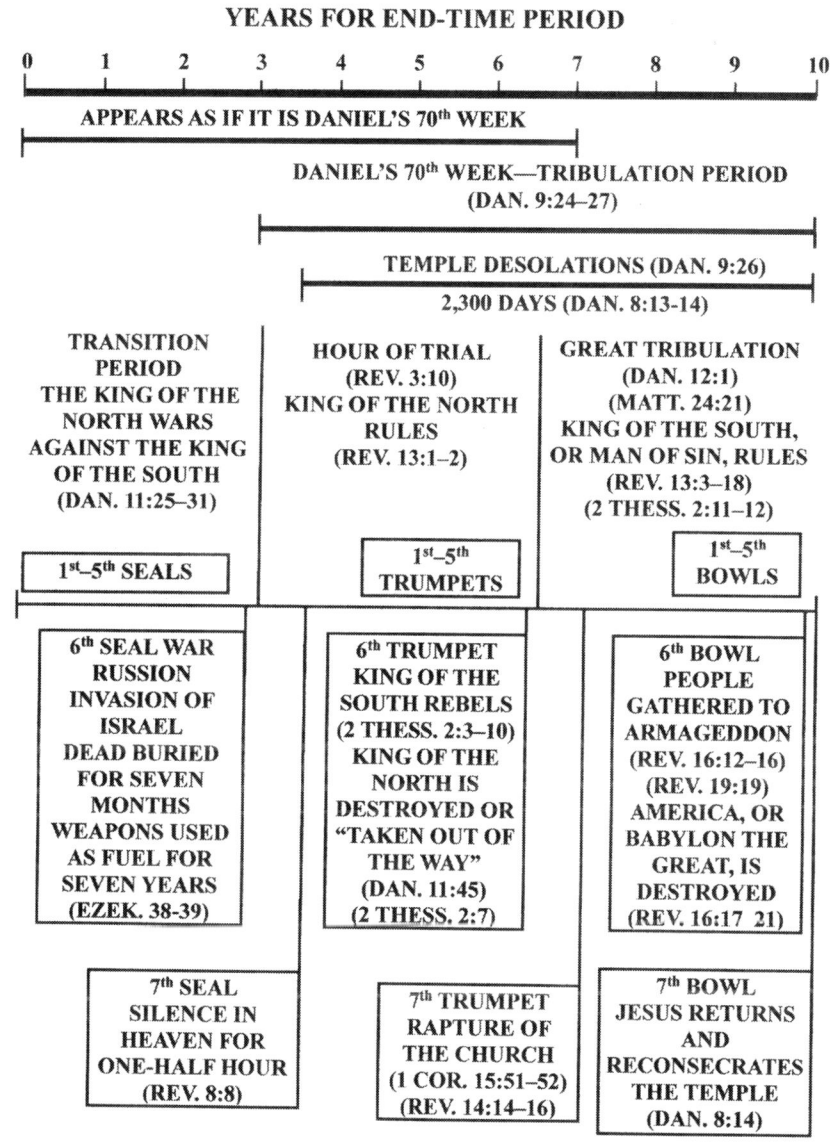

YEARS FOR END-TIME PERIOD

```
0    1    2    3    4    5    6    7    8    9    10
```

APPEARS AS IF IT IS DANIEL'S 70th WEEK

DANIEL'S 70th WEEK—TRIBULATION PERIOD
(DAN. 9:24–27)

TEMPLE DESOLATIONS (DAN. 9:26)

2,300 DAYS (DAN. 8:13-14)

TRANSITION PERIOD THE KING OF THE NORTH WARS AGAINST THE KING OF THE SOUTH (DAN. 11:25–31)	HOUR OF TRIAL (REV. 3:10) KING OF THE NORTH RULES (REV. 13:1–2)	GREAT TRIBULATION (DAN. 12:1) (MATT. 24:21) KING OF THE SOUTH, OR MAN OF SIN, RULES (REV. 13:3–18) (2 THESS. 2:11–12)
1st–5th SEALS	1st–5th TRUMPETS	1st–5th BOWLS
6th SEAL WAR RUSSION INVASION OF ISRAEL DEAD BURIED FOR SEVEN MONTHS WEAPONS USED AS FUEL FOR SEVEN YEARS (EZEK. 38-39)	6th TRUMPET KING OF THE SOUTH REBELS (2 THESS. 2:3–10) KING OF THE NORTH IS DESTROYED OR "TAKEN OUT OF THE WAY" (DAN. 11:45) (2 THESS. 2:7)	6th BOWL PEOPLE GATHERED TO ARMAGEDDON (REV. 16:12–16) (REV. 19:19) AMERICA, OR BABYLON THE GREAT, IS DESTROYED (REV. 16:17 21)
7th SEAL SILENCE IN HEAVEN FOR ONE-HALF HOUR (REV. 8:8)	7th TRUMPET RAPTURE OF THE CHURCH (1 COR. 15:51–52) (REV. 14:14–16)	7th BOWL JESUS RETURNS AND RECONSECRATES THE TEMPLE (DAN. 8:14)

FIGURE 6-1. THE POWERFUL DELUSION THAT ALLOWS SATAN TO PROCLAIM, "I AM THE CHRIST" (ISAIAH 14:12–15)